F Communism!

(A Capitalism)

By:

L. Tadeus

This book is a work of nonfiction. While every effort has been made to verify facts and historical details, some material reflects the author's interpretation and analysis. Any errors or omissions are unintentional and remain the responsibility of the author.

For information, permissions, or media inquiries, please contact:

XANANIMUUS@GMAIL.COM

Published in the United States of America

ISBN 978-1-968619-84-8 (hardcover)

ISBN 978-1-968619-86-2 (paperback)

ISBN 978-1-968619-85-5 (ebook)

Cover and interior design by L. Tadeus

DEDICATION

To my brothers and sisters in uniform,

who stood their ground against every enemy—foreign or domestic—and proved that freedom survives only when defended by those willing to bear the cost.

To the families who carried the weight beside them, quietly upholding the strength of a nation.

And to every American who understands, without apology or hesitation, that communism has destroyed more lives, crushed more hope, and poisoned more societies than any ideology in history—and that it must be rejected wherever it appears, no matter who defends it or how loudly they preach it.

This book is for all who refuse to bow to it, ever.

FOREWORD

This book is written for those who love their country but are weary of seeing it betrayed from within. It is for the citizen who senses something deeply wrong in the modern world—who sees the corrosion of virtue, the erosion of enterprise, and the quiet surrender of freedom disguised as progress. It is for the young American who has been told that capitalism is cruel, that patriotism is naïve, and that equality must be forced. It is for the parent who wants to teach truth to the next generation before the lessons of liberty are erased from our collective memory.

F Capitalism could just as easily have been called The Patriot's Quick Reference Guide to Communism. It is both a defense and a warning—a defense of the only system that has ever lifted mankind from poverty and tyranny, and a warning against the ideologies that have always dragged it back. Each page is meant to arm the reader with understanding: of what capitalism really is, of what communism always becomes, and of how the same seductive promises that enslaved half the world are once again being whispered to a new generation. Hopefully, by the end, readers will be armed with facts and feel empowered to push back against the encroachment of communist and socialist ideology in politics and academia.

This book is meant not only for those now living, but for generations across time. It is written for the generations before Millennials—to serve as a reference and teaching guide for parents, veterans, and patriots determined to educate those who follow. It is written for the generations now coming into their own suffrage—those first casting ballots and learning that freedom can be lost far faster than it is won. It is written for the generations entering college and high school, facing indoctrination from those who call themselves educators but serve ideology instead of truth. And it is written for the generations yet unborn—that they might inherit not only a free nation, but the understanding of why it must remain so.

This is not a book of theory, but of history and reality. It lays bare the contrast between two visions of the human spirit: one that trusts free individuals to build, innovate, and rise—and another that seeks to control, redistribute, and equalize by force. The first creates abundance; the second creates misery. The first honors the dignity of labor; the second reduces man to a cog in a collective machine. The first needs freedom; the second demands obedience.

The purpose of this work is simple: to remind Americans who they are, what their system represents, and why it must be defended. Capitalism is not merely an economic arrangement—it is the economic expression of liberty itself. It is the marketplace extension of the same principle that animates our Republic: that power belongs to the individual, not the state.

The goal was not to write a huge, unwieldy tome. Indeed, volumes and volumes could be filled with the stories of the failures of communism and socialism. The goal was to provide simple truths and facts for easy consumption and quick reference—and for further discussion by parents, students, and patriots. This book is filled with references to additional works for those who truly wish to dig deeper into the absolute failures of communism and socialism.

The double entendre in the title **"F Communism (A Capitalism)"** is no accident. It captures, in one stroke, the defiant spirit and unapologetic conviction that drive the entire work. The blunt "F Communism" is both a rejection and a warning—a refusal to sanitize or intellectualize the catastrophic legacy of collectivist ideology. Yet the parenthetical "A Capitalism" adds a layer of irony and purpose: what begins as condemnation transforms into affirmation. It is not just an expletive—it's an exclamation of allegiance to freedom, property, and individual enterprise. The title's wordplay forces readers to confront a choice: one system demands obedience; the other rewards initiative. In that contrast lies the essence of the book's message—bold, unfiltered, and deliberate. It is simultaneously a thumb in the eye to academia, which too often excuses tyranny in the name of theory, and an affirmation of solidarity with American patriots everywhere who still believe that liberty is worth defending.

This book is, in a sense, an inoculation against socialist and communist beliefs—a defense against what can only be described as a mind virus. These ideologies infect through emotion rather than reason, spreading envy, dependency, and resentment until they corrupt both thought and character. *F Capitalism* exposes the seductive half-truths and emotional appeals that have always been the entry points of collectivist ideology, and it arms the reader with the intellectual antibodies of history, logic, and evidence. Just as a vaccine prepares the body to recognize and repel a disease, this book prepares the mind to identify and resist the recurring infections of collectivist thought. It is written to fortify the reader against deception—to strengthen reason against propaganda and conviction against fear—so that freedom may endure in both spirit and practice.

If someone has never visited another country but has been convinced by propaganda that America is something less than the greatest nation on earth, I hope this book helps them see through that delusion. Travel the world, and you will find no freer, fairer, or more generous people than Americans. There is no greater experiment in liberty, no higher achievement of civilization. From here, there is nowhere to go but down. The only direction left for tyranny to pull is backward—away from the hard-won summit of freedom that this nation represents.

To the discerning reader who follows current events, I implore you to look closely at what you see in today's political arena. When you hear policies that promise equality through control, prosperity through redistribution, or justice through coercion—ask yourself what ideology those ideas serve. When you see hatred for success, contempt for faith, and disdain for liberty presented as moral virtue, ask yourself from which failed philosophy those notions arise. You may find that the same old specter of communism has only changed its name, not its intent. And when you do, I hope you will be emboldened to stand firm, speak truth, and challenge the creeping normalization of those ideas wherever they appear.

In that spirit, this book calls on readers to remember, to resist, and to rebuild—to take up the torch of reason and self-reliance that made America the envy of the world. F Capitalism is a call not only to reject false promises, but to rekindle faith in the system that works: one rooted in voluntary exchange, honest competition, and moral responsibility.

Freedom, after all, is not sustained by government decree but by individual conviction. If enough patriots keep that conviction alive, then capitalist republics, and Western civilization itself will endure.

Ideally, a copy of this book would rest on every coffee table, in every faculty lounge, at every family dinner table, on every bookshelf, and in every student's locker or book bag—anywhere it might provide inspiration, anywhere it might equip someone to recognize and combat the deadly ideologies of communism and socialism. For in every place truth resides, freedom has a fighting chance.

TABLE OF CONTENTS

PART I

PART II

PART IV

PART I

CHAPTER 1.
INTRODUCTION

This book begins by asking three simple but unavoidable questions:

Why do communist policies succeed nowhere?

Why do capitalist republics succeed everywhere?

And why, despite the overwhelming evidence, does anyone still believe communism is the answer?

The pages that follow attempt to answer these questions plainly, drawing not from theory but from history, reason, and lived experience. The truth is not hidden. It has simply been forgotten—or deliberately buried—by those who would prefer that new generations never learn it.

THE PROMISE, THE LIE, AND THE COST

Every generation faces the same dangerous illusion: the beliefs that freedom and prosperity can survive without vigilance and that human perfection can be engineered from above. It begins with noble words — equality, fairness, justice — and ends with chains, starvation, and mass graves. Under new names and new slogans, communism and socialism return again and again, promising a better world while erasing the very foundations of civilization.

The twentieth century was not merely a century of war — it was a century of ideological slaughter. More than one hundred million souls perished under regimes that sought to abolish private property, religion, family, competition, and individuality itself.[1] Entire nations were reduced to gray uniformity in the pursuit of "progress." Yet in the West — especially in our schools, universities, and media — these systems are still defended, rebranded, and romanticized.[2]

This project is a reckoning. It is not a partisan argument; it is a historical and moral one. It is written for those who have been told that capitalism and republicanism are "outdated," that freedom must yield to the collective, and that the individual is expendable for the "greater good." Such claims defy both reason and history. The very systems dismissed as obsolete — capitalism and constitutional republicanism — produced the most prosperous, free, and innovative nation the world has ever known. They transformed a frontier wilderness into a civilization of abundance, science, and liberty unmatched in all of human experience. To call them outdated is to deny reality itself.

> *"...would be to disregard the uniform course of human events, and to set at defiance the accumulated experience of ages."*— **John Jay**[3]

Though Jay was not speaking of communism or socialism, his words capture perfectly the arrogance of modern ideologues who imagine they can overturn the laws of human nature and succeed where every similar experiment has failed. Jay's observation reminds us that ignoring the record of human experience — and pretending history can be rewritten by ideology — is the first step toward repeating its tragedies.

> *"Society is indeed a contract... not only between those who are living, but between those who are dead, and those who are to be born."*— **Edmund Burke**[4]

Burke's counsel underscores that every generation inherits both the blessings and the responsibilities of civilization. To disregard the lessons of the past is to break that sacred contract — to cut the living off from the hard-won wisdom of those who built the very freedoms we now enjoy.

Those who escaped from such regimes understand this more clearly than anyone. Survivors of communism and socialism — from the Soviet gulags, Mao's China, Castro's Cuba, North Korea, and modern Venezuela — tell a single, unbroken story. They speak of neighbors vanishing in the night, of families torn apart, of hunger, fear, and lies presented as truth.[5] Many came to America not merely seeking opportunity but seeking freedom — that rare condition where speech, faith, and work are not dictated by the State. Their voices are not relics of the past; they are warnings to the present. To ignore them is to invite the same darkness they fled.

At the same time, this work will celebrate what does work: the Western ideals that produced prosperity, liberty, and human dignity on a scale the world had never seen — the combination of capitalism and constitutional republicanism, grounded in personal responsibility, voluntary cooperation, and moral restraint.[6]

But today, those ideals are under sustained attack — not by invading armies, but by ideological infiltration. Across America, generations of young people have been trained to distrust their own heritage. The institutions once charged with teaching truth and cultivating virtue have been turned into instruments of indoctrination. In classrooms across the country, capitalism is caricatured as greed, faith is dismissed as superstition, and patriotism is smeared as oppression. The result is not enlightenment but paradoxical resentment — a generation taught to despise the very civilization that gave it freedom.

This indoctrination must be recognized for what it is: a deliberate attempt to dismantle the moral and cultural foundations of the Republic. It seeks to produce compliant citizens rather than independent thinkers — followers rather than builders. To allow this process to continue unchecked is to surrender the future. The battle for civilization will not be fought only on foreign soil; it will be fought in the minds of our children.

To combat it, truth must once again become the standard of education. History must be taught honestly, with all its triumphs and failures intact. Young Americans must learn that prosperity, innovation, and liberty were not accidents of geography or luck but the deliberate outcomes of systems that honored work, freedom, and faith. They must understand that no government can create equality by destroying excellence — and that no nation can remain free if its citizens no longer know why it should be.[7]

THE STRUCTURE OF THIS WORK

This book is organized into four major parts, each revealing a different dimension of the ideological struggle between freedom and control. **Part I** introduces the philosophical and historical foundations of the conflict—why communism fails, why capitalism succeeds, and how the same false promises continue to seduce new generations. **Part II** examines the ten policy failures upon which communism and socialism depend, exposing why each collapses in practice and principle. **Part III** turns to the ten catastrophic outcomes those policies have produced around the world—famine, repression, and moral decay that serve as enduring warnings. Finally, **Part IV** offers the path forward, addressing propaganda, indoctrination, and the means by which liberty, faith, and truth can be restored and defended.

> *"The inherent vice of capitalism is the unequal sharing of blessings; the inherent virtue of socialism is the equal sharing of miseries."*— **Winston Churchill**[8]

Churchill's observation cuts through every false promise of socialism and communism. Equality of misery is the only equality these ideologies have ever achieved. His words serve as both a caution and a truth test: wherever collectivism reigns, freedom and prosperity perish.

Arming yourself with the facts contained in this book is an act of resistance and of patriotism. Knowledge is the antidote to propaganda, and truth is the greatest weapon against the lies of collectivism. When you hear socialism or communism spoken of as compassion, or dressed up as equality, you will know better. You will know the cost in blood and human suffering, the destruction of families and nations, and the relentless war they wage on the human spirit. With these facts in hand, you will be equipped to confront the ideology wherever it appears — in conversation, in media, or in the classroom — and to dismantle it with clarity, conviction, and courage.

The fight for liberty begins with understanding. The defense of truth begins with knowledge. And this book is written so that those who cherish freedom can speak with authority, counter deception with evidence, and stand unshaken when others waver.

> *"Freedom is never more than one generation away from extinction. We didn't pass it on to our children in the bloodstream. It must be fought for, protected, and handed on for them to do the same."*— **Ronald Reagan**[9]

Reagan's words close the circle of this introduction. Liberty is not self-sustaining — it lives only as long as free men and women defend it. Every generation must relearn why liberty matters, why truth must be defended, and why the false promises of communism and socialism always end in ruin. Forgetting these truths is how civilizations die — not from invasion, but from amnesia.

CHAPTER 2.
WHY COMMUNISM AND SOCIALISM ARE THE SAME

IDEOLOGICAL UNITY

Socialism and communism share a common origin and the same philosophical foundations. Both arise from the writings of Karl Marx and Friedrich Engels, who made no secret of their aim: the abolition of private property and the subordination of the individual to the collective. In The Communist Manifesto, they summarized their entire theory in a single line:

> *"The theory of the Communists may be summed up in the single sentence: abolition of private property."* — **Karl Marx and Friedrich Engels**[1]

This declaration exposes the heart of both ideologies. The rejection of private ownership is not an incidental feature but the central pillar upon which all socialist and communist programs rest.

The distinction between socialism and communism is therefore one of tempo, not destination. As Marx and Engels conceived it, socialism was simply the first stage on the same road toward total collectivization.

> *"The first phase of communism... is usually called socialism."* — **Vladimir Lenin**[2]

Lenin's own admission makes the connection explicit. He viewed socialism not as an alternative to communism but as its necessary foundation. The two are inseparable in both theory and intent.

CENTRALIZED CONTROL AND THE DESTRUCTION OF PRIVATE PROPERTY

At the heart of both systems lies the destruction of private property. The socialist promises gradual reform through taxation, regulation, and nationalization; the communist moves by open confiscation. Both replace voluntary exchange with political control.

> *"The economic control of the state means control of the means for all our ends."* — **Friedrich Hayek**[3]

Hayek's reflection captures the inevitable consequence of centralized planning: when the state controls production, it gains authority over every aspect of life. Economic dependence becomes political subservience.

History confirms this truth. The Soviet Union called itself a 'Union of Soviet Socialist Republics,' not a communist state. Mao's China declared itself a 'People's Republic,' committed to 'socialist construction.' Cuba, North Korea, and Venezuela all used the same language to disguise identical policies of central planning, censorship, and repression.[4]

SOCIALISM AS THE ROAD TO COMMUNISM

Marx himself divided communism into two phases. The first, socialism, would distribute goods according to contribution; the second, communism, according to need. But the bridge between them has never been crossed. Every socialist state has become a permanent dictatorship in practice.

> *"Communism is Soviet power plus the electrification of the whole country."* — **Vladimir Lenin**[5]

Lenin's phrase was not poetic; it was prescriptive. It revealed his vision of an all-encompassing state that would command both industry and ideology. The socialist 'transition' was never temporary—it was the regime itself.

CONSEQUENCES IN PRACTICE

The record of both systems is written in human suffering. Wherever the state replaces private ownership with collective control, poverty and repression follow. The Soviet Union's purges and famines, China's Great Leap Forward and Cultural Revolution, Cambodia's killing fields, and Venezuela's collapse from wealth to want all share the same origin.[6]

For the victims of these systems, the distinction between socialism and communism was meaningless. The abolition of property and the concentration of power in the hands of the state produced the same outcome: dependence, despair, and death.

THE RHETORICAL DECEPTION

If socialism and communism are one and the same in both theory and result, why do their defenders continue to separate them? The answer lies in language. 'Communism' has become synonymous with oppression, while 'socialism' retains the illusion of compassion. The same ideology is repackaged under a softer name.

> *"All animals are equal, but some animals are more equal than others."* — **George Orwell**[7]

Orwell's satire on totalitarianism perfectly describes the outcome of socialist revolutions. Promises of equality dissolve into hierarchies of privilege, where the ruling elite governs in the name of 'the people.'

The slogans change, the flags differ, but the result is constant: the replacement of freedom with control. Modern 'democratic socialism' merely repeats the same pattern under a friendlier banner.

CONCLUSION

Communism and socialism are not distinct philosophies but phases of the same experiment. Both rest on coercive redistribution, the subordination of the individual to the collective, and the eradication of private property. The only real difference lies in rhetoric and timing.

> *"Socialism is communism with better public relations."* — is widely circulated and often attributed to **Ronald Reagan**[8]

Though he likely popularized rather than coined it. Variants of the phrase appeared in conservative commentary throughout the late 1970s and 1980s, especially in editorials and speeches

The modern socialist sells the same ideology under a new label, hoping that history will forget the millions destroyed by its previous forms. Freedom and prosperity require rejecting both faces of the same totalitarian coin.[9]

CHAPTER 3.
THE GLOBAL RECORD OF FAILURE

THE ULTIMATE TEST OF IDEOLOGY

Communism, more than any modern political creed, claimed to be scientific, humane, and inevitable. It promised liberation from exploitation and a rational re-ordering of society. That promise drew in nations scarred by war, inequality, and humiliation. But everywhere it was tried, the price of the experiment was the same: the subordination of the individual to an all-powerful state. From the first decrees to the last ration card, the human person became an instrument of policy rather than the subject of rights.[1]

> *"The utopian makes the mistake of supposing that because he can imagine a perfect world, it can be made."* — **Thomas Sowell**[2]

Sowell's observation exposes the hubris of communism: the conviction that humanity can be perfected by decree. Every regime that embraced that illusion discovered that its greatest obstacle was not wealth or inequality, but human nature itself.

It is tempting to explain away the record by blaming geography, culture, or leadership. Yet the pattern is global and consistent.

WHY COMMUNIST GOVERNMENTS SUCCEED NOWHERE

Why is it that every communist experiment — regardless of culture, geography, or resources — ends in poverty, repression, and decay? The answer is not accident or circumstance; it is design.

Systems built on envy and coercion cannot produce prosperity. They smother initiative, punish success, and reward obedience. History's verdict is uniform because human nature itself — a product of hundreds of thousands of years of evolution — does not change. It cannot be switched off like a light.[3]

The same natural limitations that socialist and communist systems cite as excuses — scarcity, inequality, cultural division — were confronted and overcome by capitalist republics. Free societies faced those same human and material constraints, yet adapted, innovated, and prospered precisely because they trusted individuals rather than central planners. This reality shatters every rationalization offered by apologists for collectivism: the problem was never circumstance, but the system itself.

What follows is not theory but the historical ledger of places where communism was attempted — and failed.

THE SOVIET UNION: THE FIRST AND GREATEST COLLAPSE

The Bolshevik Revolution of 1917 created the first communist state. In the name of equality, the new regime abolished private property, outlawed opposition, and re-engineered society by decree. Under Stalin, forced collectivization shattered the countryside and triggered famine on a continental scale; purges and the gulag system devoured the regime's perceived enemies. Whole peoples were deported; fear became the glue of the state.[4]

> *"Socialism is a philosophy of failure, the creed of ignorance, and the gospel of envy; its inherent virtue is the equal sharing of miseries."* — **Winston Churchill**[5]

Churchill's words, delivered in 1948, summarize perfectly the Soviet tragedy: socialism promised equality but achieved only equal misery. The USSR's citizens shared in hunger, scarcity, and fear — not prosperity.

Even as the Soviet Union projected power abroad, its economy decayed at home. Chronic shortages, shoddy production, and the impossibility of honest price signals condemned central planning to stagnation. When Mikhail Gorbachev opened the windows with *glasnost* and *perestroika*, he revealed a system rotted through. In 1991, the empire that had dominated half the world imploded — not because it was insufficiently radical, but because it was intrinsically unworkable.

EASTERN EUROPE: REVOLT BEHIND THE IRON CURTAIN

After World War II, the Soviet Union imposed communist regimes across Eastern Europe. Secret police, party courts, and command economies kept the façade in place; the Berlin Wall was built not to keep invaders out, but to keep citizens in. Workers and intellectuals resisted — Hungary in 1956, Czechoslovakia in 1968 —only to be crushed by Soviet tanks.[6]

> *"The march of freedom and democracy will leave Marxism-Leninism on the ash heap of history."* — **Ronald Reagan**[7]

Reagan's declaration, made before the British Parliament in 1982, became the moral prophecy of a generation yearning to breathe free. The first cracks in the Iron Curtain appeared not in Moscow, but in Warsaw. The Solidarity movement in Poland, born from shipyard strikes and sustained by faith and courage, demonstrated that ordinary workers could stand against the machinery of the state.

Within a decade, Solidarity's defiance ignited revolutions across Eastern Europe. When the Soviet empire weakened, every captive nation chose liberty. Communism had survived only by coercion; once the coercion faltered, it collapsed.

CHINA: FROM FAMINE TO REFORM

When *Mao Zedong* declared the People's Republic of China in 1949, he promised to lift millions from poverty. Instead, the Great Leap Forward (1958–62) became the deadliest famine in human history. Tens of millions starved while officials falsified reports to satisfy ideological quotas. The Cultural Revolution (1966–76) followed — a decade of chaos in which China devoured its own teachers, artists, and traditions.[8]

> *"The problem with socialism is that eventually you run out of other people's money."* — **Margaret Thatcher**[9]

Thatcher's quip was prophetic: under socialism, even China exhausted the resources, morale, and humanity of its own people. The Chinese Communist Party's eventual embrace of private markets was not ideological evolution — it was survival.

After Mao's death, *Deng Xiaoping* abandoned strict Marxism in favor of private enterprise and market incentives. The prosperity that followed came not from socialism, but from its repudiation.

SOUTHEAST ASIA: IDEOLOGY AND CATASTROPHE

In Southeast Asia, communism's record was no less grim. Vietnam's reunification in 1975 brought rationing and stagnation; by the 1980s, its leaders had to reintroduce markets under *Đổi Mới*. Laos followed the same path, rediscovering private enterprise out of necessity, not conviction.[10]

> *"If it moves, tax it; if it keeps moving, regulate it; and if it stops moving, subsidize it."* — **Ronald Reagan**[11]

Reagan's humor distilled an economic truth: socialist bureaucracy kills vitality, innovation, and initiative.

In Cambodia, *Pol Pot* sought to erase modern society entirely between 1975 and 1979, driving millions into rural labor camps and killing nearly a quarter of the population. Communism there did not deliver equality — it delivered annihilation.[12]

KOREA: ONE NATION, TWO DESTINIES

Few comparisons illustrate ideological contrast more sharply than the Korean Peninsula. In the North, *Kim Il-sung's* Stalinist model produced a hereditary dictatorship, economic collapse, and famine. In the South, constitutional republicanism and market reform produced one of the world's most dynamic economies.[13]

> *"Freedom is never more than one generation away from extinction. We didn't pass it to our children in the bloodstream."* — **Ronald Reagan**[14]

Reagan's caution finds vivid expression in the Korean experiment: one half enslaved by tyranny, the other flourishing in liberty. Their shared language and culture reveal that the difference between famine and prosperity is not fate — it is freedom.

Their divergent destinies — one imprisoned by collectivism, the other liberated by capitalism — remain one of history's clearest verdicts.

LATIN AMERICA: ROMANTIC REVOLUTION, REAL COLLAPSE

When *Fidel Castro* seized Cuba in 1959, he promised social justice and dignity. What followed was dictatorship, censorship, and dependence on Soviet aid. When those subsidies vanished in 1991, Cuba's "Special Period" exposed the bankruptcy of command economics.[15]

> *"The more the state 'plans,' the more difficult planning becomes for the individual."* — **Friedrich A. Hayek**[16]

Hayek's principle, articulated in *The Road to Serfdom* (1944), played out in Cuba and beyond. The more control communist regimes exercised, the less room their citizens had to act, think, or hope. Chile's socialist experiment under *Salvador Allende* (1970–73) ended in chaos and hyperinflation. Across Latin America, central planning led inevitably to collapse.

AFRICA: MARXISM AND MISERY

In post-colonial Africa, Marxism masqueraded as a shortcut to modernization. In Ethiopia, *Mengistu Haile Mariam's* Derg regime (1974–91) imposed collectivization, triggering famine and civil war. In Angola and Mozambique, Soviet-backed governments devastated their economies while fighting decades-long insurgencies.[17]

> *"You cannot help the poor by destroying the rich. You cannot strengthen the weak by weakening the strong."* — **Abraham Lincoln**[18]

Lincoln's timeless principle, echoed by Ronald Reagan, exposes the moral failure of socialism in Africa: by punishing success, regimes ensured poverty for all. Prosperity emerged only where markets were restored, and individuals were allowed to build their own futures.

Wherever Marxism took root in Africa, it brought hunger instead of hope. Only when nations embraced markets and private initiative did recovery begin.

THE MIDDLE EAST AND SOUTH ASIA: IMPORTED IDEOLOGY, IMPORTED FAILURE

Communism never found fertile soil in the Middle East or South Asia. In Afghanistan, the Soviet invasion of 1979 plunged the region into a decade of war and destruction. South Yemen — the Arab world's lone Marxist state — collapsed into poverty before merging with its northern neighbor in 1990.[19]

> *"The great danger is that we forget that freedom is fragile and must be defended anew by each generation."* — **Margaret Thatcher**[20]

Thatcher's warning, given in 1986, captures the lesson of the region: freedom is not inherited — it must be renewed. India's experiments with socialism produced the same failures of inefficiency and stagnation until liberalization unleashed the country's latent potential.

Only economic liberalization lifted hundreds of millions from poverty — proof that prosperity follows freedom, not central planning.

THE VERDICT OF HISTORY

Communism was not merely a philosophy; it was a century-long experiment repeated across cultures and continents. Every version — Leninist, Maoist, Castroist, or African — ended in repression, scarcity, and decay. Its failure was not the fault of geography or circumstance, but of principle.[21]

> *"The trouble with our liberal friends is not that they're ignorant; it's just that they know so much that isn't so."* — **Ronald Reagan**[22]

Reagan's remark from *A Time for Choosing* (1964) defines the tragedy of the modern Left: the refusal to learn from reality. Even after a century of ruin, many continue to believe that socialism failed only because the "wrong people" tried it.

On paper, communism and socialism seem compassionate and rational. Their promises of equality and fairness look irresistible in theory, especially to those who have never endured their practice. But they have failed everywhere they have been tried. The same policies that appear humane on paper produce misery in reality — because they deny the truths of human nature: that people respond to incentives, that freedom is the engine of innovation, and that prosperity cannot be coerced into existence.

Despite this record, the ideology endures in insulated enclaves, where its theoretical elegance floats free of consequence. It works only in seminar rooms. The world outside has already delivered its verdict.

CHAPTER 4.
CONTEMPORARY FAILURES OF SOCIALISM AND COMMUNISM

The century changed; the creed did not. Communism merely exchanged the hammer and sickle for hashtags and slogans about equity and justice. Across continents, its newest heirs repeat the same old arithmetic: control in, collapse out. Wherever the state attempts to replace human choice with command, the result is decay—moral, economic, and civic. What follows are ten living proofs that the lessons of the last hundred years remain unlearned.[1]

CASE STUDY 1 – CUBA: REVOLUTION WITHOUT RESULTS

Six decades after Castro's "triumph", the island still rations bread and blames the embargo.[2] Tourism props up a system that produces nothing but slogans. The "New Man" the revolution promised turned out to be the same exhausted citizen waiting for fuel, food, and permission. Even Cuba's doctors—once the pride of socialism—now moonlight abroad to earn real wages.

> *"Good intentions will always be pleaded for every assumption of authority. It is hardly too strong to say that the Constitution was made to guard the people against the dangers of good intentions."* — **Daniel Webster**[3]

Webster's words foretold Havana's tragedy: a revolution founded on idealism hardened into an oligarchy of excuses. Every "temporary" ration becomes permanent, every decree another lock on enterprise. Cuba demonstrates that poverty can be centrally planned.

CASE STUDY 2 – NORTH KOREA: THE LABOR CAMP NATION

No communist state has carried collectivism to greater extremes. Private life is treason; worship is reserved for the ruling bloodline.[4] The border is a prison wall, and the population survives on propaganda and smuggled grain. While elites dine in Pyongyang's showcase towers, the countryside starves in silence.

> *"When people lose the capacity to dream of freedom, they lose the capacity to be fully human."* — **Václav Havel**[5]

Havel's insight captures North Korea's central horror: it has criminalized the imagination. By extinguishing hope, the regime maintains control, but at the cost of its own soul. Even in the twenty-first century, it reminds the world that socialism's purest form is slavery with a flag.

CASE STUDY 3 – CHINA: CONTROL AS CAPITAL

China's "miracle" rests on contradiction. Markets are permitted, but only at the pleasure of the Party. Success is tolerated until it threatens authority, at which point innovation yields to intimidation. A housing collapse, mounting debt, and a shrinking workforce now expose the fragility beneath the façade of growth.[6]

> *"To live in truth costs more than to live in lies, but it is the only way to remain alive inside."* — **Aleksandr Solzhenitsyn**[7]

Solzhenitsyn's words speak to a nation that thrives on false statistics and forced optimism. When truth itself is censored, markets become mirrors—reflecting only what the state demands to see. The illusion of prosperity may endure for a time, but illusions cannot pay interest forever.

CASE STUDY 4 – VIETNAM: A MARKET IN MANACLES

After decades of collectivization and famine, Vietnam embraced limited reform through Đổi Mới. Private businesses re-emerged, foreign investment arrived, and living standards rose. Yet the Party's grip on expression and religion remains absolute. Citizens may own shops, but not opinions.[8]

> *"The greatest danger to liberty is the belief that it can be preserved without courage."* — **Pericles**[9]

Vietnam's prosperity depends on the courage of those who dare to innovate under watchful eyes. So long as fear governs thought, reform will stall. Economic liberalization without moral liberty is a transaction, not a transformation.

CASE STUDY 5 – LAOS: THE LEASED COUNTRY

Laos mirrors Vietnam's economic experiment but lacks its scale or momentum. To fund growth, it borrowed heavily from China, pledging land and infrastructure as collateral. Entire provinces function as foreign franchises, while domestic poverty deepens. A nation that once promised independence now lives on imported capital and imported control.[10]

> *"The liberty of a people is not secure when the transactions of their rulers may be concealed from them."* — **Patrick Henry**[11]

Behind every deal signed in secret lies another inch of lost sovereignty. Laos's socialism has become a brokerage of dependence, proving that when the state owns everything, foreign creditors soon own the state.

CASE STUDY 6 – VENEZUELA: REVOLUTION OF RUINS

The Bolivarian Revolution began with chants of equality and ended with ration cards. Oil revenues funded subsidies, nationalizations, and corruption until the wells ran dry and the treasury followed. Today, Venezuela exports its citizens instead of its wealth.[12]

> *"Political power, once it has become absolute, knows no limits but those it imposes upon itself—and it rarely does."*
> — **Anne Applebaum**[13]

Maduro's regime illustrates Applebaum's argument perfectly: the bureaucracy that claimed to defend the poor now defends only its privileges. Inflation is measured in wheelbarrows, and socialism survives only because starvation is cheaper than freedom.

CASE STUDY 7 – BOLIVIA: PROMISES IN THE PIT

Bolivia nationalized its gas fields and mines under the banner of "people's ownership." Revenues swelled, but productivity fell. The state spent windfalls on patronage instead of progress, and when global prices dipped, the economy sank with them. Disillusionment spread faster than the subsidies could.[14]

> *"Every revolution evaporates and leaves behind only the slime of a new bureaucracy."* — **Franz Kafka**[15]

Kafka's cynicism has become Bolivia's realism. A movement born to liberate the worker now chains him to paperwork. Ideology cannot extract ore, and committees cannot refine it.

CASE STUDY 8 – RUSSIA: RED EMPIRE, BLACK MARKET

Russia abandoned Marx but not monopoly. The state decides who may profit and who must perish. Oligarchs serve at the pleasure of power, not the discipline of law.[16] What once failed in the name of the proletariat now fails in the name of patriotism.

"Truth is treason in an empire of lies." — **Ron Paul**[17]

The Soviet archives opened; the habits remained. Corruption became heritage, and censorship evolved into a business model. Communism died, but command survived—proof that tyranny outlives its textbooks.

CASE STUDY 9 – ARGENTINA AND GREECE: THE DEBT UTOPIA

Neither nation calls itself socialist, yet both practice the arithmetic of redistribution without production. In Argentina, perpetual deficits and currency controls strangle investment. In Greece, decades of public hiring and subsidies culminated in a national bankruptcy under the euro's rigid rules.[18]

"You may delay, but time will not." — **Benjamin Franklin**[19]

Debt defers pain, but it does not erase it. These democracies reveal that socialist policy, even when wrapped in populism, ends where mathematics begins—at zero.

CASE STUDY 10 – THE WESTERN PARADOX: SOCIAL DEMOCRACY AT THE EDGE

In the wealthy democracies of Europe, socialism survives not by success but by inertia. The National Health Service in Britain groans under shortages; Scandinavian welfare models quietly privatize to remain solvent. Citizens still trust the state to provide everything, though the state can barely maintain itself.[20]

"The welfare of humanity is always the alibi of tyrants."
— **Albert Camus**[21]

Camus's discovery now describes the bureaucratic class as well as the dictator. Compassion enforced by taxation breeds resentment instead of unity. As populations age and debts climb, even the mildest forms of socialism reveal their terminal flaw: they consume the freedom that once made generosity possible.

EPILOGUE – THE LIVING DEAD

From Havana to Helsinki, ideology still outruns reality. Communism no longer conquers by armies; it seeps through policies and slogans. Yet its results are constant—rationed ambition, regulated conscience, and moral fatigue.

The truth is that communism never truly dies. It survives as a creed without a conscience—the living dead of political thought—feeding on envy, fear, and ignorance wherever liberty grows weak. Its banners may fade, but its habits endure: the belief that control can replace character, that equality can substitute for excellence, that bureaucracy can impersonate compassion.

The world does not need another revolution to prove its failure. The proof is already governing.

CHAPTER 5.
WHY CAPITALIST REPUBLICS ARE SO SUCCESSFUL

Every society rises or falls on how it answers two simple questions:

Who decides what is produced? and *Who decides who rules?*

For most of human history, the answers were the same: a small group of elites. Kings commanded production through decree, and peasants had little say in either government or economy. The marriage of capitalism and republicanism shattered that pattern. For the first time, both political and economic power were decentralized—disciplined not by dogma but by feedback: the consent of the governed and the choices of free individuals.[1]

VOLUNTARY EXCHANGE AND POLITICAL CONSENT

> *"The liberty of the individual must be thus far limited; he must not make himself a nuisance to other people."* — **John Stuart Mill**[2]

Mill's simple statement captures the genius of freedom tempered by responsibility. Capitalism and republicanism both rest on voluntary participation balanced by moral restraint.

In markets, every transaction is an act of consent—each party must agree or it doesn't happen. In republican government, every law derives legitimacy from the consent of the governed. Together they create a moral equilibrium: liberty guided by accountability.[3]

INCENTIVES AND VIRTUE

"Men are qualified for civil liberty in exact proportion to their disposition to put moral chains upon their own appetites." — **Edmund Burke**[4]

Burke's comment captures the moral core of capitalist republics. They assume that human beings are imperfect but capable of self-restraint. Profit in capitalism and power in republicanism are both fenced by law and conscience.

The system channels self-interest into productivity rather than plunder. It makes virtue profitable and corruption costly. Where socialism requires saints to run it, capitalism and republicanism flourish among ordinary people willing to work, trade, and govern themselves.[5]

INNOVATION THROUGH FREEDOM

"Discovery consists of seeing what everybody has seen and thinking what nobody has thought." — **Albert Szent-Györgyi**[6]

Freedom allows societies to aim higher. When individuals can imagine, invent, and experiment, they transform entire civilizations. The capitalist republic thrives on failure turned into discovery.

The Industrial and digital revolutions were born in free economies, not command economies. They arose where property was secure, and ideas could be tested without permission. Innovation is simply the practical expression of freedom.[7]

EQUALITY OF OPPORTUNITY, NOT OUTCOME

"Do not wish to be anything but what you are, and try to be that perfectly." — **St. Francis de Sales**[8]

True equality lies in the freedom to develop one's own potential. Capitalist republics reject both hereditary privilege and enforced uniformity. They guarantee equality before the law, not sameness of result.

By contrast, every ideology that seeks to equalize outcomes must seize control over individuals' choices. That is not equality—it is servitude disguised as fairness. Freedom does not promise equal destinies, only equal dignity.

THE MORAL DIVIDEND

"Liberty cannot be preserved without general knowledge among the people." — **John Adams**[9]

Adams's words speak directly to the moral dividend of freedom. Capitalism and republicanism succeed not because they indulge selfishness, but because they cultivate responsibility.

They foster habits of learning, thrift, and self-discipline. Citizens who must earn their living learn the link between effort and reward; voters who must choose their leaders learn the link between liberty and duty. Together, these systems elevate the human character along with the human condition.

THE HISTORICAL RECORD

"History is a vast early warning system."—**Norman Cousins**[10]

The record is clear. Nations that embraced free markets and self-government became prosperous and humane. Those that rejected them became impoverished and cruel.

Britain, the United States, Switzerland, South Korea, and Japan rose through liberty. The Soviet Union, Maoist China, and Venezuela sank under central control. Every generation forgets this at its peril; history exists to remind us what happens when it's ignored.[11]

SELF-CORRECTION AND RENEWAL

"It is the mark of an educated mind to be able to entertain a thought without accepting it."—**Aristotle**[12]

The genius of capitalist republics is that they can question themselves without collapsing. Free speech and free markets act as self-correcting mechanisms. Mistakes become lessons, not permanent scars.

When free citizens are allowed to debate and compete, error is exposed and corrected quickly. Totalitarian regimes, by contrast, preserve their lies until collapse. The republic and the market both turn truth into the ultimate regulator.

THE REAL "SYSTEMIC" ADVANTAGE

"The most dangerous phrase in any language is: 'We've always done it this way.'" — **Grace Hopper**[13]

Admiral Hopper's quip about innovation applies equally to freedom. Both capitalism and republicanism thrive on discovery and change. They rely on distributed wisdom—the countless daily decisions of ordinary people.

No central planner can replace that spontaneous order. Freedom doesn't require omniscience; it harnesses the intelligence already dispersed among millions of minds. That humility before human complexity is the true systemic advantage of the free world.[14]

THE GREAT EXPERIMENT ENDURES

"The test of progress is not whether we add more to the abundance of those who have much; it is whether we provide enough for those who have too little." — **Franklin D. Roosevelt**[15]

Roosevelt reminds us that liberty and compassion are not enemies. The free republic survives because it can reform itself without tyranny. It is flexible where despotism is brittle, honest where totalitarianism must lie.

It has survived wars, depressions, and upheavals precisely because it is built on self-correction and civic virtue, not force. It remains the most adaptable form of human civilization ever created.[16]

THE MIGRATION TEST: WHERE PEOPLE ACTUALLY WANT TO LIVE

"If you have to fence people in, it's probably not paradise."
— **Modern proverb (anonymous)**[17]

There is no stronger proof of success than where people go when they are free to choose. No one risks death crossing oceans to reach Cuba, North Korea, or the remnants of the Soviet bloc. Even nations that softened communism—like Vietnam or China—see their citizens striving to leave, not enter.

The migration tide flows unmistakably toward Western civilization, toward capitalist republics, and most of all toward the United States of America. Every year, millions seek entry not for promises of equality, but for the right to pursue their own destiny.

This is the verdict of the human race rendered without speeches, propaganda, or ideology. People run from tyranny and race toward freedom. The vote with the feet is the world's most honest election—and it proves beyond doubt the failure of communism and the triumph of the capitalist republic.[18]

CONCLUSION

"Freedom is not a gift bestowed upon us by other men, but a right that belongs to us by the laws of God and nature."
— **Benjamin Franklin**[19]

Capitalism and republicanism succeed because they take human nature as it is and elevate it through liberty and responsibility. They transform self-interest into progress, competition into cooperation, and freedom into civilization.

Every other system—monarchy, fascism, socialism, communism—has tried to replace voluntary order with coercive control, and all have failed. The free world grows stronger because it rests not on fear, but on faith in the dignity of the individual.

That is why people risk their lives to reach capitalist republics, and why none risk them to escape.

PART II

CHAPTER 6.
TEN POLICIES THAT MUST WORK FOR SOCIALISM/ COMMUNISM TO SUCCEED

Every communist experiment in history has shared a single fatal flaw: it depends on ten policies that cannot work in the real world. Each of these policies rests on a utopian vision of human nature and assumes the state can override the forces that drive prosperity—private property, free exchange, faith, family, and individuality. For communism to succeed, these ten pillars would all have to hold. They never do. Why? Because Utopia, like any form of perfection, is aspirational and can never be achieved. Because communism is counter to human nature itself.

ABOLITION OF PRIVATE PROPERTY

Karl Marx's first and most essential commandment was to abolish private property. The communist state must own all land, factories, and capital goods. The promise is equality; the result is deprivation. When individuals can no longer own what they produce, they lose the incentive to produce it. In the Soviet Union, this led to chronic shortages and a black market that mocked the official system.[1]

Property is not a flaw of capitalism—it is the foundation of liberty. Without it, every person becomes a servant of the state.

"Property is the guardian of every other right." — **James Madison**[2]

Madison understood that liberty depends on the tangible ability to own, use, and defend what one creates. Property is not merely economic—it is moral, a recognition of the individual's sovereignty. Once the state controls ownership, it controls the person.

CENTRALIZED ECONOMIC PLANNING

Communism replaces the free market with a bureaucratic machine. Prices, production, and distribution are determined not by supply and demand but by decree. The planners assume they can outthink millions of independent decisions made every day by citizens in a free economy. They never can.

The Soviet Gosplan and Mao's Five-Year Plans became monuments to inefficiency and waste.[3] No government can compute the infinite data of human wants and resources. As Friedrich Hayek warned, central planning inevitably leads to tyranny because only force can enforce economic conformity.

> *"Nothing is so permanent as a temporary government program."* — **Milton Friedman**[4]

Friedman revealed how state control grows beyond its promises and never retreats. What begins as reform becomes permanence, and the bureaucracy that was meant to serve soon demands obedience. Central planning breeds stagnation precisely because it cannot admit error or relinquish power.

FORCED ECONOMIC EQUALITY

Communism seeks to equalize wealth by redistributing income until everyone is the same. This destroys the link between effort and reward. When doctors, farmers, and factory workers receive the same compensation regardless of output, excellence withers.

Even Lenin conceded that once "everyone gets the same pay," the incentive to work vanishes.[5] The inevitable result is a decline in productivity followed by coercion to make people work harder. Equality by force breeds only resentment and decay.

"A society that puts equality before freedom will get neither. A society that puts freedom before equality will get a high degree of both." — **Milton Friedman**[6]

Friedman grasped that freedom is the soil from which fairness grows. When governments attempt to manufacture equality through compulsion, they destroy the very freedom that makes prosperity possible. True equality is earned through opportunity, not decree.

ABOLITION OF PROFIT AND COMPETITION

Profit in a free-market signals value. It tells producers what consumers want and drives innovation. Communism abolishes profit as "exploitation" and replaces it with political quotas. Without profit or competition, mediocrity flourishes.

In every planned economy, from Cuba to North Korea, productivity collapsed once profit was outlawed.[7] Competition disappears, and with it, the motivation to improve.

"If you see a man approaching you with the obvious intent of doing you good, you should run for your life." — **Henry David Thoreau**[8]

Thoreau's cynicism speaks directly to the danger of benevolent tyranny. Those who claim to perfect society through control often end up crippling it. Human progress depends on voluntary exchange and ambition, not forced altruism.

COLLECTIVE OWNERSHIP OF AGRICULTURE

Communists believe pooling land into collective farms will yield abundance through "scientific" cooperation. Instead, collectivization has always led to famine. The Ukrainian Holodomor, Mao's Great Leap Forward, and Cambodia's killing fields all proved that forced collectivism starves the people it claims to serve.[9]

Farmers who own nothing have no reason to plant, cultivate, or innovate. Food production plummets, and the state must resort to terror to seize grain from starving peasants.

"You can't eat slogans." —**Aleksandr Solzhenitsyn**[10]

Solzhenitsyn laid bare the futility of ideology divorced from reality. No amount of revolutionary rhetoric can substitute for personal effort or ownership. When the plow is politicized, hunger follows.

SUPPRESSION OF RELIGION AND FAMILY LOYALTY

To control the soul, communism must destroy the institutions that nourish it. Faith and family anchor the conscience and stand as rival authorities to the state. The Bolsheviks outlawed church schools and persecuted clergy. Mao's Red Guards forced children to denounce their parents. The result was moral desolation.[11]

Without faith and family, people become easier to manipulate but harder to inspire. Communism produces conformity, not community.

"When men forget God, tyrants forge their chains." — **Patrick Henry**[12]

Henry captured the truth that moral freedom begins with spiritual allegiance, not political loyalty. A people that ceases to look upward inevitably bows to earthly masters. Communism replaces reverence with fear and destroys the moral spine of society.

ELIMINATION OF FREE EXPRESSION AND DISSENT

Because communism depends on ideological unity, it must silence those who disagree. Truth becomes whatever the Party says it is. Censorship, secret police, and propaganda replace open debate. In the USSR, speaking one's mind could mean a one-way trip to the Gulag.[13]

Free speech is not merely a political right—it is the safety valve of civilization. Without it, corruption festers and reality itself becomes a lie.

> *"To learn who rules over you, simply find out who you are not allowed to criticize."*—**Voltaire (attributed)**[14]

The sentiment reminds us that tyranny thrives on silence. When speech is restricted, truth becomes contraband. A society that fears honest words will soon lose the capacity for honest thought.

CREATION OF THE "NEW SOCIALIST MAN"

Communist theory insists that human beings can be remade—stripped of self-interest and made to serve the collective. Marx called this the birth of a "new man." But the human spirit is not clay. It resists manipulation. Every attempt to remake mankind has led to psychological collapse, fear, and rebellion.[15]

The "new man" never appears; only broken people remain, haunted by the impossible standards of the ideology that crushed them.

> *"Human nature must be taken as we find it, not as we might wish it to be."* — **James Madison**[16]

Madison saw that systems must adapt to humanity, not the reverse. The effort to perfect mankind through politics leads only to suffering. Liberty accepts imperfection; tyranny demands transformation.

PERMANENT CLASS WARFARE

Because communism depends on the idea of an eternal struggle between oppressors and oppressed, it must continually invent new enemies to justify its power. The revolution never ends—it only turns inward. The "bourgeoisie" become "kulaks," then "counterrevolutionaries," then anyone who doubts the Party line.[17]

Every purge strengthens the state but weakens the nation. A society perpetually at war with itself cannot build or endure.

"Those who make peaceful revolution impossible will make violent revolution inevitable." — **John F. Kennedy**[18]

Kennedy's words reveal the self-destructive logic of total control. When reform and dissent are outlawed, rebellion becomes the only language left. Suppression breeds the very chaos it claims to prevent.

BELIEF IN UTOPIA THROUGH COERCION

Communism promises paradise but delivers prison. It assumes perfection can be forced into existence by the state's power. In practice, coercion becomes the only way to maintain "equality." Surveillance, censorship, and violence replace freedom and faith.[19]

Utopia through coercion is a contradiction in terms. The more force applied, the farther the dream recedes.

"Utopias rest on the belief that we can make heaven on earth—but we cannot even make peace on earth." — **Winston Churchill**[20]

Churchill understood that human progress depends on humility before the limits of man. The attempt to build heaven by force turns earth into a graveyard. Freedom, not perfection, is the highest political good.

For communism to succeed, these ten policies must function perfectly and simultaneously. Not one has ever done so. Each requires a denial of human nature, freedom, and the moral order on which civilization depends. The ruins of the Soviet Union, Mao's China, and countless smaller experiments all bear witness to this truth: wherever these policies take root, liberty dies and misery spreads.

This chapter sets the foundation for what follows—the ten great failures of communism and socialism in practice. The dream collapses under its own weight, leaving behind a warning to every generation that freedom, not force, is the only system that endures.

CHAPTER 7.
WHY THE ABOLITION OF PRIVATE PROPERTY WILL NEVER WORK

Few ideas have promised paradise and delivered ruin as reliably as the abolition of private property. From Marx's proclamations in the Communist Manifesto[1] to the collectivist experiments of Lenin, Mao, and Pol Pot, each attempt to erase ownership has ended in destruction, famine, and tyranny. The pattern is neither accidental nor cultural—it is the inevitable result of denying human nature, economic law, and moral truth.

THE PSYCHOLOGICAL DIMENSION: HUMAN NATURE AND OWNERSHIP

Private property is not a social invention; it is a reflection of human instinct. The desire to own, to protect, and to improve what is one's own runs deeper than any political theory. It binds effort to reward and gives dignity to labor. When ownership is stripped away, so too is the sense of responsibility that drives human progress.

> *"The utopian schemes of leveling and redistribution... only make the rich poor and the poor more miserable."* — **Frédéric Bastiat**[2]

Bastiat's observation uncovers the moral vanity of forced equality. His warning reminds us that redistribution cannot create happiness—it only spreads despair. From childhood, human beings recognize what is theirs. They fight to protect it and take pride in creating value. When a system seeks to erase that bond by declaring everything "collective," it erases a vital piece of human identity. The Soviet collective farms[3] and Mao's "people's communes"[4] both failed for precisely this reason. When effort and reward are severed, care and productivity vanish. Psychologically, the abolition of property demands the abolition of the self. Yet no regime, however ruthless, has ever managed to rewire human nature. People will always cling to what is theirs because ownership is part of who they are.

THE ECONOMIC DIMENSION: INCENTIVES AND EFFICIENCY

An economy without private property cannot function because it destroys the very mechanism of motivation. When everything belongs to the state, no one has a reason to work harder, innovate, or maintain quality. The result is not equality but universal poverty.

"You cannot multiply wealth by dividing it."—**Adrian Rogers**[5]

Rogers' words strike at the heart of socialist folly. Wealth cannot be created by redistribution; it must be produced. When property is abolished, markets disappear, and with them, the prices that measure supply and demand. Ludwig von Mises called this the "economic calculation problem."[6] Without private ownership, a planner has no way to know what to produce, how much, or at what cost. That is why every socialist experiment—whether in the Soviet Union, Maoist China, or Cuba[7]—has led to the same result: scarcity and stagnation. Even under threat of punishment, black markets spring to life because people instinctively rebuild the private exchanges they were denied. Property is not an economic preference; it is an economic necessity.

THE HISTORICAL DIMENSION: LESSONS FROM FAILURE

Every major attempt to abolish private property has ended in coercion and bloodshed. The Soviet Union's "War Communism" starved millions[8] before Lenin was forced to retreat through limited private ownership under the New Economic Policy. Mao's collectivization of agriculture produced the deadliest famine in recorded history.[9] Cambodia's Khmer Rouge eliminated money, markets, and property entirely—along with a quarter of its population.[10]

> *"Property rights and personal rights are the same thing."* — **Calvin Coolidge**[11]

Coolidge's statement gets to the core of what history teaches: the destruction of property always leads to the destruction of freedom. When a government claims the right to confiscate what its citizens own, it inevitably claims the right to control their lives. America's 19th-century utopian communes like New Harmony and Brook Farm collapsed not because their members lacked idealism, but because their ideals ignored the law of human incentive. In contrast, the societies that respected ownership—Britain, the United States, and postwar West Germany—built prosperity and stability. The right to own is inseparable from the right to live freely.

THE MORAL DIMENSION: PROPERTY AS LIBERTY

To abolish private property is not only impractical—it is immoral. Ownership forms the moral boundary between the individual and the state. Without it, every person becomes a ward of government, dependent and powerless.

> *"The right to life has little meaning if the right to property is denied."* — **Margaret Thatcher**[12]

Thatcher's statement lays bare the hypocrisy of socialist compassion. A government that seizes what people earn in the name of "equity" robs them of the ability to sustain and define their own lives. Communism claims to lift humanity up, yet it reduces the citizen to a servant of the collective. The slogan "From each according to his ability, to each according to his needs" only masks the power of those who decide what ability and need mean. John Locke understood centuries earlier that property is an expression of liberty: the moment a man's labor ceases to be his own, his freedom ceases as well.[13]

CONCLUSION: THE INESCAPABLE LAW OF OWNERSHIP

The abolition of private property will never work because it defies both human nature and divine order. It severs the link between effort and reward, authority and responsibility, liberty and dignity. Every attempt to erase property has required force, deception, and terror—and still, people resist.

> *"Property must be secured, or liberty cannot exist."* — **John Adams**[14]

Adams' words summarize the lesson of every failed socialist experiment: the protection of property is the first defense of freedom. Where property is secure, citizens are free. Where it is abolished, tyranny fills the void. Private ownership is not a barrier to equality; it is the foundation of civilization itself.

CHAPTER 8.
WHY CENTRAL PLANNING WILL NEVER WORK

THE ILLUSION OF CONTROL

Every generation is tempted by the same promise: that if only the right experts ran the economy, they could design prosperity. Central planning offers order, fairness, and efficiency by replacing millions of individual choices with a single blueprint. It appeals to the intellectual vanity of those who believe society can be engineered as easily as a machine.

But it fails because no one knows enough. An economy is not a mechanism to be wound and measured; it is a living web of human action. Replace voluntary exchange with commands, and the system begins to decay.

> *"He seems to imagine that he can arrange the different members of a great society with as much ease as the hand arranges the different pieces upon a chess-board; he does not consider that...the pieces upon the chess-board have no other principle of motion besides that which the hand impresses upon them; but that, in the great chess-board of human society, every single piece has a principle of motion of its own."* — **Adam Smith**[1]

The examination is timeless. Central planners see people as pieces, not as self-directing beings. Yet every individual acts according to personal judgment, ambition, and circumstance. The moment that freedom is denied, the vitality of a nation dies with it.

THE INFORMATION PROBLEM

In a free economy, prices are signals. They carry within them the hidden knowledge of scarcity, demand, and opportunity. When governments fix prices or dictate production, those signals vanish. Guesswork replaces discovery.

> *"Where there is no free market, there is no pricing mechanism; without a pricing mechanism, there is no economic calculation."* — **Ludwig von Mises**[2]

That truth exposes the fatal blindness of command economies. When the state abolishes markets, it abolishes the only language through which economic reality can be known. Without authentic prices, planners cannot tell whether they are creating value or wasting resources. History's record of empty shelves and false statistics is not the result of bad luck—it is the unavoidable consequence of planning without knowledge.

THE INCENTIVE PROBLEM

Markets reward accuracy and punish error. Central planning rewards obedience. Bureaucrats climb by loyalty, not merit. Managers meet quotas that measure effort but not usefulness. When all risk is socialized, mediocrity becomes policy.

> *"It is hard to imagine a more stupid or more dangerous way of making decisions than by putting those decisions in the hands of people who pay no price for being wrong."*
> — **Thomas Sowell**[3]

The quote encapsulates the moral vacuum at the core of every planned system. When error carries no cost, truth becomes irrelevant. Decisions multiply without accountability until the entire structure serves itself rather than the people it claims to protect.

Those who make decisions under central planning pay no personal price for being wrong. The bureaucratic machine learns nothing, because it cannot fail honestly. Without responsibility, truth becomes irrelevant, and productivity gives way to performance theater.

THE COMPLEXITY AND TACIT-KNOWLEDGE PROBLEM

Most of what keeps an economy running is tacit knowledge—the unspoken skill of workers, farmers, builders, engineers, and entrepreneurs who adapt minute-by-minute to new conditions. Their judgment cannot be written into a five-year plan or captured by a central computer.

> *"We can know more than we can tell."*—**Michael Polanyi**[4]

That insight destroys the planner's conceit. Data can be collected; wisdom cannot. The success of free societies lies in their ability to let millions act on what they know locally and personally. The more a system relies on central command, the less it can adapt. The economy becomes brittle precisely because it is over-controlled.

THE MORAL AND POLITICAL COST

To make one plan binding on all, the state must extend its control from production to property, from property to speech, and from speech to conscience. Economic power and political power merge into one. The result is uniformity enforced by fear.

> *"The poor have houses but not titles; crops but not deeds."*
> — **Hernando de Soto**[5]

The tragedy behind that truth is that without ownership, there is no freedom. When the state owns everything, the citizen owns nothing—not his labor, not his home, not even his silence. Property is more than an economic institution; it is the moral boundary between the individual and the state.

The right to own, to choose, and to dissent are inseparable from the right to live as a free person.

THE HISTORICAL VERDICT

Across cultures and continents, command economies have followed the same grim path—shortages, corruption, stagnation, and collapse. From Moscow to Havana to Caracas, the pattern never changes.

"The socialist economy is a shortage economy." — **János Kornai**[6]

That was not a metaphor but a diagnosis. Shortage is not a temporary flaw of socialism—it is its natural condition. When prices are fixed and production is dictated, demand always exceeds supply. Black markets thrive, connections replace competence, and cynicism becomes survival. Only when nations abandon the plan do they recover. Britain, India, and China all discovered that prosperity returns only when liberty returns with it.[7]

THE NEW TECHNOLOGICAL TEMPTATION

Today's social engineers claim that new technology will finally make central planning work. With artificial intelligence, big data, and endless surveillance, they believe they can process the information that confounded their predecessors. But the same law still holds: no system, no matter how sophisticated, can anticipate the infinite creativity of free people.[8]

Algorithms describe the past; liberty invents the future. A society that trades freedom for coordination gains neither. Technology can amplify freedom, but it cannot redeem coercion.[9, 10]

CONCLUSION: WHY IT WILL NEVER WORK

Central planning will never work because it denies the nature of humanity itself. It assumes people are predictable, knowledge is static, and virtue can be commanded. Markets may appear messy, but they learn. Plans appear tidy, but they break.

Freedom is not disorder; it is self-ordering. It is the only system flexible enough to absorb change without violence. Every nation that has trusted the planner has found poverty; every nation that has trusted its people has found progress.

The only sustainable plan is the plan for liberty itself.

CHAPTER 9.
WHY FORCED ECONOMIC EQUALITY WILL NEVER WORK

Every revolution that promises equality begins with noble words and ends with force. The dream of economic sameness has always sounded humane—a world without envy or want—but it can only be achieved through government compulsion. When the state takes it upon itself to level outcomes, it must first seize control of who earns, who keeps, and who spends. That is not justice; that is tyranny disguised as virtue.[1]

> *"The man who builds a factory builds a temple; the man who works there worships there."* — **Calvin Coolidge**[2]

Coolidge understood that productive work is sacred, not shameful. To confiscate its reward is to desecrate that temple. Equality enforced by law does not elevate the worker; it merely tears down the builder.

THE DESTRUCTION OF INCENTIVE

Forced equality kills the will to achieve. When success is punished and failure subsidized, human energy withers. People work less, risk less, and dream smaller because the fruits of their labor no longer belong to them.[3]

> *"Envy was once considered one of the seven deadly sins—before it became one of the most admired virtues under its new name, 'social justice.'"*— **Thomas Sowell**[4]

Sowell's judgment describes the moral decay at the heart of enforced equality. What begins as compassion soon becomes legalized envy, stripping incentive from the very people whose ambition sustains a nation's prosperity.

THE ILLUSION OF PLANNING

Every centralized scheme rests on the fantasy that a handful of bureaucrats can know what millions of free citizens need and desire. But the economy is not a machine—it is a living network of human choices. Once government interferes to engineer equality, it breaks the very mechanisms that create abundance.[5]

> *"The curious task of economics is to demonstrate to men how little they really know about what they imagine they can design."*— **Friedrich Hayek**[6]

Hayek's admission reminds us that arrogance, not ignorance, drives collectivism. Planners cannot design prosperity because prosperity is the product of freedom, not direction.

THE MYTH OF SAMENESS

Human beings are not interchangeable. Each possesses different talents, desires, and levels of effort. To force identical outcomes is to deny human nature itself.

> *"It is not from the benevolence of the butcher, the brewer, or the baker that we expect our dinner, but from their regard to their own interest."*— **Adam Smith**[7]

Smith's insight remains economic scripture. People contribute most when allowed to pursue their own goals. Erase self-interest, and production collapses; reward it, and prosperity spreads. Forced equality punishes the very impulses that make progress possible.

THE RISE OF A NEW ELITE

Equality enforced by power always creates new masters. When the state gains authority to decide what is "fair," it also gains authority to decide who is deserving. Bureaucrats, party officials, and favored groups rise above the masses they claim to defend.

> *"Men are seldom guilty of a deliberate choice of evil; but when they fail in understanding, they mistake evil for good."*— **Alexis de Tocqueville**[8]

Tocqueville anticipated that democratic societies could slide into "soft despotism," where leaders impose equality for the people's supposed good. Their intentions may sound moral, but the result is servitude in the name of fairness.

THE RECORD OF REALITY

Every nation that has tried to legislate economic equality has suffered the same fate: stagnation, scarcity, and oppression. The Soviet Union promised fairness and delivered famine. Mao's China promised dignity and delivered death. Cuba and Venezuela promised justice and delivered poverty.[9] The lesson is universal—when government tries to equalize wealth, it equalizes despair.

> *"The natural progress of things is for liberty to yield and government to gain ground."*— **Thomas Jefferson**[10]

Jefferson's suspicion explains the pattern. Equality by decree demands control, and control consumes liberty until nothing remains but dependence.

FREEDOM, NOT FORCE

True equality in a free republic is equality of opportunity—equal rights under the law and before God. That equality is the soil in which merit, industry, and charity can grow. Government should guard that soil, not plow it under in pursuit of utopia.

"The end of law is not to abolish or restrain, but to preserve and enlarge freedom."— **John Locke**[11]

Locke's principle remains the heart of Western liberty. The purpose of law is protection, not provision. When law becomes the instrument of redistribution, it ceases to preserve freedom and begins to erase it.[12]

CONCLUSION

Forced economic equality will never work because it must destroy freedom to exist. It demands obedience in place of effort, envy in place of excellence, and sameness in place of justice. History has rendered its verdict, and human nature will never overturn it. True equality is moral equality—our shared dignity before the Creator and the law. Everything beyond that must be earned, or it ceases to have value. Freedom, not force, is the only foundation on which prosperity and justice can stand.

CHAPTER 10.
WHY SUPPRESSION OF COMPETITION AND PROFIT WILL NEVER WORK

> *"Competition is not only the basis of protection to the consumer, but is the incentive to progress."*— **Herbert Hoover**[1]

Herbert Hoover's assertion remains timeless. He understood that competition is not cruelty—it is protection. It guards the consumer from exploitation and keeps the producer honest. Where competition thrives, so does progress. Where it is suppressed, corruption and stagnation follow. His words frame the lesson that this chapter proves again and again: freedom in commerce is inseparable from freedom itself.[2]

THE ILLUSION OF A WORLD WITHOUT GREED

Throughout history, there has been a recurring temptation to imagine that mankind could build a just society by abolishing profit and suppressing competition. From the outside, this dream looks merciful and humane. If no one could "win" more than anyone else, surely no one would "lose." To its advocates, profit represents greed, and competition represents cruelty.[3]

But this dream is a mirage. When profit is outlawed and competition is smothered, what follows is not harmony but decay. In every nation that has tried to abolish the incentives that drive human progress, production has slowed, innovation has ceased, and the pursuit of excellence has been replaced with the pursuit of permission.[4] Profit and competition are not corruptions of human nature; they are its natural expressions—the economic equivalents of free speech and free thought. They are how a free people discover, adapt, and improve.

PROFIT: THE SIGNAL THAT KEEPS CIVILIZATION RUNNING

Profit, despite being despised by those who misunderstand it, is not merely a reward—it is a message. Every profit earned in a free market is an encoded signal that someone has created something others value. Losses, by contrast, are warnings that resources are being wasted or misused. Together, these signals form an intricate feedback system that no government, planner, or committee can ever replicate.[5]

When that feedback is suppressed, the system begins to fail. Factories produce what nobody wants, while real needs go unmet. Workers labor harder and earn less, because there is no measure of efficiency or value left to guide them. It is not morality that disappears when profit vanishes—it is meaning.

Economist Friedrich Hayek called this the "knowledge problem." The vast information required to coordinate an economy—the preferences of consumers, the costs of materials, the possibilities of technology—exists only in millions of separate minds. Prices and profits communicate that knowledge faster than any planner could collect it. When those signals are silenced, ignorance becomes official policy.[6]

> *"When men are free to compete, progress is guaranteed."*—
> **Barry Goldwater**[7]

Barry Goldwater's comprehension connects directly to this truth. He recognized that competition is the engine of discovery, not a moral evil. When freedom and enterprise are joined, progress is inevitable; when they are separated, decline soon follows.

COMPETITION: THE DISCIPLINE OF FREEDOM

Competition, like freedom itself, can be uncomfortable. It exposes weakness, punishes laziness, and rewards those willing to work harder and think smarter. But in that discomfort lies the strength of civilization. It is the only force that continuously weeds out inefficiency and rewards ingenuity. Without it, complacency and privilege take root.[8]

When a government suppresses competition, it does not remove rivalry—it merely changes its form. People still compete, but no longer to serve the public; they compete to please bureaucrats. Influence replaces innovation, and advancement becomes a function of loyalty, not merit. The result is a society where corruption is not an aberration—it is the system itself.[9]

History offers the same verdict time and again: in the absence of competition, quality declines, productivity falters, and the spirit of enterprise is replaced by the obedience of the ruled. There can be no genuine progress where failure is impossible and success is punished.[10]

WHEN MARKETS ARE TURNED OFF, POLITICS TAKES OVER

To suppress competition and profit is to declare that economics must be ruled by politics. Once that line is crossed, the measure of worth ceases to be productivity and becomes proximity to power. Instead of entrepreneurs, a new class of courtiers emerges—those who thrive not by creating wealth, but by redistributing it to the politically favored.[11]

This is why every society that has sought to eliminate market forces has ended up erecting political hierarchies even more unjust than the economic ones they replaced. The new elites are not the most efficient producers or the most imaginative creators; they are the best at maneuvering through the maze of privilege. In this way, socialism and communism never abolish inequality—they merely sanctify it under another banner.

"If you want to make the poor richer, you don't make the rich poorer—you make the system freer."— **Milton Friedman**[12]

Milton Friedman's point could serve as the summary of this entire section. Prosperity cannot be decreed into existence; it must be earned through freedom. The poor do not rise when others are pulled down—they rise when opportunity expands, and only competition and profit make such expansion possible.

THE KNOWLEDGE PROBLEM MADE FLESH

The philosopher's dream of perfect equality runs aground on an unchangeable fact: no single person or council can ever possess enough knowledge to allocate resources for millions.[21] What should be produced, how much, where, and for whom—these are not static questions. They change daily with every human need and invention.[13]

In market economies, prices and profits perform this impossible coordination automatically. In planned economies, it must be done by command. The result, inevitably, is mismatch: overproduction of some goods, shortages of others, and endless queues for necessities.[14] Hayek's insight remains undefeated—knowledge in society is decentralized, and only freedom allows it to function.

HISTORY'S REPEATED LESSON

The twentieth century stands as the most expensive experiment in human history. The Soviet Union, in abolishing private profit and outlawing competition, proved not that socialism could build utopia, but that it could only build scarcity. Its factories produced weapons of war but not enough bread to feed its people. Hungarian economist János Kornai described it as a "shortage economy"—a system where queues were permanent and progress was prohibited.[15]

Venezuela followed the same road a generation later, imposing price controls and confiscating private enterprises in the name of equality. The result was hyperinflation, starvation, and mass emigration. Millions fled the very paradise they had been promised.[16]

Even in mixed economies, whenever profit is punished or competition is strangled by overregulation, vitality fades. When innovators are told their reward will be confiscated, they stop innovating. When businesses cannot compete freely, productivity declines. And when productivity declines, it is the working class—not the wealthy—that suffers most.

> *"Freedom and free enterprise are not values to be traded for comfort; they are the conditions of human dignity."*— **William F. Buckley Jr.**[17]

Buckley's reflection defines the moral dimension of this truth. Freedom is not a negotiable convenience; it is the condition that allows human dignity to exist. When enterprise is strangled in pursuit of comfort, both prosperity and dignity disappear together.

INNOVATION CANNOT SURVIVE WITHOUT UPSIDE

Every great leap forward in human progress has been driven by someone willing to risk failure for the chance of success. Profit is the mechanism that rewards that courage. When states cap rewards or seize the fruits of enterprise, they extinguish the very fire that powers civilization. Innovation becomes dangerous, and conformity becomes safe.[18]

Modern research confirms what common sense already knows: competition fosters better management, productivity, and adaptability. The more freely people can compete, the faster societies grow. Suppress profit, and you suppress the very incentive that turns imagination into reality.[19]

THE MORAL COST OF SUPPRESSION

Beyond economics, there lies a deeper moral cost. When a state controls who may profit and who may compete, it controls who may live freely. People cease to be citizens and become clients. Permission replaces opportunity. Freedom becomes conditional, granted or withdrawn by the ruling class.[20]

This is the true cruelty of systems that suppress competition and profit: they not only impoverish the body but also enslave the mind. The man who cannot choose his work, his price, or his reward is not a free man—he is property of the state.

> *"The great danger to freedom is the concentration of power—economic or political—in the hands of the few."*— **Ronald Reagan**[21]

Reagan's warning explains why suppression always decays into tyranny. When economic control and political power merge, there are no checks left—only masters and dependents. Competition disperses power; socialism concentrates it. The more tightly power is held, the more freedom withers.

CONCLUSION: THE LAW OF LIBERTY

The suppression of competition and profit is not merely an economic mistake—it is a rebellion against human nature. It denies the reality that people are not identical, that creativity is unpredictable, and that ambition, when channeled through freedom, lifts everyone. Every attempt to erase those forces ends not in equality, but in misery.[22]

Profit and competition, rightly understood, are the law of liberty applied to economics. They are the invisible constitution of free societies—the guarantors that effort will be rewarded and failure will not be final. They keep government honest by giving citizens the means to build without permission. They keep society dynamic by ensuring that tomorrow need not be like yesterday.[23]

Communism and socialism try to cage these forces, believing they can direct them better than the millions of minds that create them. But the law of liberty always reasserts itself. Markets reopen, entrepreneurs return, and freedom revives—because no ideology, however disciplined, can suppress forever the human desire to strive, to improve, and to create.[24]

CHAPTER 11.
WHY FORCED COLLECTIVIZATION WILL NEVER WORK

Every collectivist revolution begins with the same promise: that by pooling all property and labor, humanity will finally abolish inequality and waste. Yet every forced collectivization ends in failure, hunger, and despair. The reason is not poor execution but a fatal misunderstanding of human nature. Productivity, initiative, and stewardship cannot be commanded from above; they flourish only where freedom and ownership meet.[1]

> *"The urge to save humanity is almost always only a false-face for the urge to rule it."* — **H. L. Mencken**[2]

Mencken's revelation exposes the true impulse behind collectivization. Its advocates cloak control in compassion. What begins as a promise to "save" the people ends as a mechanism to rule them.

THE INCENTIVE AND KNOWLEDGE PROBLEM

In a free economy, every farmer acts on intimate local knowledge—soil, weather, experience, and need. Collectivization severs this lifeline. When distant bureaucrats dictate what to plant and when to harvest, they replace millions of adaptive minds with one rigid will.[3] The result is predictable: waste, low yields, and apathy. When everyone receives the same reward regardless of effort, the incentive to excel disappears.

RESISTANCE, SABOTAGE, AND THE COLLAPSE OF TRUST

No people willingly surrender the fruits of their labor. When collectivization arrives, farmers resist—some hide grain, others slaughter livestock rather than surrender it to the state.[4] The Soviet Union's peasants did exactly that in 1930–31.[5] Stalin answered with arrests, deportations, and terror.[6] The result was social disintegration. Families turned on one another, neighbors informed on neighbors, and the moral cohesion of the countryside dissolved.

EXTRACTION OVER PRODUCTION

The stated goal of collectivization is efficiency; its real outcome is extraction.[7] The state demands quotas of grain to feed cities, armies, or export contracts, while leaving rural families to starve. When quotas are unmet, punishment follows. Crops are seized for "the common good," even if it means the farmers themselves perish.[8] Such extraction does not create wealth—it consumes it. The Soviet, Chinese, and Cambodian experiences all proved the same rule: when a government confiscates the means of survival, it soon confiscates survival itself.

> *"We have learned that when a government declares a war on poverty, it is usually the poor who lose."* — **Ronald Reagan**[9]

Reagan's thought portrays the tragedy perfectly. Every "war on poverty" waged by collectivist regimes has ended by destroying the very people it claimed to save.

THE HUMAN COST

Forced collectivization is not merely inefficient—it is lethal. In Ukraine, Stalin's policies produced the Holodomor, a famine that killed millions.[10] In Kazakhstan, collectivization obliterated nomadic life and reduced the population by nearly one-third.[11] Mao's Great Leap Forward repeated the tragedy, killing tens of millions more through famine and policy error.[12] Each catastrophe followed the same pattern: the plan was perfect on paper, and therefore reality had to be wrong. Those who questioned it were imprisoned or executed.

> *"When plunder becomes a way of life for a group of men in society, they create for themselves a legal system that authorizes it and a moral code that glorifies it."* — **Frédéric Bastiat**[13]

Bastiat's words display the moral inversion at the heart of collectivization. It sanctifies theft and calls it justice. What was once crime becomes law; what was once virtue becomes resistance.

BUREAUCRACY, CORRUPTION, AND FEAR

Collectivization requires an army of administrators—inspectors, quota-setters, and enforcers. Paper replaces productivity. Every failure adds another layer of oversight. Corruption spreads: officials falsify reports to protect themselves; citizens falsify output to survive.[14] The bureaucratic state becomes both parasite and jailer, feeding on the very people it claims to serve. It grows not by producing but by punishing—tightening its grip each time results fall short.

MORAL AND CULTURAL EROSION

Beyond economics lies moral decay. The family farm teaches responsibility, thrift, and pride of ownership. Collectivization replaces those virtues with dependency and fear. When all property belongs to the state, gratitude supplants ambition; initiative gives way to obedience. Over time, the collectivized village forgets how to work for itself. The tragedy of the fields becomes the tragedy of the soul. A people who once lived by their own labor now survive only by permission.

THE MYTH OF BETTER IMPLEMENTATION

Apologists insist collectivization could succeed "if only it were done right." Yet the contradiction cannot be resolved.[15] You cannot abolish private ownership and still expect private diligence. You cannot erase local knowledge and expect efficiency. You cannot rule by threat and expect creativity. The system fails not because it was poorly applied but because it is conceptually impossible. Men who imagine they can design perfection always end by designing oppression.

COMPARATIVE LESSONS

Wherever collectivization was imposed—the Soviet Union, China, Eastern Europe, or Cambodia—it produced hunger, decline, and eventual retreat.[16] Even in Poland and Hungary, where resistance was widespread, collectivization collapsed once coercion eased. The moment property was restored to families, yields and morale recovered. Freedom, not force, proved to be the fertilizer of prosperity.[17]

CONCLUSION

Forced collectivization violates every law of human nature and economics.[18] It extinguishes incentive, destroys trust, and replaces voluntary cooperation with terror. No ideology can overcome the truth that people care most for what they own. Liberty, not compulsion, remains the only lasting foundation of plenty.

> *"It is easy to be conspicuously compassionate when others are forced to pay the cost."* — **Murray N. Rothbard**[19]

Rothbard's assessment defines the collectivist paradox—compassion by compulsion is not virtue; it is theft disguised as mercy. The lesson is eternal: no state that robs individuals of ownership can ever feed them, much less free them.

CHAPTER 12.

WHY SUPPRESSION OF RELIGION AND FAMILY LOYALTY WILL NEVER WORK

Communist regimes, from the Soviet Union to Maoist China, have always sought to replace religion and family with the Party.[1] The reasoning seems simple enough: loyalty divided between the State and other institutions—especially moral and spiritual ones—threatens total control. But the deeper truth, rooted in human nature itself, is that such suppression is doomed to fail. Religion and family are not artificial constructs that can be engineered away; they are organic extensions of human identity. Attempts to destroy them always end up destroying the societies that try.[2]

THE RELIGIOUS INSTINCT: HUMANITY'S UNQUENCHABLE FLAME

Humans are meaning-seeking creatures. Every culture that has ever existed—no matter how primitive or advanced—has formed some belief in a higher order. Whether called God, the divine, nature's law, or moral truth, this instinct for transcendence cannot be legislated out of existence.

> *"When men choose not to believe in God, they do not thereafter believe in nothing, they then become capable of believing in anything."* — **G.K. Chesterton**[2]

Chesterton's acuity cuts to the heart of why communist suppression of religion always backfires. When faith in God is destroyed, faith in something else—often the State—rushes to fill the void. The Soviet and Chinese attempts to eliminate religion did not yield atheism in its pure sense; they simply created new religions of political idolatry, where Marx replaced Moses and Lenin replaced Christ.[3]

> *"Freedom prospers when religion is vibrant and the rule of law under God is acknowledged."* — **Ronald Reagan**[4]

Reagan's words reflect a timeless truth: the vitality of freedom depends on the vitality of faith. Religion reminds citizens that moral authority does not begin and end with government. A society that rejects God must either descend into chaos or elevate the State as a substitute deity.

THE FAMILY: HUMANITY'S FIRST AND LAST INSTITUTION

Before there was a State, there was a family. The family unit—father, mother, and children—is the original network of loyalty and love. It's where morality, trust, and cooperation are learned. For that reason, collectivist systems have always viewed it as a rival.[5]

> *"As the family goes, so goes the nation, and so goes the whole world in which we live."* — **Pope John Paul II**[6]

Pope John Paul II, who saw communism's destruction of family life firsthand in Poland, understood that civilization rises and falls on the strength of its families. When communism replaces parental love with ideological loyalty, it severs the very bonds that teach compassion and responsibility.

> *"Communism has never concealed the fact that it wants to abolish the family."* — **Karl Marx, The Communist Manifesto**[7]

Marx admitted openly that the family must be abolished for communism to succeed. The Party could not command full loyalty while citizens still owed love and duty to their own kin. But that policy proved fatal. When the family disintegrates, society disintegrates.

THE MORAL LAW: OLDER THAN THE STATE

Religious and familial bonds are not arbitrary—they express something ancient and moral within human nature. Even people who claim to reject religion instinctively appeal to moral principles.

> *"A nation that forgets its past has no future."* — **Winston Churchill**[8]

Churchill's wisdom applies here: a society that forgets the moral and spiritual foundations of its past cannot endure. Communism tried to erase that past—its faith, its moral codes, its traditions—and in doing so, severed itself from the very roots of civilization.

THE HUMAN COST OF SUPPRESSION

The attempt to suppress religion and family loyalty leaves psychological and cultural ruins. In the USSR, generations grew up with a hollow sense of purpose. In China and North Korea, attempts to replace God and family with ideology have only bred despair and blind worship of the State.[9]

> *"Those who seek absolute power, even though they seek it to do what they regard as good, are simply demanding the right to enforce their own version of heaven on earth. And let me remind you, they are the very ones who always create the most hellish tyranny."* — **Barry Goldwater**[10]

WHY IT CAN NEVER WORK

You can outlaw churches, but you can't outlaw belief. You can dissolve families, but you can't dissolve love. You can indoctrinate children, but you can't erase the longing for truth.

> *"If you will not fight for right when you can easily win without bloodshed, you may come to the moment when you will have to fight with all the odds against you and only a precarious chance of survival."* — **Winston Churchill**[11]

Churchill's words are not merely about war—they are about moral courage. The defense of faith and family is the defense of civilization itself. If we will not stand for them when it is easy, we may find ourselves fighting for their remnants when it is nearly impossible.

CHAPTER 13.
WHY ELIMINATION OF FREE EXPRESSION WILL NEVER WORK

THE HEARTBEAT OF A FREE SOCIETY

Free expression is the heartbeat of every free society. It is not simply a political right or a constitutional guarantee — it is the natural outlet of human thought, conscience, and creativity. Every totalitarian regime that has attempted to eliminate free expression has discovered the same inescapable truth: human beings cannot be silenced without consequence.[1] Suppress the voice, and the mind rebels; control the language, and thought itself finds new, subversive ways to break through.

> *"Freedom is the right to tell people what they do not want to hear."* — **George Orwell**[2]

Orwell's advice reminds us that liberty only exists when people are free to offend those in power. A society that restricts speech to what is comfortable or popular ceases to be free at all.

Communist systems, in particular, have always seen free expression as an enemy.[3] Marxist theory teaches that ideas are determined by material conditions — that "bourgeois" thought must be replaced with "revolutionary consciousness." To enforce this transformation, regimes from Lenin's Russia to Mao's China to Castro's Cuba have placed speech under strict ideological control.[4] Art, journalism, religion, literature, even private conversation — all must conform to the Party's narrative. Yet every time, the same pattern emerges: intellectual stagnation, hypocrisy, and eventual rebellion.[5]

THE TRUTH ALWAYS FINDS A VOICE

In Stalin's Soviet Union, writers like Boris Pasternak and Aleksandr Solzhenitsyn were harassed, imprisoned, or exiled for telling simple truths about the human condition.[6] Their works, Doctor Zhivago and The Gulag Archipelago, circulated in secret across the world because truth has a way of surviving censorship. In Mao's China, entire generations of thinkers were forced into "self-criticism," denouncing their own thoughts to survive. Universities turned into indoctrination centers, and creativity withered under political conformity.[7]

> *"The truth is not for all men but only for those who seek it."* — **Ayn Rand**[8]

Rand's comment explains why tyrannies fear thinkers: those who seek truth cannot be ruled by lies. Attempts to silence them only drive truth deeper underground until it erupts uncontrollably.

If anyone doubts that suppression can happen here, they need only look at what occurred in the United States in recent years. During and after the COVID-19 outbreak, the Biden administration coordinated with major media platforms and social-media companies to label dissenting opinions as "misinformation." Independent journalists, doctors, and citizens who questioned official narratives were censored, demonetized, or de-platformed.[9] Algorithms buried inconvenient facts, and sympathetic legacy outlets amplified government talking points while discrediting dissent.[10]

These were not acts of open tyranny but of quiet coercion — phone calls, pressure campaigns, and "guidelines" delivered behind closed doors.[11] It was an attempt to shape reality by limiting what the public could say or hear. Yet, as history always proves, the truth resurfaced. Leaked communications, congressional investigations, and testimony from technology executives have since revealed how far the effort to silence Americans went — and how quickly it began to unravel once exposed.[12]

Today, many of those same platforms are beginning to reverse course, re-platforming voices they once silenced and admitting that political pressure influenced their actions.[13] It stands as a modern American reminder that censorship, whether imposed by decree or by social coercion, cannot hold back reality. The truth finds its way through every crack in the wall built to contain it.

And while Joe Biden and his allies attempted to style him as a modern FDR, his legacy will not be one of courage or renewal but of suppression and fear.[14] Like Mao, Lenin, and every other ruler who sought to control thought and language, history will remember him not for what he built, but for what he tried to silence. The attempt to manage truth through force or manipulation always ends the same way — with the truth standing and the tyrant forgotten.

The attempt to eliminate free expression always backfires because it misunderstands the nature of truth. Truth does not depend on permission to exist. It can be ignored or punished, but it cannot be destroyed. When governments ban certain words, people invent new ones. When they suppress books, people read them in secret. When they silence the press, rumors, networks, and later the internet carry information across borders faster than any censor can stop it. The very act of suppression exposes the weakness of the system — it reveals that the regime fears what people might say more than it trusts what it claims to be true.

CENSORSHIP DESTROYS THE MIND THAT CREATES

Censorship erodes the intellect of a society. When people are not allowed to debate, question, or contradict the state, they lose the habits that sustain reason itself.[15] Science, philosophy, and art all depend on the freedom to challenge assumptions. Without free expression, the human mind turns inward and the culture begins to rot. That is why every authoritarian state eventually must import innovation from freer nations — because creativity cannot survive under fear.

"The remedy for speech that is false is speech that is true."
— Justice Louis D. Brandeis[16]

Brandeis described the essence of the free market of ideas: the answer to bad speech is not censorship, but better speech. When expression is open, truth corrects falsehood naturally; when it is closed, lies metastasize unchallenged.

Censorship replaces truth with fear and replaces thought with obedience. It can produce conformity, but never conviction. History shows that even under the harshest regimes, forbidden ideas live on — in whispers, in manuscripts, in coded messages, and now in encrypted networks.[17]

THE NEW TYRANNY OF "OFFENSE"

Incredibly, even nations that once stood as beacons of liberty are beginning to forget this truth. In England — the birthplace of the Magna Carta, John Locke, and the common-law tradition of individual rights — people are being arrested merely for hurting someone's feelings or for expressing opinions deemed "offensive." Police have visited citizens' homes over social-media posts, comedians have been investigated for jokes, and ordinary people now measure their words for fear of prosecution under so-called "hate-speech" laws.[18]

> *"To forbid thought is to destroy freedom itself."* — **John Locke**[19]

Locke's statement, written centuries ago, speaks directly to this modern decay. When the state claims authority over what people may think or feel, it dismantles the very foundation of liberty it once enshrined.

What began as an effort to promote civility has turned into a tool of soft authoritarianism — one that punishes emotional discomfort rather than genuine harm.[20] This erosion of liberty abroad should serve as a dire warning to Americans: if the right to free expression can wither in the land of Churchill, it can vanish anywhere.

> *"The price of freedom is eternal vigilance."* — **Thomas Jefferson**[21]

Jefferson's timeless reminder reinforces that freedom of speech must be defended constantly, not assumed permanently. Once people grow complacent, censors move in to fill the silence.

A WARNING TO NEW GENERATIONS

For Millennials and Gen Beta, who have grown up in an era of social media, algorithmic control, and "cancel culture," this lesson is more urgent than ever. The old Soviet-style censorship has reappeared in digital form — not always through government decree, but through social pressure, corporate conformity, and ideological policing of speech.[22] The methods are new, but the goal is the same: to make people afraid to say what they think. Yet history has already proven that such control always collapses. People yearn to speak, to create, to tell the truth. It is an instinct that cannot be trained out of humanity.

> *"If liberty dies in the hearts of men and women, no constitution, no law, no court can save it."* — **Justice Learned Hand**[23]

Hand's alarm underscores that legal protections mean nothing if citizens themselves lose the courage to speak. The defense of liberty begins not in courts but in conscience.

Free expression is not chaos — it is the safety valve that keeps societies honest. Once you remove that valve, pressure builds until it explodes. The fall of the Berlin Wall, the collapse of the Soviet Union, and the continuing underground dissent in China, North Korea, and Cuba are all reminders that silence never lasts.[24] The truth, once buried, rises again — usually with a vengeance.

THE HUMAN SPIRIT CANNOT BE SILENCED

The elimination of free expression fails because it tries to rewrite human nature itself. To speak one's mind is as natural as breathing. To hear differing opinions is how we grow. And to forbid speech is to declare war on the human spirit. That war cannot be won.[25]

"I disapprove of what you say, but I will defend to the death your right to say it." — **Voltaire**[26]

Voltaire's sentiment embodies the moral courage that sustains every free civilization. True freedom requires defending even the speech we despise, for only then do we prove that liberty belongs to all and not just the favored few.

CHAPTER 14.
WHY THE "NEW SOCIALIST MAN" DOCTRINE WILL NEVER WORK

INTRODUCTION

The idea of the New Socialist Man (or New Soviet Man, Homo Sovieticus in its ironic actuality) is one of the most ambitious and revealing parts of Marxist–Leninist ideology. It presupposes that socialism will not only restructure economics but will transform human nature itself—creating a new kind of being who is selfless, cooperative, and collectively oriented. This chapter argues that such a transformation is impossible. The doctrine collapses under the weight of human psychology, evolutionary incentives, and historical experience. Far from creating a higher moral species, it has repeatedly produced conformity, fear, and cynicism.[1]

> *"The line dividing good and evil cuts through the heart of every human being."* — **Aleksandr Solzhenitsyn**[2]

Solzhenitsyn's words attack the core of the socialist fantasy. Evil, he reminds us, is not a defect of systems but a condition of the soul. Any ideology that imagines it can eradicate evil by reorganizing society must either deny human nature or destroy human freedom. The Soviet effort to "perfect" mankind failed because it tried to legislate moral purity—an act that inevitably multiplied hypocrisy and cruelty.[3]

THE DOCTRINE AND ITS CLAIMS

Socialist thinkers from Lenin to Che Guevara envisioned a new moral and social archetype: a person freed from "bourgeois egoism" and motivated solely by the collective good.[4] Guevara, in his 1965 essay Socialism and Man in Cuba, called for the conscious creation of this new being through education, example, and revolutionary culture.[5] Soviet ideology pursued similar aims through propaganda, literature, and institutional design, teaching citizens to value social duty over personal ambition. In theory, the New Socialist Man would be the human embodiment of communism's moral superiority—a species elevated above greed and competition. In practice, it required a wholesale remolding of human instincts.[6]

> *"Freedom is the freedom to say that two plus two make four."* — **George Orwell**[7]

Orwell's augury from Nineteen Eighty-Four captures the psychological violence required to create the "New Man." When a government forces citizens to deny plain truth, it destroys their capacity for integrity. The Soviet and Cuban attempts to cultivate a "collective conscience" demanded exactly this kind of moral self-betrayal—requiring citizens to parrot what they knew to be false in order to survive. A person trained to lie for the Party cannot become a moral ideal; he becomes its victim.[8]

THE PROBLEM OF HUMAN NATURE

Marxist theory assumes that human nature is infinitely adaptable to material conditions.[9] Yet modern psychology, evolutionary biology, and behavioral economics contradict this assumption. While context shapes behavior, core drivers such as selfinterest, reciprocity, statusseeking, and the desire for recognition persist.[10] Attempts to erase them merely redirect them: ambition becomes political loyalty; greed turns into corruption; competition reappears as a scramble for privilege within the Party hierarchy.[11]

> *"Of all tyrannies, a tyranny sincerely exercised for the good of its victims may be the most oppressive."* — **C. S. Lewis**[12]

Lewis uncovers the moral inversion at the heart of socialist idealism. The leaders who claim to coerce for the people's "own good" justify limitless intrusion into every aspect of life. Believing themselves moral saviors, they cannot imagine the evil of their methods. The result is a state that punishes dissent not out of cruelty but out of moral certainty—a tyranny wrapped in virtue.[13]

THE PARADOX OF COERCIVE VIRTUE

The doctrine demands voluntary moral transformation, yet it enforces it through compulsion.[14] To build the New Man, socialist states monopolized education, art, and media, punishing deviation and dissent. But coerced virtue is not virtue; it is submission. The Soviet writer Alexander Zinoviev observed that the result was the opposite of its goal: citizens publicly obedient but privately cynical. Outward conformity replaced inner conviction. Polish philosopher Leszek Kołakowski described the outcome as a culture of hypocrisy.[15]

> *"Emergencies have always been the pretext on which the safeguards of individual liberty have been eroded."* — **F. A. Hayek**[16]

Hayek's contemplation explains the political mechanism that sustained socialist utopianism. Every failure of the revolution became a new "emergency" requiring more control. The perpetual crisis of "building socialism" justified censorship, rationing, and surveillance in the name of virtue. The New Man could exist only under permanent martial law of the soul.[17]

HISTORICAL REALITY: HOMO SOVIETICUS

Instead of the promised New Man, socialism produced Homo Sovieticus—a figure dependent on the state, fearful of initiative, adept at doublethink, and detached from moral agency.[18] In the USSR, claims of altruism clashed with shortages, bureaucracy, and corruption; survival depended on bending rules and cultivating connections. In Maoist China, the Cultural Revolution's campaign to purge "selfish" thinking yielded mass denunciations and moral terror. Across cases, the pattern repeats: when ideology collides with human nature, human nature wins.[19]

THE ETHICAL COST

The New Socialist Man doctrine is not just unrealistic—it is dangerous. By claiming to define what "true humanity" should be, it authorizes the persecution of those who fall short. Dissenters, religious believers, independent thinkers, and ordinary people pursuing private goals are cast as moral defects. The demand for a single ideal soul justifies censorship, imprisonment, and purges.[20]

CONCLUSION

The "New Socialist Man" doctrine fails because it misunderstands the nature of human beings. People are not blank slates to be rewritten by ideology, nor are they latent collectivists awaiting the right economy. They are complex, selfinterested, creative, and fallible. A system that suppresses these realities ends by corrupting them. The result is not the New Man, but a demoralized citizen—cynical, fearful, and disillusioned. Real moral progress arises from freedom, pluralism, and personal responsibility—not from stateimposed virtue.[21]

CHAPTER 15.
WHY CLASS WARFARE WILL NEVER WORK

THE MYTH OF THE OPPRESSOR AND THE OPPRESSED

Every communist revolution begins by dividing society into two camps—the "oppressors" and the "oppressed." Karl Marx insisted that history itself was nothing more than a record of class struggle. Yet this vision denies what human nature and experience both confirm: that people are not locked into permanent classes, but constantly moving, trading, building, and rising.[1]

> *"The moment you make property the slave of the community, instead of the community being the protector of property, liberty is destroyed, and class war is inaugurated."* — **Lord Acton**[2]

Acton's caveat strikes at the heart of Marxist theory. When government ceases to protect property and instead subordinates it to "the community," freedom collapses. Property rights are the foundation of individual autonomy; once they are politicized, envy becomes law, and society enters an endless cycle of resentment and retaliation.[3]

THE POLITICS OF ENVY

Class warfare thrives on envy—the belief that someone else's success must have caused one's own hardship. But envy cannot sustain civilization. It poisons motivation and transforms ambition into bitterness.[4]

"Class hatred is one of the most evil passions of the human heart. It will not build up; it can only tear down." — **Ayn Rand**[5]

Rand comprehended that envy is inherently destructive. It motivates people to destroy wealth rather than to create it, to resent the productive rather than to emulate them. When governments weaponize envy—through confiscatory taxes, forced redistribution, or propaganda vilifying the successful—the creative engine of society grinds to a halt.[6]

DIVISION AS POLICY

Marxist rhetoric promised unity through revolution, yet in practice it institutionalized division. By branding one class as permanently guilty and another as perpetually victimized, communist regimes made social conflict their governing principle.[7]

"Those who stir up hatred between rich and poor, employer and worker, sow dragons' teeth from which armed men will spring." — **William E. Gladstone**[8]

Gladstone's metaphor is chillingly accurate. The seeds of hatred sown for political gain inevitably germinate into violence. Every regime that has institutionalized class struggle—Lenin's Russia, Mao's China, Castro's Cuba—reaped not equality but bloodshed. When citizens are taught that their neighbor's prosperity is their oppression, peace becomes impossible.[9]

THE DEATH OF MERIT AND FAIRNESS

Class warfare policies pretend to restore fairness, yet they destroy it. When the state rewards one group and penalizes another based on ideology, the very concept of justice is inverted.[10]

"When people get used to preferential treatment, equal treatment seems like discrimination." — **Thomas Sowell**[11]

Sowell's meditation explains why class politics never ends: once a society normalizes favoritism, equality before the law feels unjust. That is why communist regimes must continually invent new privileged and oppressed groups—because once their initial injustices lose momentum, resentment must be kept alive artificially. The more a state claims to fight inequality, the more inequality it creates.[12]

THE ILLUSION OF PROGRESS THROUGH CONFLICT

Communist theory insists that progress can only come through struggle between classes. Yet the history of successful nations proves the opposite: progress comes from cooperation, voluntary exchange, and respect for law.[13]

> *"The engine of progress is cooperation, not conflict; and the notion that society can be improved by setting one class against another is a dangerous illusion."* — **Herbert Hoover**[14]

Hoover's sagacity reveals the fatal flaw of permanent revolution. Conflict may energize mobs, but it cannot build institutions. The farms, factories, and universities that drive advancement depend on trust and collaboration, not hatred. Societies that replace cooperation with coercion soon find themselves impoverished in both wealth and spirit.[15]

HUMAN NATURE REJECTS PERMANENT WAR

Ultimately, human beings desire stability and dignity. Class warfare denies both. A government that thrives on grievance must keep its citizens divided, afraid, and dependent. Yet wherever people are free to trade and to speak, they re-create cooperation from the ground up. Underground markets in Soviet Russia, family enterprises in Maoist China, and black-market networks in Venezuela all testify to humanity's instinct to rebuild where ideology destroys.[16]

regime tries to rewire these natural drives, it collides with the hard walls of biology, psychology, and conscience.[4]

> *"The road to hell is paved with good intentions."* — **Saint Bernard of Clairvaux**[5]

The utopian begins with noble aspirations, but the pursuit of perfection through force inevitably drifts toward oppression. The more power centralized in the name of virtue, the more swiftly virtue is corrupted.[6]

COERCION DESTROYS AUTHENTIC BELIEF

True belief can never be compelled. You can make a man speak the words, but you cannot make him mean them. Every attempt at enforced faith produces hypocrisy, not harmony.[7]

Under Stalin, Soviet citizens sang hymns to the Party while whispering jokes in their kitchens. Under Mao, millions waved the Little Red Book by day and feared their own children by night.[8] The outward uniformity of belief — the "unanimous enthusiasm" broadcast on state media — was pure theater. Beneath it lay exhaustion, cynicism, and quiet hatred.[9]

> *"Those who promise us paradise on earth never produced anything but a hell."* — **Karl Popper**[10]

Popper's words sum up the tragic irony of coercive utopianism: in striving to eliminate evil, it destroys good; in chasing paradise, it manufactures despair. The result is not heaven on earth but a living purgatory.[11]

THE IRON LAW OF VIOLENCE

Because coerced utopias depend on obedience rather than persuasion, they must constantly escalate their use of force. Every deviation, every act of doubt, becomes a threat to the dream itself.

Dissent cannot be tolerated because it reveals the utopia is not universal — and therefore, not real.[12]

> *"Utopias appear to be much more realizable than we formerly believed. Now we find ourselves faced with a much more frightening question: how can we prevent their final realization?"* — **Nikolai Berdyaev**[13]

Berdyaev's question exposes the ultimate horror: utopia is not impossible, it is terrifyingly possible — and every attempt to bring it about ends in servitude.[14]

The result is predictable: the ideology consumes its own children. The French Revolution turned on the Girondins. The Bolsheviks purged the Mensheviks. Mao's Red Guards devoured their teachers.[15] The pattern repeats because coercion is not a stage on the road to utopia — it is the road, and it never ends.[16]

THE EROSION OF RESPONSIBILITY AND MEANING

A coerced society eliminates the individual as a moral agent. When obedience replaces conscience, people stop thinking for themselves. They surrender personal responsibility to the collective or the State.[17]

In such a system, good and evil are redefined by decree. The bureaucrat who signs the order for deportations, the soldier who enforces the ration, the neighbor who denounces a friend — all can claim virtue, because they act "for the greater good."[18] The dream of utopia absolves them of guilt.

> *"All utopias are dystopias. The term 'dystopia' was not coined until later, but every utopia that has been realized has become a nightmare."* — **Ayn Rand**[19]

Rand grasped that when personal freedom is sacrificed to collective fantasy, the supposed dream society becomes indistinguishable from a nightmare. The machinery of perfection grinds down the soul.[20]

THE UTOPIA THAT CANNOT BE SEEN

The coercive utopian always insists that suffering today will bring bliss tomorrow. "You must sacrifice now," they say, "so that your children will live in the perfect world." But the horizon of perfection keeps retreating.[21]

After decades of sacrifice, shortages, censorship, and executions, no paradise ever arrives. What remains are the ruins of societies that tried to perfect man by breaking him.[22]

> *"The most terrifying words in the English language are: 'I'm from the government, and I'm here to help.'"* — **Ronald Reagan**[23]

Reagan's humor conceals a profound warning: when power is concentrated in the name of salvation, coercion soon follows. Every utopian scheme ends where freedom dies — at the hands of those convinced they know what is best for everyone else.[24]

THE ONLY REAL UTOPIA

If there is such a thing as a "utopia," it cannot be imposed from above. It must arise from the inside out — from the choices of free individuals guided by conscience, faith, and love.[25]

Every great civilization that has endured understood this balance: the law restrains evil, but liberty nourishes good. When coercion replaces persuasion, when the State claims authority over the human soul, it destroys the very material it seeks to perfect.[26]

A humane society is not one without flaws, but one that allows people to seek betterment without fear — to disagree, to create, to err, to believe. That kind of world can never be built with bayonets and propaganda. It must be cultivated through freedom and truth.[27]

The coercive utopian dreams of a garden, but wields a hammer. And the more he swings it, the less he understands why all he builds are ruins.[28]

CHAPTER 17.
YOU CAN'T BE A COMMUNIST OR SOCIALIST AND BE A...

FAITH AND MORALITY

... CHRISTIAN (OR PERSON OF FAITH)

Communism and socialism demand faith in the State, not in God. Every society that embraced them sought to replace the church with the Party and to make morality a matter of political convenience.[1]

> *"Religion is the sigh of the oppressed creature, the heart of a heartless world."* — **Karl Marx**[2]

Marx meant that religion should be abolished because it comforted people in suffering rather than ending suffering through revolution. Yet Christianity teaches that suffering can have meaning and that dignity comes from the image of God, not the decree of a committee. A Christian cannot bow to both Christ and the collective. History proves it—wherever communism gained power, the cross was torn down, and the Bible burned.[3] Faith and freedom live or die together.

... MORAL PERSON

To be moral is to distinguish right from wrong; to be a communist is to erase that line in service of the cause. The ideology excuses any cruelty if it claims to serve equality.

> *"The end may justify the means as long as there is something that justifies the end."* — **Leon Trotsky**[4]

A moral person knows that murder, theft, and deceit remain evil regardless of intent. But socialism baptizes envy and calls it justice. It converts covetousness into policy and violence into virtue. In doing so, it severs the conscience from the act and leaves only the will to power disguised as compassion.

... BELIEVER IN GOOD AND EVIL

Communism cannot accept objective good or evil, for that would imply a higher law than the State. It insists that morality is relative—useful when it advances the revolution, disposable when it does not.

> *"If God does not exist, everything is permitted."* — **Fyodor Dostoevsky**[5]

The totalitarian regimes of the twentieth century tested that idea and proved it terrifyingly true. When leaders declared themselves the authors of right and wrong, gulags and killing fields followed.[6] To believe in absolute good is to place limits on human power; communism destroys those limits and calls it liberation.

... HUMANITARIAN

The humanitarian seeks to relieve suffering; communism multiplies it.

> *"The road to hell is paved with good intentions."* — **Proverb (English, 17th century)**[7]

Every socialist experiment begins with promises of compassion—free bread, free medicine, free equality—and ends in ration cards and repression.[8] Compassion without accountability becomes tyranny in disguise. True humanitarianism values each human life as sacred; communism values only the collective and discards the individual as expendable material for its utopia.

FREEDOM AND IDENTITY

... PATRIOT

Communism cannot coexist with patriotism. To the socialist mind, love of country is tribalism to be outgrown, loyalty to be redirected toward the Party.[9]

> *"The heritage of freedom must be guarded by the spirit that won it."* — **Calvin Coolidge**[10]

Coolidge expressed what every patriot knows: liberty survives only when citizens love their nation more than they envy one another. Communism feeds envy until gratitude dies. The patriot sees his flag as a covenant of duty and sacrifice; the communist sees it as a rival banner to the red one. No man can serve both.

... LOVER OF FREEDOM

Freedom is not merely the absence of chains but the presence of choice. Socialism abolishes both. It promises liberation from want, yet delivers bondage to bureaucracy.[11]

> *"None are more hopelessly enslaved than those who falsely believe they are free."* — **Johann Wolfgang von Goethe**[12]

Goethe's insight illuminates the cruelest illusion of socialism: it teaches dependence while calling it freedom. Citizens obey ration cards and decrees but congratulate themselves for their "collective will." True liberty allows the individual to rise or fall by his own decisions; socialism forbids both and calls the stagnation equality.

... FREE THINKER

To think freely is to question received truth. Under communism, the only heresy is independent thought.

"The most dangerous of all falsehoods is a slightly distorted truth." — **Georg Christoph Lichtenberg**[13]

The socialist censors rarely erase facts—they distort them just enough to make obedience seem rational. A free thinker insists on evidence over emotion; the Party insists on narrative over evidence. When truth becomes conditional, thinking freely becomes impossible, and error reigns unchallenged.

... INDIVIDUAL

The individual is the smallest minority on earth—and the one collectivism seeks to erase.

"Collectivism means the submergence of the individual in the group." — **Ludwig von Mises**[14]

Mises understood that every central plan requires the sacrifice of personal plans. In exchange for guaranteed equality, the citizen surrenders ownership, ambition, and voice. What remains is a managed population—equal only in its powerlessness.

... NONCONFORMIST

A nonconformist refuses to chant the slogans of the day. Under socialism, such refusal is a crime.

"The most subversive people are those who ask questions." — **Jostein Gaarder**[15]

Every tyranny fears the question more than the answer. The nonconformist's curiosity exposes contradictions the ideology cannot explain. Socialism survives only through repetition and intimidation; inquiry breaks both. When a society must punish curiosity to preserve peace, it has already lost both truth and peace.

CITIZENSHIP AND CIVILIZATION

… CONSTITUTIONALIST

To be a constitutionalist is to believe that government must be bound by law. To be a communist is to believe that law must serve the Party.[16]

> *"The Constitution is not an instrument for the government to restrain the people, it is an instrument for the people to restrain the government."* — **Patrick Henry**[17]

Communism reverses this principle. It binds the citizen and unleashes the state. Under its rule, the constitution—if it exists at all—is merely a weapon of control. The true constitutionalist holds that freedom is safest when power is caged; the communist insists that power must be absolute to perfect society. One guards liberty through limits, the other destroys liberty through promises.

… AMERICAN

The American idea is that rights come from God and that government exists only to secure them. Communism denies both the divine source and the limited purpose.[18]

> *"The liberties of our country, the freedom of our civil constitution, are worth defending against all hazards."* — **Samuel Adams**[19]

To be American is to live by self-government and personal responsibility. To be socialist is to live by central command and collective guilt. The two creeds cannot occupy the same heart. The American bows to law under God; the socialist bows to government above all.

… STUDENT OF HISTORY

History is the most unforgiving teacher—its lessons repeat until learned. The communist refuses to learn them.[20]

"The one thing we learn from history is that we learn nothing from history." — **Georg Wilhelm Friedrich Hegel**[21]

Hegel's irony became prophecy. Every generation of revolutionaries believes that their version of socialism will finally succeed. Each discovers, too late, that human nature has not changed. The student of history respects consequence; the ideologue despises it. Thus, failure becomes doctrine and suffering becomes progress.

... DEFENDER OF HUMAN RIGHTS

To defend human rights is to defend the individual. Communism recognizes only the collective.

"It is in justice that the ordering of society is centered." — **Aristotle**[22]

When justice is defined by equality of outcome, it ceases to be justice. True rights belong to persons; socialist rights belong to classes. Under communism, some are silenced for the "greater good," and others die for the "common future." No ideology that destroys the person can claim to defend humanity.[23]

... JUST PERSON

Justice begins with truth and ends with accountability. Communism allows neither.

"Justice cannot be for one side alone, but must be for both." — **Eleanor Roosevelt**[24]

Socialism preaches fairness while institutionalizing favoritism. It divides citizens into oppressors and oppressed, assigning guilt by category instead of conduct. The just person seeks impartiality; the socialist seeks advantage. In a society ruled by envy, justice becomes impossible because innocence itself is a privilege.

... DEMOCRAT (SMALL-D)

A true democrat believes in the consent of the governed; a socialist believes in the command of the planners.

> *"Democracy and socialism have nothing in common but one word, equality. But notice the difference: while democracy seeks equality in liberty, socialism seeks equality in restraint and servitude."* — **Alexis de Tocqueville**[25]

Tocqueville foresaw that socialism would mimic democracy while dismantling it. The ballot becomes theater once outcomes are predetermined. The democrat trusts persuasion; the socialist trusts coercion. Where freedom votes, communism dictates. What?

FAMILY AND COMMUNITY

... PARENT

A parent's first duty is to nurture and protect; a communist state's first impulse is to control.[26]

> *"The family is the first essential cell of human society."* — **Pope John XXIII**[27]

Every totalitarian movement understands that if it can claim the child, it can rule the future. Communism replaces parental guidance with political indoctrination, teaching loyalty to ideology over love of family. When the state educates children to distrust their parents, the home ceases to be a refuge and becomes an outpost of propaganda.[28]

... FAMILY MEMBER

To be a true family member is to cherish bonds formed by affection, not assignment. Communism seeks to dissolve those bonds into collective duty.

"The strength of a nation derives from the integrity of the home." — **Confucius**[29]

Socialism treats such devotion as a distraction from production. In its zeal to equalize society, it trivializes kinship until blood means nothing and ideology means everything. Yet civilization itself began with families, not factories. The heart that serves the state before its own household soon forgets how to love anyone at all.

... CHILD OF GOD

Faith teaches that each life possesses divine worth. Communism teaches that worth is measured by usefulness to the plan.

"Man is not the creature of circumstances; circumstances are the creatures of men." — **Benjamin Disraeli**[30]

Disraeli's wisdom affirms human agency under moral law. Socialism denies both, insisting that the environment must shape the soul. The believer sees destiny guided by Providence; the communist sees it programmed by policy. Where man is no longer sacred, he becomes expendable.

... COMMUNITY BUILDER

A genuine community is born of cooperation and voluntary service; a socialist society is manufactured through compulsion.

"The smallest act of kindness is worth more than the grandest intention." — **Oscar Wilde**[31]

Communism replaces kindness with quotas, charity with taxation, and belonging with surveillance. It claims to unite neighbors but breeds suspicion instead. The true community builder knows that trust cannot be legislated—only earned. When fellowship is forced, friendship dies.[32]

WORK, REWARD, AND REASON

... WORKER

The worker is the pride of every free economy, but under communism he becomes its prisoner.[33]

"The worker has become a slave, though he imagines himself free." — **Alexis de Tocqueville**[34]

Tocqueville foresaw a system where men would be "worked" for equality rather than rewarded for excellence. In socialism, the dignity of labor is lost because the fruits of labor no longer belong to the one who earned them. The worker is reduced to a tool in the machinery of the state—managed, monitored, and discarded when no longer useful.[35]

... ENTREPRENEUR OR CREATOR

The entrepreneur embodies the spirit of innovation, courage, and self-reliance. Communism destroys all three.

"Where men cannot freely transact, they cannot freely think." — **Thomas Sowell**[36]

Sowell's rebuke cuts to the heart of creative freedom: invention thrives only when property is secure. Socialism smothers creativity under regulation and redistributes the rewards of risk to those who took none. Without incentive, invention dies, and the well of prosperity runs dry.[37]

... MERITOCRAT

A meritocrat believes in achievement based on effort and excellence. Communism abolishes both and calls the void fairness.

"In a system where all are rewarded equally, excellence becomes an act of rebellion." — **Anonymous (20th-century maxim)**[38]

Socialism exalts mediocrity because it fears comparison. It cannot celebrate success without betraying its creed of envy. The meritocrat seeks justice through opportunity; the socialist demands equality through limitation. In the end, everyone becomes equally unrewarded.

... REALIST

The realist accepts human nature as it is; the socialist insists on rewriting it.

> *"Utopias appear possible only to those who ignore reality."*
> — **Friedrich A. Hayek**[39]

Hayek observed that socialist planning depends on imaginary perfection. Realism, by contrast, confronts imperfection honestly and works to improve within it. When ideology replaces observation, policy becomes delusion. The realist builds progress; the socialist dreams it—and punishes those who wake up.

... SCIENTIST OR SCHOLAR

Science advances through skepticism; communism survives through censorship.

> *"Science can flourish only in an atmosphere of free speech."*
> — **Albert Einstein**[40]

In communist states, research bends to ideology. Facts that contradict doctrine vanish into archives, and scholars who question the narrative vanish into prisons. Truth becomes a servant of politics, and knowledge decays into propaganda. Where inquiry must ask permission, discovery ends.[41]

... ARTIST

Art is the voice of the soul; communism mutes it with propaganda.

"Art is freedom—the ability to say the unsayable." — **Salman Rushdie**[42]

The artist lives by expression, not permission. Yet socialism assigns art a purpose: to glorify the state. Creativity turns into obedience; imagination becomes a slogan. In every communist nation, color fades into gray because the artist no longer paints from truth but from fear. Only free men can make beautiful things.[43]

CONCLUSION

Communism and socialism promise harmony, but they demand surrender. They contradict faith, destroy family, silence conscience, and punish success. You cannot be a Christian, patriot, individual, parent, or creator—and still serve an ideology that denies the worth of the soul. Freedom and collectivism are not two sides of one coin; they are the coin and its counterfeit. One enriches the human spirit, the other bankrupts it.

PART III

CHAPTER 18.
THE TEN WORST OUTCOMES OF COMMUNISM AND SOCIALISM

MASS DEATH

No single feature defines communism's legacy more starkly than the human cost. From Stalin's Holodomor and purges to Mao's Great Leap Forward and Pol Pot's killing fields, socialist regimes have slaughtered their own citizens in numbers exceeding 100 million in the 20th century alone. These deaths were not incidental—they were instrumental, resulting from the belief that utopia could be engineered through force.[1]

PERMANENT POLITICAL REPRESSION

Every communist and socialist state has required censorship, surveillance, imprisonment, and torture to preserve "unity." The totalitarian apparatus—secret police, informants, reeducation camps—was not an accident but a necessity to suppress dissent against a system that cannot survive free speech.[2]

ECONOMIC COLLAPSE AND CHRONIC SHORTAGES

Central planning and price control destroy the feedback loops that make markets work. The result: empty shelves, worthless currency, and black markets that become the only functioning economy. The USSR, Maoist China, Cuba, and Venezuela all followed this script to the letter.[3]

FORCED COLLECTIVIZATION AND FAMINE

When governments seize private farms "for equality," agriculture collapses. Individual initiative disappears, efficiency plummets, and millions starve while bureaucrats falsify production numbers. Ukraine's 1930s famine alone killed millions under Stalin's "scientific socialism."[4]

DESTRUCTION OF FAMILY, RELIGION, AND CIVIC LIFE

Communism demands allegiance to the state above all else. Families, churches, and voluntary associations are branded "bourgeois relics." Children are indoctrinated to spy on their parents. Faith is outlawed. The spiritual and moral fabric of society unravels.[5]

ELIMINATION OF PRIVATE PROPERTY

By abolishing ownership, socialism abolishes responsibility. When nothing belongs to anyone, no one maintains, repairs, or innovates. Land, factories, and infrastructure decay. Property rights are not merely economic—they are civilizational glue.[6]

LACK OF INNOVATION AND TECHNOLOGICAL STAGNATION

Socialism smothers the incentive to create. Scientists and engineers become state employees with no reward for ingenuity. The Soviet Union could copy, but rarely invent. Communist China innovated only after abandoning Marxist economics and embracing markets.[7]

CULTURAL AND INTELLECTUAL DECAY

Wherever socialism takes hold, art and scholarship become propaganda. Literature and science must serve "the people's revolution." Fear replaces curiosity; mediocrity replaces excellence. Independent thought is labeled "counter-revolutionary."[8]

ENVIRONMENTAL DEVASTATION

Despite their "anti-capitalist" posturing, socialist states have produced some of the worst pollution in history. Central planning prizes output quotas, not sustainability. The Aral Sea disaster and Chernobyl are not market failures—they are products of bureaucratic secrecy and contempt for accountability.[9]

DEMORALIZATION AND LOSS OF HUMAN DIGNITY

When the state dictates what you may say, own, earn, or believe, the human spirit atrophies. Citizens become cynical, dependent, and fearful. Freedom is replaced by quiet despair—a nation of people who survive, but no longer truly live.[10]

LOOKING AHEAD

Each of the ten consequences outlined above warrants deeper examination. In the next ten chapters, we will explore these outcomes one by one—tracing their origins, mechanisms, and devastating results across nations and generations. From the unspeakable toll of mass death to the silent stagnation of innovation, these chapters will reveal how every aspect of human life—moral, material, and intellectual—has suffered under the banner of collectivist ideology.

CHAPTER 19.
MASS DEATH

THE ULTIMATE CONSEQUENCE

Of all the failures of communism and socialism, none is more horrifying than their record of mass death.[1] Across the twentieth century, regimes claiming to serve equality and liberation produced the greatest slaughter of civilians in recorded history. What began as dreams of a classless paradise ended in famine, terror, and the mechanized destruction of human life. In every nation where Marxist or socialist revolutions seized total power—from Russia to China, Cambodia to Ethiopia—the same grim pattern emerged: utopia built on graves.

Mass death is not a historical accident of communism; it is its logical conclusion when theory meets absolute power. Once the state claims the right to redesign humanity, to sacrifice individuals for "the greater good," and to silence dissent in the name of progress, human life loses all inherent value. The result is predictable: labor camps, purges, starvation, and the slow erasure of millions of souls who refused to fit the plan.[2]

> *"Communist regimes turned mass crime into a full-blown system of government."* — **Stéphane Courtois**[3]

Courtois, editor of The Black Book of Communism, summarized the very essence of the communist tragedy: murder institutionalized. Violence was not a deviation from socialist theory—it became its instrument of enforcement. Wherever communism took hold, mass death was not the by-product of failure; it was the measure of success in eliminating opposition.

CONCEPTUAL FRAMEWORKS AND DEFINITIONS

Before the statistics and testimonies, one must define the phenomenon. Political scientist Rudolph Rummel coined the term democide—the intentional killing of civilians by their own governments.[4] This includes executions, forced labor, starvation, and deliberate neglect. Under communist regimes, democide was often justified as revolutionary necessity or class warfare.

Other scholars describe classicide—the systematic extermination of an entire social class, such as Stalin's campaign against the kulaks—or politicide, the murder of political opponents. In all such cases, the state replaces law with ideology, and the individual becomes expendable material in the construction of history.

> *"Power kills; absolute power kills absolutely."* — **R. J. Rummel**[5]

Rummel's observation compacts the deadly logic of centralized power. When the state monopolizes every decision—political, economic, and moral—there is no restraint against its will. Under communism, absolute power was not a risk; it was the design.

MECHANISMS AND DYNAMICS OF MASS DEATH

The means of destruction were varied but followed consistent logic. Revolutionary upheaval and total control dismantled every existing institution—church, family, property, law—and replaced them with one party and one ideology. The purge of "enemies" never ended. Collectivization and famine followed. Central planners seized farms, outlawed markets, and requisitioned grain regardless of human cost. Entire regions starved while the state exported food or hid shortages.[6] The secret police, gulag systems, and "re-education" camps became the machinery of fear. Millions perished through overwork, exposure, or execution. Because dissent was treason, bad news was suppressed. Famines were denied, disasters concealed, and the suffering of millions erased from official history.

"In our country, the lie has become not just a moral category but a pillar of the State." — **Aleksandr Solzhenitsyn**[7]

Solzhenitsyn's words unmask the foundation on which all totalitarian killing rests: the lie. By forcing entire populations to live within falsehood, communist states destroyed the moral immune system of society. Once truth dies, justice follows—and people soon after.

THE SOVIET UNION UNDER STALIN

The Soviet Union became the proving ground for communism's most catastrophic social experiments. Joseph Stalin's rise to power marked a total transformation of Marxist theory into an instrument of terror. His Five-Year Plans aimed to industrialize a peasant nation overnight, and collectivization of agriculture was enforced with military precision. Peasants who resisted surrendering their land were labeled 'kulaks,' enemies of the people, and sent to forced labor camps or executed outright. Entire regions were stripped of food as quotas rose beyond human reach. The resulting famine in Ukraine—the Holodomor—left millions dead, their suffering hidden behind official lies.[8]

The Great Purge of the late 1930s deepened the nightmare. Millions of citizens—party officials, soldiers, intellectuals, even ordinary workers—were accused of imagined disloyalty and either executed or imprisoned. Fear became the air people breathed; denunciation was the path to survival. Stalin's gulag archipelago stretched across the frozen wastes of Siberia, consuming lives in the name of socialist progress. Death came from starvation, exposure, exhaustion, and despair.[9] Yet the propaganda machine portrayed this as triumph—the necessary cleansing of enemies to build paradise on earth.

The Soviet experiment revealed the inescapable truth of totalitarianism: when the state becomes both master and god, it demands not obedience but worship. Those who refused to bow were erased from existence, and their silence became the price of order.

CHINA UNDER MAO ZEDONG

In China, Mao Zedong sought to outdo Stalin not only in ideology but in scope. The Great Leap Forward of 1958 promised to transform China from an agrarian society into a communist utopia of steel and grain. Peasants were forced into 'people's communes,' traditional farming was outlawed, and steel furnaces appeared in backyards as families were commanded to melt their tools and pots for the revolution. Harvest reports were falsified to please the Party, leading officials to seize crops that did not exist. When the truth emerged, it was already too late.[10]

As starvation spread across the countryside, Mao refused to acknowledge the failure. Villages resorted to eating bark, grass, and even the dead. The famine that followed claimed tens of millions of lives—an atrocity not of nature but of willful blindness.[11] During the Cultural Revolution that followed, Mao unleashed China's youth against teachers, parents, and history itself. Ancient art was destroyed, churches and temples ransacked, and countless citizens beaten or executed in a frenzy of ideological purity. Families were torn apart by loyalty to the Party, and truth itself was redefined by political decree.

Mao's China stands as the ultimate warning of collectivist delusion: when truth is sacrificed to ideology, and humanity to the state, progress becomes indistinguishable from destruction.

CAMBODIA UNDER THE KHMER ROUGE

When the Khmer Rouge seized power in Cambodia in 1975, Pol Pot announced the beginning of 'Year Zero'—the complete erasure of history, class, and individuality. Cities were emptied at gunpoint; millions were forced into the countryside to labor in collective farms. Money, markets, schools, and religion were abolished. Even wearing glasses could mark one as an intellectual—and thus an enemy of the revolution. Families were separated, and confession under torture became a daily ritual of survival. The fields themselves became mass graves.[12]

In less than four years, a quarter of Cambodia's population perished through execution, starvation, and disease. The killing fields that dot the countryside remain silent memorials to a movement that sought to create purity through annihilation. As the regime collapsed under its own madness, the world glimpsed the inevitable end of radical equality: the destruction of the human spirit itself.

Pol Pot's experiment stripped communism of all pretense. There were no imperial powers to blame, no natural disasters to excuse the deaths—only ideology turned inward until it consumed the nation that believed in it.

OTHER COMMUNIST ATROCITIES

Though smaller in scale, other communist regimes repeated the same tragedy with chilling consistency. In North Korea, the Kim dynasty built a hereditary totalitarian state where dissent is punished by generations, and mass starvation became a tool of control. In Ethiopia, the Derg regime imposed collectivization and political purges that slaughtered hundreds of thousands under the guise of socialist renewal. Eastern Europe under Soviet domination lived in a shadow of fear—secret police, prison camps, and show trials serving as constant reminders of the price of disobedience.

Each of these societies differed in culture, geography, and history, yet they shared a single creed: that the state could perfect man by force. The result was always the same—fear, hunger, and death. No environment, no leader, no century could redeem the lie at the heart of communism.[13, 16]

DEBATES AND REFLECTIONS

Even sympathetic historians concede that no other modern ideology produced such systematic, peacetime killing of its own citizens. Estimates of total deaths vary—from 60 million on the conservative side to over 100 million in The Black Book of Communism—but the pattern is unmistakable.[14]

Critics sometimes argue that these outcomes were not "true socialism." Yet every government that attempted full collectivization and one-party control, without exception, generated repression, famine, and fear. The moral failure lies not only in execution but in the premise: that human beings can be perfected by coercion.

> *"No other political movement of our time has proved so ruthless in its disregard for human life."* — **George F. Kennan**[15]

Kennan's assessment, written at the dawn of the Cold War, has only grown truer with hindsight. From Moscow to Beijing to Phnom Penh, communist regimes proved that ideology unchecked by morality leads inevitably to the degradation of human life itself.[17]

THE COST OF AMERICAN LIVES IN THE FIGHT AGAINST COMMUNISM

The story of communism's mass death is not only written in the suffering of those who lived under its rule, but also in the blood of those who fought to stop its spread. Millions of Americans served—and hundreds of thousands died—defending freedom on foreign soil so that others might never endure the chains of totalitarianism.[18]

In the Korean War, over thirty-six thousand Americans lost their lives halting the advance of communist forces across the peninsula.[19] They fought in brutal conditions, often against overwhelming odds, to preserve the independence of South Korea—a nation that now stands as one of the world's most prosperous democracies.[20]

In Vietnam, more than fifty-eight thousand Americans were killed resisting the expansion of communism in Southeast Asia.[21] The war divided the nation, but its moral core was clear: a refusal to yield the world to a system that had already enslaved half of humanity. Many who returned were met not with gratitude but with scorn, yet their sacrifice remains a testament to the enduring American belief that liberty is worth defending—even at great cost.

Beyond these wars, countless American servicemen stood guard through decades of Cold War tension, in Germany, Japan, and across the world. Their presence deterred Soviet aggression and gave oppressed peoples hope that freedom had not been forgotten.

These men and women did not fight for conquest or ideology, but for principle—the belief that individual life has infinite worth and that tyranny, no matter how it disguises itself, must be resisted. Their sacrifice forms part of the great human toll exacted by communism—not as its victims, but as its opponents who died so others might live free.

ALLIED SACRIFICE IN THE FIGHT AGAINST COMMUNISM

America did not stand alone. The struggle to contain communism cost the lives of **hundreds of thousands of soldiers from allied nations** who stood shoulder to shoulder with the United States across decades of conflict.

In the **Korean War (1950–1953)**, the United Nations coalition lost more than **137,000 soldiers** in defense of South Korea.[22] The British, Canadians, Australians, Turks, and soldiers from seventeen other nations fought together under one banner of freedom. Tens of thousands of South Korean troops also fell defending their homeland. Together with American forces, they halted communist expansion at the 38th parallel and preserved one of the world's most enduring democracies.

In the **Vietnam War (1955–1975)**, soldiers from **South Vietnam, South Korea, Australia, New Zealand, Thailand, and the Philippines** fought alongside U.S. troops. South Vietnam alone lost an estimated **250,000 men**, and America's allies together sacrificed more than **60,000** additional lives resisting the communist North and its Soviet and Chinese backers.[23]

Across **Cold War flashpoints**—in Berlin, in the jungles of Laos, in the mountains of Afghanistan where Western arms aided those resisting Soviet invasion—the price of opposing communism was counted in lives, limbs, and generations scarred by tyranny's shadow.

These allied dead represent more than national service; they embody a shared moral conviction that liberty transcends borders. Together with American soldiers, they formed a shield for the free world. Their courage bought time for democracy to survive and for half the world to remain unshackled from the totalitarian night that descended elsewhere.

WHY WESTERN CIVILIZATION AND CAPITALIST–REPUBLICAN SYSTEMS DO NOT PRODUCE MASS DEATH

In Western republics, no authority is absolute. Constitutions, elections, and courts distribute power so that no ideology can command unchecked obedience. From the Judeo-Christian conception of the soul to Enlightenment natural rights, Western civilization defines life as sacred and individual. Property, speech, and conscience are extensions of that dignity.

Capitalist markets decentralize decision-making. When harvests fail or industries collapse, innovation and competition produce solutions rather than starvation. Free societies tolerate opposition because dissent is information. Newspapers, civic groups, and elections expose corruption and force reform.

> *"The tragedy of modern man is not that he knows less and less about the meaning of his own life, but that it bothers him less and less."* — **Václav Havel**[24]

Havel advised that moral indifference—the quiet submission of the individual conscience—is what allows tyranny to thrive. Western civilization resists this through open faith, free speech, and moral responsibility. The preservation of conscience is the preservation of life.

Western nations have confronted grave injustices—slavery, inequality, war—but they have corrected them through open debate and democratic reform, not mass extermination. Capitalist prosperity funds medicine, welfare, and education. Liberal democracies have never engineered a famine against their own citizens.[25]

THE ADAPTIVE TRIUMPH OF FREE SOCIETIES

The same challenges that communism claimed only revolution could solve—industrialization, inequality, and poverty—were actually overcome by adaptive, capitalist republics. Free enterprise harnessed innovation rather than suppressing it. Private ownership encouraged efficiency instead of waste.

Through opportunity, education, and mobility, wealth became dynamic, not hereditary. Living standards rose across all classes without violence.[26] Democratic reforms—unions, labor laws, and social insurance—tempered capitalism's excesses while preserving freedom.

Western civilization proved that progress and liberty are compatible. Its genius lay in adaptation: institutions flexible enough to reform without collapsing, markets resilient enough to recover, and citizens free enough to question power. Communism promised heaven on earth and delivered mass graves. Capitalist republicanism promised only freedom—and from that freedom came science, prosperity, and the longest sustained expansion of human life in history.[27, 28]

CHAPTER 20.
PERMANENT POLITICAL REPRESSION

THE INEVITABLE SUPPRESSION OF DISSENT

Every communist and socialist regime, regardless of its national flavor or stated ideals, has ultimately been sustained by repression. Because central authority replaces personal liberty as the organizing principle of society, the state must silence those who question its legitimacy. Dissent becomes treason; independent thought becomes counterrevolutionary. From the earliest years of Lenin's Soviet Union to the modern single-party dictatorships of Cuba, China, and North Korea, the machinery of government has been turned inward—against its own people—to maintain obedience through fear.[1]

"Whenever law ends, tyranny begins." — **John Locke**[2]

Locke's misgiving predates communism by centuries, yet his words precisely capture its essence. Where the rule of law is replaced by the rule of ideology, tyranny inevitably follows.

Political repression is not a temporary flaw that can be corrected through reform. It is a permanent condition of any system that subordinates individual rights to collective ideology. When the state controls property, labor, and speech, it must also control conscience. The leaders of such regimes may speak of equality and progress, but they cannot tolerate the diversity of opinion that genuine equality requires.[3]

FROM UTOPIA TO POLICE STATE

Communism and socialism begin with promises of liberation: the end of exploitation, the abolition of class, and the birth of a "new man" free from greed and selfishness. Yet because these goals demand the restructuring of human nature itself, they can only be pursued through coercion. Once the population resists or even questions the state's utopian program, repression follows inevitably.[4]

> *"A government that violates the rights of even one individual is not truly secure."* — **Andrei Sakharov**[5]

Sakharov, who risked his life challenging Soviet tyranny, understood that regimes built on repression cannot survive indefinitely. The very act of denying liberty undermines the foundation of government itself.[6]

The Bolsheviks replaced the Tsar's secret police with the Cheka; Mao Zedong's Cultural Revolution empowered masses of indoctrinated youth to denounce their parents and teachers; Castro's Committees for the Defense of the Revolution turned neighbors into informants. In every case, idealism decayed into surveillance and terror. What began as a dream of equality ended as a system of permanent control.[7]

THE MECHANICS OF CONTROL

Permanent repression under socialism operates through three interlocking mechanisms:

1. Control of Information. Independent media, free universities, and religious institutions are dismantled or co-opted. The press becomes an organ of propaganda, redefining truth as whatever serves the Party's interests.[8]
2. Control of Expression. Citizens learn to censor themselves. Literature, art, and humor are policed for ideological purity. The result is cultural stagnation—the death of creativity that threatens the regime's myth of progress.[9]

3. Control of Opportunity. Economic privilege is redistributed not according to merit but according to loyalty. To question authority is to risk one's livelihood, ration allotment, or even access to medical care.[10]

"He that would make his own liberty secure must guard even his enemy from oppression." — **Thomas Paine**[11]

Paine's counsel reminds us that oppression tolerated against one group will soon ensnare all others. Once repression becomes a political tool, it knows no limits.

Together these mechanisms ensure that political repression is not merely episodic but systemic. The dictator may die, but the system endures because fear has been institutionalized.[12]

CASE STUDY: THE SOVIET UNION – THE PURGES AND THE GULAG

Under Joseph Stalin, repression reached a mechanized scale. The secret police executed over a million people during the Great Purge, while millions more were condemned to the frozen hell of the Gulag. The entire apparatus of the state existed to instill fear and extinguish dissent. Political opponents, writers, scientists, and even loyal party members were branded "enemies of the people."[13] Repression became not a policy but a way of life.

"The most radical revolutionary will become a conservative the day after the revolution." — **Hannah Arendt**[14]

Arendt's insight condenses the transformation of Lenin's revolution into Stalin's empire of fear. Once power was seized in the name of liberation, it had to be preserved through terror.[15]

CASE STUDY: MAO'S CHINA – CULTURAL REVOLUTION AND THOUGHT CONTROL

In China, Mao Zedong sought to purify society through the Cultural Revolution. Millions were humiliated, imprisoned, or killed as the Red Guards turned neighbor against neighbor. Professors, artists, and religious leaders were destroyed in the name of ideological purity.[16] China's ancient culture was nearly obliterated so that a new socialist orthodoxy could take its place.

What began as a "revolution of the mind" became a system of permanent fear.[17] The lesson was clear: in a society that worships conformity, everyone becomes a suspect.

CASE STUDY: NORTH KOREA – THE PERFECTION OF TOTAL CONTROL

Nowhere has repression been made more complete than in North Korea. Loyalty to the regime is enforced from birth, and entire families are condemned for the alleged crimes of one relative. Three generations can share the same sentence in the same camp. Informants fill every neighborhood, and even whispers of doubt are fatal.[18]

The regime survives not by prosperity or innovation but by total domination of human thought. It represents the logical endpoint of socialism's obsession with control—an unending police state that exists only to sustain itself.[19]

Even in less extreme socialist systems, repression persists in subtler forms: censorship, blacklists, and bureaucratic punishment for ideological dissent. The names change—"social credit," "re-education," "de-platforming"—but the instinct is the same: silence the individual in favor of the collective.[20]

THE ADAPTIVE TRIUMPH OF FREE SOCIETIES

History proves that liberty outlasts repression. The Iron Curtain fell not because the West invaded, but because the truth could not be contained indefinitely.[21] Individuals in every age yearn to speak, create, and worship freely; systems that deny these instincts must rely on terror until terror exhausts itself.

> *"The price of freedom may be high, but never so costly as the loss of it."* — **Lech Wałęsa**[22]

Wałęsa's words reflect the hard-won lesson of those who tore down communism from within. Freedom's price is vigilance, not submission.[23]

The enduring lesson is clear: communism and socialism require permanent political repression to survive, but freedom requires only vigilance to endure.[24] A society that respects individual conscience will always regenerate; one that fears its own citizens must eventually collapse under the weight of its lies.[25]

CHAPTER 21.
ECONOMIC COLLAPSE AND CHRONIC SHORTAGES

THE INEVITABLE CONSEQUENCE OF CENTRAL PLANNING

Economic collapse under communism and socialism is not an accident—it is the direct and predictable outcome of suppressing the mechanisms that make a market function: supply, demand, price signals, and private ownership.[1] When governments take control of production and distribution in the name of "equality," they destroy the very incentives that generate abundance.

> *"The first lesson of economics is scarcity: there is never enough of anything to fully satisfy all those who want it."*
> — **Thomas Sowell**[2]

This truth lays bare the fatal flaw of socialism. Every central planner believes he can overcome scarcity through decree, yet scarcity is a fact of life. Denying it guarantees chronic shortages, black markets, and collapse.

In a capitalist republic, every price in the marketplace conveys information. It tells producers what people want and tells consumers what it costs to make it. When this information system is abolished—as it always is under socialism—the economy becomes blind.[3] Central planners, no matter how intelligent or well-intentioned, cannot possibly know how to allocate millions of products, services, and resources efficiently. The result is always the same: economic paralysis.

The Soviet Union, Maoist China, North Korea, Cuba, and Venezuela all followed this path.[4] Each began with promises of fairness and equality, and each ended with hunger, deprivation, and despair.

THE DEATH OF INCENTIVE

Socialist systems abolish profit under the assumption that self-interest is immoral. Yet profit is simply the measure of how well one serves others in a free market. When profit is outlawed, motivation disappears. Productivity collapses.[5]

In the Soviet Union, workers quickly learned that whether they worked hard or not, their pay remained the same. Factories met quotas by producing useless goods or shoddy materials to satisfy bureaucratic metrics.[6] Soviet farmers, stripped of their land, saw no reason to labor for a collective that would confiscate their harvest. By contrast, tiny private garden plots—barely three percent of Soviet farmland—produced nearly onethird of the nation's food.[7]

Without incentives, the economy devolves into stagnation. When citizens realize that hard work gains them nothing, apathy replaces ambition, and a nation once rich in potential becomes destitute.

CHRONIC SHORTAGES AND EMPTY SHELVES

Wherever socialism is implemented, chronic shortages follow. Food, fuel, medicine, clothing, and even basic household goods become scarce.[8] This is not bad luck—it is the natural outcome of a command economy that cannot adjust to reality.

> *"As a rule, panics do not destroy capital; they merely reveal the extent to which it has been previously destroyed by its betrayal into hopelessly unproductive works."* — **John Stuart Mill**[9]

Mill's remark perfectly describes what happens when socialist economies implode. Collapse doesn't create ruin—it merely unmasks the waste, inefficiency, and corruption long concealed by propaganda.

When prices are fixed by decree rather than by market competition, shortages are inevitable. Low prices cause overconsumption and underproduction.[10] Factories stop producing because they cannot afford to operate, while consumers line up for goods that no longer exist.

> *"In times of crisis human beings don't have it in them to be rational."* — **Larry McMurtry**[11]

Socialist regimes prove this repeatedly. Faced with economic failure, they don't reform—they blame enemies, tighten control, and print money, deepening the catastrophe.

Black markets emerge, corruption flourishes, and the very inequalities socialism claimed to abolish reappear in their ugliest form—favoritism, rationing, and bribery.[12]

CASE STUDY: THE SOVIET UNION AND THE GREAT SHORTAGE ECONOMY

From the 1930s through the 1980s, the Soviet Union lived in a constant state of shortage. Stores were notorious for long queues, bare shelves, and rationed goods.[13] The saying "You pretend to pay us, and we pretend to work" captured the economic absurdity.

Under central planning, entire sectors collapsed due to misallocation. Factories produced massive surpluses of nails of the wrong size or shoes that didn't fit, all to meet arbitrary production quotas.[14] Basic foodstuffs like bread, sugar, and meat were rationed, while refrigerators and televisions required years on a waiting list.

By the 1980s, Soviet citizens spent an average of two hours a day waiting in line—economists called it the "economy of the queue."[15] Even vodka—so vital to Russian culture that it was used as an informal currency—became scarce during lateera reforms. The system finally imploded under its own inefficiency, unable to provide even the most basic necessities.

CASE STUDY: MAOIST CHINA AND THE GREAT LEAP FAMINE

Mao Zedong's Great Leap Forward (1958–1962) sought to transform China into an industrial powerhouse through collectivized agriculture and backyard steel production. Instead, it led to one of the deadliest famines in human history.[16]

Private farming was abolished, and peasants were forced into "People's Communes." Local officials, fearful of punishment, exaggerated harvest numbers to meet impossible quotas. The state seized grain based on those false reports, leaving villagers to starve.[17]

> *"By collapse, I mean a drastic decrease in human population size and/or political/economic/social complexity ... for an extended time."* — **Jared Diamond**[18]

Diamond's definition could serve as a clinical description of Mao's China. The Great Leap Forward destroyed both population and complexity—obliterating the very social and economic networks that sustain civilization.

Tens of millions died—estimates range from 30 to 45 million.[19] Yet the regime blamed "bad weather" and "counterrevolutionaries" rather than its own policies. Meanwhile, Mao's government exported food abroad to maintain appearances.

CASE STUDY: CUBA'S "SPECIAL PERIOD"

When the Soviet Union collapsed in 1991, Cuba lost its primary source of subsidies and trade. The island entered what the government called the "Special Period in Peacetime," a euphemism for economic collapse.[20]

Food and fuel vanished almost overnight. Public transportation ground to a halt. The average Cuban's caloric intake dropped by nearly onethird.[21] Power outages lasted sixteen hours a day, and bicycles replaced cars as the main form of transport.

The government responded by rationing, issuing libreta booklets that entitled citizens to small monthly allocations of rice, beans, and sugar.[22] Black markets flourished as people traded or stole goods to survive.

Even today, after decades of reform promises, Cuba still imports up to eighty percent of its food.[23] Chronic shortages remain a fact of daily life—proof that socialism cannot sustain itself even on a small island.

CASE STUDY: VENEZUELA'S HYPERINFLATION AND STARVATION

Once one of South America's richest nations, Venezuela collapsed into ruin after embracing socialism under Hugo Chávez and Nicolás Maduro.[24] The government expropriated farms, factories, and oil assets in the name of "social justice." Predictably, production plummeted.

When price controls made it impossible to profit, store owners closed. Shelves emptied. Medicine disappeared.[25] Citizens lined up for hours in hopes of buying basic items like flour or diapers. By 2018, inflation exceeded one million percent.[26] People carried backpacks full of worthless currency just to buy a loaf of bread.

> *"If the economy has collapsed in a country, success is to put the whole burden of the collapse on those who disrupted the economy, and to restore the economy without putting any burden on those who have no blame in the economic collapse!"* — **Mehmet Murat İldan**[27]

The lesson is moral as well as economic. Under socialism, those responsible for ruin—the ruling elite—never bear its weight. The innocent always suffer while the architects of failure remain in power.

THE DESCENT INTO ECONOMIC DESPAIR

Once shortages become chronic, a socialist economy enters a death spiral. Productivity declines, infrastructure decays, and the state resorts to printing money to cover its failures.[28] Inflation spirals out of control. Savings evaporate. Citizens turn to barter, foreign currency, or crime to survive.

Venezuela's collapse in the twentyfirst century mirrors the Soviet Union's in the twentieth.[29] A nation blessed with vast oil reserves became a land where bread, toilet paper, and insulin disappeared. Meanwhile, the ruling elite enriched themselves while ordinary citizens scavenged for food. Socialism always begins with confiscation and ends with desperation.[30]

THE MIRACLE OF FREE MARKETS

In stark contrast, capitalist and republican systems recover from crises precisely because they allow individuals to adapt, innovate, and respond to changing circumstances.[31] Private ownership and free exchange unleash creativity and resilience.

When the United States faced the Great Depression, it did not descend into starvation or permanent collapse.[32] Private enterprise, combined with constitutional governance, eventually restored prosperity. When postwar Germany embraced Ludwig Erhard's social market economy, its recovery was so rapid it was called the Wirtschaftswunder—"economic miracle."[33]

Free societies selfcorrect because they are guided not by decrees, but by millions of voluntary choices. Each buyer and seller acts on real information, creating a living, selfadjusting system that no central committee could ever replicate.[34]

THE ADAPTIVE TRIUMPH OF FREE SOCIETIES

Economic collapse is not merely the failure of a policy—it is the exposure of a lie: the lie that equality can be engineered, that the human spirit can be subordinated to bureaucracy, and that prosperity can exist without freedom.[35]

Free societies triumph because they recognize that human beings are fallible yet capable, selfinterested yet cooperative, and competitive yet compassionate. When individuals are allowed to create, trade, and profit within a framework of law and liberty, prosperity follows.[36]

The record of history is absolute: communism and socialism destroy economies; capitalism and republicanism restore them.[37]

CHAPTER 22.
FORCED COLLECTIVIZATION AND FAMINE

THE PROMISE OF ABUNDANCE AND THE REALITY OF STARVATION

Communist leaders promised that collectivizing the land would end hunger forever. The peasants, they said, would no longer toil for themselves but for the good of all. In practice, the "collective" quickly became a mechanism of confiscation. Fields once full of life turned into wastelands patrolled by bureaucrats and guarded by fear. The plow and sickle became instruments not of harvest, but of control.[1]

In the name of communal justice, the fields were stolen—and in the name of equality, the people starved. The slogan of justice had become the excuse for theft. What began as a social revolution ended as organized starvation.[2]

CASE STUDY: THE SOVIET UNION AND THE HOLODOMOR

When Joseph Stalin launched his campaign to "liquidate the kulaks as a class," he declared it a necessary step toward socialist progress. In truth, it was a war on the very people who fed the nation. Independent farmers were branded enemies of the state, their livestock seized, and their grain requisitioned to meet impossible quotas.[3] Those who resisted were deported or executed; those who obeyed often starved anyway.

> *"A famine is not a natural disaster, it is a political one."*— **Robert Conquest**[4]

Historian Robert Conquest seized the essence of this horror with those words. Stalin's famine was not born of drought or blight—it was engineered by decree. Entire villages in Ukraine were sealed off and stripped of food; even gathering wild herbs was a punishable crime.[5]

> *"People ate rats and tree bark, yet the granaries were full—reserved for the state."* — **Anne Applebaum**[6]

Anne Applebaum's reflection exposes the grotesque contradiction of communist rule: plenty existed, but it was hoarded as proof of ideological triumph while millions died in silence.[7] The Soviet state weaponized food, turning sustenance itself into a tool of submission and control.

When the state takes both your land and your food, your death is not accidental—it is engineered. Starvation became not a consequence but an instrument of power—a lesson to those who dared to remember freedom.[8]

CASE STUDY: CHINA AND THE GREAT LEAP FORWARD

A generation later, Mao Zedong launched his "Great Leap Forward," promising to surpass the industrial powers of the West.[9] Communes replaced villages, family plots were abolished, and citizens were forced into collective dining halls where food was rationed by political favor. Officials falsified production reports to appease superiors, who in turn demanded even higher quotas. The result was catastrophe.

> *"The communes became prisons without walls; the fields, their killing grounds."* — **Jasper Becker**[10]

Jasper Becker's words depict the suffocating reality of life under Mao's collectivization: peasants were trapped in their own villages, forbidden to move, as grain was exported abroad to display socialist success.[11]

"The result was the greatest man-made famine in history, a famine that killed tens of millions." — **Frank Dikötter**[12]

Frank Dikötter's research illuminates the moral bankruptcy of the system—one that valued ideological pride over human life.[13] The famine that followed was not a miscalculation, but the logical outcome of central control and the deliberate silencing of truth.

They dubbed it a struggle for progress; it was the slow genocide of the peasantry. The same revolution that claimed to liberate the poor instead devoured them.[14]

CASE STUDY: OTHER COMMUNIST FAMINES

The same pattern unfolded across the communist world. In Cambodia, the Khmer Rouge emptied cities to create an agrarian utopia; in Ethiopia, Mengistu's Marxist regime collectivized farms and triggered another wave of famine; in North Korea, decades of isolation and central planning left the population perpetually malnourished.[15]

Each believed it could command nature and man alike into obedience. Each discovered that ideology cannot grow crops, and slogans cannot fill stomachs.

Under communist rule the famine is never famine—it is silence, concealment, and control. The suffering is hidden behind numbers, the dead behind rhetoric.[16]

THE POLITICS OF SILENCE

Perhaps the most chilling feature of these famines is not the hunger itself, but the silence that followed. Records were destroyed, journalists were banned, and survivors forbidden to speak.[17]

"The starvation of a people is the surest sign of absolute power—it is hunger imposed by decree." — **Aleksandr Solzhenitsyn**[18]

Solzhenitsyn's perceptiveness reveals the final cruelty of totalitarianism: starvation as policy, hunger as discipline, and death as proof of loyalty.[19] The state that controls food controls life itself.

Even as corpses lined the roads, officials proclaimed victory. The slogans of progress grew louder as the people grew thinner. Truth was the first crop to die, and the last to be buried.[20]

CAPITALISM'S TRIUMPH IN FEEDING THE WORLD

In contrast, capitalist and republican systems unleashed the productive power of free individuals.[21] From the American Midwest to post-war Europe, private ownership and open markets transformed scarcity into surplus. Incentives drove innovation—mechanization, fertilizers, hybrid crops, and global trade networks that fed billions.[22]

While socialist nations endured rationing and famine, capitalist nations produced abundance. The free farmer, rewarded by the fruits of his own labor, became both the backbone of national prosperity and the guarantor of food security.[23]

Where socialism sought equality through confiscation, capitalism achieved plenty through freedom. It was not coercion but competition, not quotas but ingenuity, that conquered hunger. Liberty fills the granaries; tyranny empties them.[24]

THE LESSON OF HISTORY

The story of collectivization and famine is not merely a chapter in the past—it is a warning to the future. Whenever a government asserts that it knows better than those who work the land, hunger follows. The more absolute the state's control, the more absolute the misery of its subjects.[25]

The graves of Ukraine, China, Cambodia, and Ethiopia remind us that utopian dreams enforced by violence yield dystopian realities. History makes the pattern unmistakable: where freedom is denied, famine thrives; where men are free, the earth yields plenty.[26]

As Conquest and Applebaum showed, as Solzhenitsyn and Becker recorded, famine under communism was never an accident of nature. It was an act of governance—deliberate, systemic, and defended by ideology.[27]

Freedom, not force, feeds the world.[28]

CHAPTER 23.
DESTRUCTION OF FAMILY, RELIGION, AND CIVIC LIFE

FOUNDATIONS OF A FREE SOCIETY

Every enduring civilization rests upon three indispensable pillars: the family, religion, and civic community. These are the sources of moral formation, social trust, and voluntary cooperation—the fabric that holds a free people together. In contrast, totalitarian ideologies, particularly communism and socialism, have consistently sought to dissolve these natural institutions.[1] For the collectivist state to be supreme, all rival sources of loyalty must be eradicated. The individual must not look to God, family, or community for meaning, but only to the State.[2]

> *"All that is necessary for evil to triumph is for good men to do nothing."* — **Edmund Burke**[3]

Burke's timeless advisory underscores the danger of moral complacency. When families cease to teach virtue, when churches are silenced, and when citizens retreat from civic duty, evil advances unchallenged. Communism thrives not in a moral society, but in one that has grown indifferent to truth and responsibility.

Marx himself described the family as a bourgeois construct meant to perpetuate property relations, calling for its "abolition" along with religion—the "opiate of the masses." Lenin and Stalin followed suit, treating family life as a reactionary obstacle to the creation of the "new socialist man."[4] What they built in its place was a generation uprooted from the moral traditions that make freedom possible.[5]

THE POLITICS OF UNREALITY: GENDER AS IDEOLOGICAL WEAPON

> *"Freedom is the freedom to say that two plus two make four. If that is granted, all else follows."* — **George Orwell**[6]

The denial of biological reality is not merely a cultural fad—it is a political strategy. When citizens can be compelled to "blackwhite"(Orwell) or affirm what they know to be false, they are no longer free in mind or conscience.[7] The modern obsession with gender identity is thus the ultimate test of submission: whether people will obey ideology over evidence, the collective over the self, the narrative over the truth.[8]

By severing human identity from nature, Marxist thought achieves what brute force never could—the redefinition of reality itself.[9] If "male" and "female" are social constructs, then so are all distinctions upon which civilization rests: parent and child, husband and wife, right and wrong. The family becomes fluid, morality becomes negotiable, and the State becomes the sole authority left to define both.[10]

The tragedy is not confusion but compulsion. A society that forces its citizens to deny the obvious has already surrendered to tyranny in principle. The goal is not acceptance but obedience. When the mind is trained to call unreality truth, it will call servitude freedom—and believe it.[11]

CASE STUDY – THE SOVIET "NEW MAN" PROJECT

In the 1920s and 1930s, Soviet planners sought to remake human nature itself.[12] The "New Soviet Man" was to be selfless, atheistic, and entirely loyal to the Party. Traditional roles were dismissed as "bourgeois relics." Families were encouraged to send children to state boarding schools; church weddings were discouraged; and the concept of personal property within the household was condemned. The project failed disastrously, producing not enlightened citizens but fearful, hollow individuals dependent on the State for identity and purpose.[13]

ATTACK ON THE FAMILY

Under communism, the family was seen as a competing institution that divided loyalty and interfered with state control.[14] In the Soviet Union, early Bolsheviks encouraged communal child-rearing, easy divorce, and the devaluation of motherhood. Marriage was reduced to a civil arrangement subject to Party oversight. In Maoist China, children were urged to denounce their parents as "class enemies." Similar policies appeared in Cuba and Cambodia, where regimes tore children from their homes to be "re-educated" in collective institutions.[15]

> *"The most important thing a father can do for his children is to love their mother."* — **Theodore Hesburgh**[16]

Hesburgh's truth emphasizes the irreplaceable moral foundation of family life. The love between husband and wife is the first school of loyalty, trust, and compassion. Communism undermined this sacred bond, replacing it with loyalty to the State. The destruction of the family therefore did not merely attack tradition—it severed the transmission of virtue from one generation to the next, leaving only dependence and despair in its wake.[17]

CASE STUDY - CHINA'S CULTURAL REVOLUTION (1966–1976)

During Mao's Cultural Revolution, family life was upended by state-orchestrated paranoia. Children were instructed to inform on their parents for "counterrevolutionary" behavior; wives denounced husbands to prove their loyalty to Mao. Millions of families were destroyed as love, trust, and kinship gave way to fear and betrayal. By the time the campaign ended, Chinese society had been psychologically shattered, and an entire generation had grown up without the experience of a functioning home.[18]

SUPPRESSION OF RELIGION

Communism has always viewed religion as a rival authority. To the atheist materialist, faith in God must be replaced by faith in the State. Churches were shuttered or turned into museums of atheism; priests, monks, and pastors were imprisoned or executed; believers were mocked, surveilled, and driven underground.[19]

> *"Despotism may govern without faith, but liberty cannot."*
> — **Alexis de Tocqueville**[20]

Tocqueville understood that faith is not an enemy of freedom but its precondition. A society grounded in religious belief teaches self-restraint and moral accountability. When communism outlawed religion, it removed the very source of the virtues necessary to sustain liberty. In its place, it substituted an empty ideology demanding total obedience.[21]

CASE STUDY - THE PERSECUTION OF THE RUSSIAN ORTHODOX CHURCH

After the Bolshevik Revolution, Lenin declared war on religion, calling priests "black crows." Between 1918 and 1941, nearly 100,000 clergymen were executed or sent to gulags. Thousands of churches were desecrated, turned into warehouses, or demolished outright. Only after World War II, when Stalin sought to rally patriotic support, were a few churches reopened under state control. The faithful endured decades of terror simply for professing belief in God—a crime in the eyes of the communist state.[22]

EROSION OF CIVIC LIFE

Beyond family and faith lies the third foundation of freedom: civic life—the voluntary associations, charities, schools, clubs, and local institutions that form the living tissue of a healthy society. Communism systematically dismantled this realm as well. Independent organizations were banned; all collective action had to flow through the Party. Even friendship itself was subordinated to ideology. Citizens learned to distrust one another, for every conversation might be overheard, every gathering infiltrated by informants.[23]

"Our Constitution was made only for a moral and religious people. It is wholly inadequate to the government of any other." — **John Adams**[24]

Adams' statement exposes the fatal flaw of communism: without moral self-government, no system can endure freedom. Civic life depends on the internal discipline that faith and family provide. When communism destroyed those sources of virtue, it had to replace them with surveillance and coercion. The void left by moral collapse was filled by the police state.[25]

CASE STUDY - EAST GERMANY AND THE STASI

The German Democratic Republic maintained one of the most extensive surveillance networks in history. By the 1980s, the Stasi had nearly one informant for every 60 citizens. Ordinary life became impossible: neighbors spied on neighbors, friends turned in friends, and even family members reported on one another. The destruction of civic trust was complete, and when the Berlin Wall finally fell, it revealed a nation spiritually exhausted and socially hollowed out by decades of suspicion.[26]

THE CONSEQUENCES

The psychological and cultural consequences of destroying family, religion, and civic life are staggering. Birth rates collapse, substance abuse rises, suicide rates soar, and a pervasive sense of meaninglessness spreads through society. The communist "utopia" becomes a gray wasteland of disconnected individuals, each dependent upon the State for survival and identity.[27]

"If we lose faith in the future, we have lost everything." — **Ronald Reagan**[28]

Reagan's words encapsulate the ultimate outcome of communism's war on the human spirit. A people stripped of family, faith, and community lose not only their freedom but their hope.

The result is not progress but despair—a society where meaning is replaced by obedience, and purpose by survival.

CASE STUDY – THE COLLAPSE OF SOVIET SOCIETY (1980S–1990S)

By the late 1980s, decades of ideological control had left the USSR morally bankrupt. Families were fragmented, alcoholism was rampant, and civic trust was nonexistent. When the system finally imploded, it did so not only economically but spiritually. Millions suddenly faced a world without faith, identity, or purpose. The social vacuum that communism created outlasted the regime itself, leaving behind a legacy of cynicism and moral fatigue that still plagues post-Soviet life.[29]

THE ADAPTIVE TRIUMPH OF FREE SOCIETIES

Western civilization, founded upon the sanctity of the family, the freedom of conscience, and the voluntary cooperation of citizens, has proven resilient precisely because it honors these institutions. The American experiment thrives when parents educate their children in virtue, when churches teach moral restraint, and when communities act through voluntary associations rather than coercive bureaucracy.[30]

> *"Of all the dispositions and habits which lead to political prosperity, religion and morality are indispensable supports."* — **George Washington**[31]

Washington, in his Farewell Address, identified the two pillars upon which republican government rests. Remove either, and liberty collapses. His insight stands as a timeless refutation of communism's moral vacuum.

> *"The foundations of our society and our government rest so much on the teachings of the Bible that it would be difficult to support them if faith in these teachings should cease."* — **Calvin Coolidge**[32]

Coolidge reminds us that freedom is not self-sustaining—it must be nourished by belief in eternal truths. A society that forgets its moral roots forgets itself.

> *"Freedom consists not in doing what we like, but in having the right to do what we ought."* — **John Paul II**[33]

John Paul II spoke these words as he stood against communism in Eastern Europe. True freedom, he taught, is ordered liberty—rooted in duty, conscience, and divine truth.

Where communism sought to replace love with loyalty to the State, freedom reclaims the truth that human dignity begins in the family, is sanctified by faith, and flourishes in civic friendship.[34] These are the sources of strength that no ideology can permanently destroy.

CHAPTER 24.
THE DESTRUCTION OF PRIVATE PROPERTY

THE FOUNDATION OF FREEDOM

Private property is not merely a material possession—it is the cornerstone of liberty, responsibility, and civilization itself. From the smallest plot of land to the largest enterprise, ownership confers stewardship: the incentive to maintain, improve, and pass something better to the next generation. The right to own what one earns is inseparable from the right to think, act, and live as an independent being. Destroy that right, and the entire edifice of freedom collapses.

Communism and socialism, in all their forms, begin with the assault on private property. Karl Marx declared that

> *"The theory of the Communists may be summed up in the single sentence: abolition of private property."* — **Karl Marx**[1]

This declaration is the ideological root of every subsequent attempt to centralize power under collectivist rule. Marx saw private ownership as the foundation of inequality, but in destroying it, he also destroyed the foundation of liberty.

CASE STUDY: THE SOVIET UNION AND THE WAR ON OWNERSHIP

When Lenin and the Bolsheviks seized power in 1917, one of their first acts was the nationalization of all land.[2] Farmers, once the proud stewards of their own plots, became "laborers for the collective." The state confiscated property under the pretense of serving the "people," but it was the Party that controlled every acre and every harvest.

By 1930, Stalin's collectivization campaign had destroyed millions of small farms.[3] Those who resisted were branded kulaks—enemies of the people—and either executed or exiled to the gulags.[4] Entire villages starved as the state seized grain quotas to meet industrial goals. The peasant class, once Russia's backbone, was annihilated.

> *"What belongs to everyone belongs to no one."* — **Aristotle**[5]

Aristotle's timeless admonition describes the moral vacuum of collectivism. When ownership is erased, so is accountability, and what was once cared for under personal responsibility decays under communal neglect.

CASE STUDY: MAO'S CHINA AND THE GREAT LEAP BACKWARD

In 1958, Mao Zedong launched the "Great Leap Forward," forcing rural Chinese into massive collective farms.[6] Private ownership of land, tools, or even cooking pots was forbidden. Peasants were told to eat in communal mess halls and surrender their grain to the state.

Without property rights, there was no accountability—and thus no production. Local officials, desperate to meet impossible quotas, inflated numbers to avoid punishment.[7] The state then confiscated the nonexistent "surplus," leaving millions to starve. Between 1958 and 1962, an estimated forty-five million people perished.[8]

> *"Where there is no private property, there is no liberty."* — **Lord Acton**[9]

Acton's intuition captures the essence of Mao's tragedy: a society without property rights cannot be free because individuals have no independent means to live. Where everything belongs to the state, the citizen becomes property himself.

CASE STUDY: CUBA'S CONFISCATION AND DEPENDENCE

When Fidel Castro came to power in 1959, he promised reform, not revolution. Yet within two years, he had nationalized all private businesses, banks, and industries.[10] Property was seized, homes were "redistributed," and entrepreneurs fled by the thousands.[11] Cuba's once-thriving economy—second only to the United States in the Caribbean—collapsed into permanent stagnation.[12]

> *"Property is the fruit of labor; property is desirable; it is a positive good in the world. That some should be rich shows that others may become rich."* — **Abraham Lincoln**[13]

Lincoln's defense of property is a defense of opportunity itself. In protecting what a person earns, society encourages ambition and rewards hard work—principles that vanish when the state becomes master of every wage and every home.

CASE STUDY: VENEZUELA'S NATIONALIZATION NIGHTMARE

In the early 2000s, Hugo Chávez followed the socialist script to the letter—seizing industries, farms, and even supermarkets under the banner of "economic justice."[14] By 2010, Venezuela had nationalized over 1,000 private enterprises.[15] Once one of Latin America's richest nations, it soon could not feed its people or keep the lights on.[16]

> *"It is not inequality that is the real misfortune, it is dependence."* — **Voltaire**[17]

Voltaire's observation speaks directly to Venezuela's downfall: socialism replaced self-reliance with dependency, making citizens servants to the state rather than masters of their own fate.

THE AMERICAN MIRACLE OF OWNERSHIP

The American experiment was founded on the exact opposite principle. The Founders understood that private property is the guardian of all other rights. John Adams wrote, "Property must be secured, or liberty cannot exist." James Madison declared that "government is instituted to protect property of every sort."[18]

It was private ownership that transformed a vast wilderness into the most prosperous nation on earth. Free men and women, secure in their right to the fruits of their labor, built farms, towns, and industries unmatched in productivity or generosity. The right to own was the right to dream—and to make those dreams real.

"A man's house is his castle." — **Sir Edward Coke**[19]

Coke's assertion became a cornerstone of Anglo-American law. It affirms that the home is a sanctuary from tyranny—an inviolable space where the individual's rights stand higher than the whims of power.

THE ADAPTIVE TRIUMPH OF FREE SOCIETIES

History proves that societies which defend private property are the only ones capable of growth and renewal.[20] Ownership breeds accountability, innovation, and investment—the essential engines of progress. The freedom to own also creates the freedom to fail and to try again, which is the very definition of resilience.

Under capitalism, resources flow naturally toward productive use because individuals have the incentive to act wisely. When property rights are secure, even the poorest citizen has a path to prosperity through hard work and enterprise.[21] When those rights are denied, all paths lead only to dependency.

In every era, free societies have adapted to new challenges because they protect the individual's right to own, trade, and build.[22] The dynamism of free ownership continually corrects the failures of policy and circumstance. Communism and socialism, by contrast, are static systems—they cannot evolve, because they deny the freedom that makes adaptation possible.

The endurance of private property is not an accident; it is civilization's greatest innovation.[23] It converts ambition into progress, self-interest into cooperation, and independence into prosperity. That is why free societies survive, and socialist ones collapse.

LESSONS OF HISTORY

The lesson is unmistakable. Every society that abolished private property abolished prosperity with it.[24] Every government that sought to equalize outcomes by seizing what others built has produced misery and dependence.

Ownership is the foundation of freedom. To lose it is to lose the means of self-determination. To defend it is to defend civilization itself.[25]

CHAPTER 25.
LACK OF INNOVATION AND TECHNOLOGICAL STAGNATION

Communism and socialism claim to engineer equality. What they engineer instead is paralysis. When governments own the means of production and dictate what must be invented, discovery dies. Without freedom of thought, the laboratory becomes a factory floor, and the dreamer becomes a functionary.[1]

> *"It is not from the benevolence of the butcher, the brewer, or the baker that we expect our dinner, but from their regard to their own interest."* — **Adam Smith**[2]

Smith's insight explains why innovation thrives only where personal effort can yield personal reward; collectivism severs this incentive and suffocates invention.[3]

WHY INNOVATION DIES UNDER COMMUNISM

Communism replaces initiative with obediencc. The bureaucrat determines priorities; the citizen obeys. Under socialism, there is no incentive to excel, because excellence is treated as inequality. The state decides what counts as "useful," and imagination retreats into silence.[4]

> *"Intellectual freedom is the only guarantee of progress in science."* — **Andrei Sakharov**[5]

Sakharov highlights the fatal contradiction of communist systems: when inquiry must conform to politics, science and technology cannot advance.[6]

CASE STUDY — THE SOVIET UNION: MILITARY BRILLIANCE, CIVILIAN BACKWARDNESS

The USSR proved a nation can launch a satellite while its citizens queue for bread. Technical triumphs concentrated in defense and propaganda; agriculture and consumer goods stagnated.[7] Factories met quotas, not quality; feedback loops from free consumers did not exist, so improvement never compounded.

This divergence was structural: resources flowed to command priorities (weapons), while everyday life—housing, food, appliances—remained starved of innovation. Even late Soviet leaders conceded that central planning had exhausted its capacity to generate progress outside the military sphere.[8]

CASE STUDY — CHINA: THEFT IN PLACE OF INVENTION

Contemporary China's growth arrived with limited market openings, yet genuine, original innovation still lags where speech and enterprise remain constrained. To fill the gap, the Party-state has repeatedly leaned on intellectual-property theft and coercive technology transfer from the United States and other free nations—an implicit admission that fear and censorship cannot substitute for curiosity and risk-taking.[9]

Without secure property rights and free inquiry, talent is channeled toward compliance and replication, not discovery. Surveillance and ideological vetting signal that political loyalty outranks independent thought—the opposite of an innovative culture.[10]

CASE STUDY — CUBA: A REVOLUTION THAT FROZE TIME

Pre-revolution Cuba was among Latin America's most modern economies. After mass nationalizations, engineers emigrated, private workshops vanished, and technology ossified.[11] Mid-century automobiles still rumble through Havana not as retro chic, but because innovation and capital formation stopped where profit and ownership were outlawed.

Bureaucratic rationing and party permission replaced entrepreneurial upgrade cycles; maintenance became heroic, and progress became rhetorical.[12]

CAPITALISM: THE ENGINE OF INNOVATION

Capitalism alone aligns freedom, ownership, and ambition. Markets function as continuous experiments: ideas compete, failures teach quickly, and successes scale. From electricity to the microchip to the internet, breakthroughs emerged from individuals and firms free to test, pivot, and profit.[13]

> *"The fundamental impulse that sets and keeps the capitalist engine in motion comes from the new consumers' goods, the new methods of production or transportation, the new markets..."* — **Joseph Schumpeter**[14]

Schumpeter names the mechanism—creative destruction—by which free economies constantly replace the old with the new, compounding progress.[15]

> *"Innovation is the specific instrument of entrepreneurship."*
> — **Peter Drucker**[16]

Drucker ties invention to enterprise: where entrepreneurship is free and rewarded, innovation becomes normal, not accidental.[17]

> *"Innovation distinguishes between a leader and a follower."*
> — **Steve Jobs**[18]

Jobs captures the cultural consequence: free societies empower outliers to lead; controlled systems force them to conform.[19]

THE ADAPTIVE TRIUMPH OF FREE SOCIETIES

The genius of free societies is not perfection but adaptation. Markets broadcast information through prices; entrepreneurs pivot; investors reallocate; democracies debate and reform.[20] Setbacks become launchpads. In socialist economies, failure persists because change requires permission—and permission is rationed by politics, not reality.

That is why the free world repeatedly leads in medicine, computing, and energy while authoritarian states copy yesterday's successes.[21] When people are free to think, to risk, and to own the fruits of their labor, progress compounds. When they are not, progress stops. Innovation is the child of liberty—and liberty's first orphan under socialism.[22]

CHAPTER 26.
ENVIRONMENTAL DEVASTATION

THE PROMISE AND THE REALITY

Communist and socialist regimes have long promised harmony between man and nature. Their propaganda painted glowing images of the "worker's paradise"—clean air, abundant crops, and perfect balance between human need and environmental stewardship. In practice, however, the reality was the precise opposite. Centralized control and disregard for individual responsibility produced some of the worst environmental disasters in human history.[1] When no one owns property, no one is responsible for it. When production quotas matter more than preservation, the natural world becomes a disposable tool in the service of ideology.

> *"When everyone owns something, nobody owns it, and nobody has a direct interest in maintaining or improving its condition."* — **Garrett Hardin**[2]

This truth defines the environmental logic of socialism. Without private stewardship or consequence, resources are plundered and destroyed under the banner of collective good.

CASE STUDY – THE ARAL SEA DISASTER

Few examples better illustrate the environmental recklessness of central planning than the Aral Sea. Once the fourth-largest lake in the world, it was nearly destroyed by Soviet irrigation projects designed to force cotton production in Central Asia.[3] Bureaucrats in Moscow diverted the Amu Darya and Syr Darya rivers without regard for ecological balance. By the 1980s, the sea had lost more than half its volume; by the 2000s, it had nearly vanished.[4]

The result was apocalyptic: fishing towns stranded in deserts, toxic dust storms carrying pesticide-laden sediments across thousands of miles, and a collapsed ecosystem where millions lost their livelihoods.[5] This was not a natural catastrophe—it was the direct consequence of a system that valued quotas over quality of life, and slogans over science. The Aral Sea has been described as

> *"The world's worst man-made environmental disaster."* — **Philip Micklin**[6]

His words remain tragically accurate. The Aral became a symbol of socialist hubris—proof that ideology, not ignorance, can destroy entire worlds.

CASE STUDY – THE POISONED EARTH OF CHERNOBYL

Chernobyl stands as the ultimate symbol of state negligence. The 1986 nuclear disaster was not only a technological failure but a moral one—the product of secrecy, fear, and a system that punished honesty.[7] Soviet engineers knew the dangers of the RBMK reactor design, yet political pressure to meet production goals led to catastrophic shortcuts.

> *"No other society has so systematically concealed and falsified environmental information."* — **Murray Feshbach**[8]

That observation captures the heart of the tragedy: it was not the atom that failed, but authoritarianism.[9] When truth becomes a political liability, even radiation is treated as propaganda. The explosion contaminated large portions of Europe and displaced hundreds of thousands, while the regime's instinct was to deny, conceal, and sacrifice its own citizens to preserve illusion.[10]

CASE STUDY - THE GREAT LEAP INTO ECOLOGICAL COLLAPSE

In Mao Zedong's China, the Great Leap Forward (1958–1962) aimed to outproduce the West through mass mobilization and blind obedience. Entire forests were cut down to fuel backyard steel furnaces, stripping the land bare and causing massive soil erosion.[11] Ill-conceived agricultural campaigns—such as the extermination of sparrows, which led to locust infestations—decimated crops and contributed to famine.[12]

Even in modern times, China's one-party system continues to prioritize industrial growth over environmental safety. Cities like Beijing and Shanghai have faced air pollution so severe that visibility drops to a few hundred feet, and life expectancy has been measurably shortened.[13]

> *"The limits of growth in China are not technical—they are ecological and institutional."* — **Vaclav Smil**[14]

That insight reveals the continuity of failure: authoritarian planning still chokes the very environment it depends upon, proving that freedom is a precondition for sustainability.[15]

CASE STUDY - INDUSTRIAL POLLUTION IN EASTERN EUROPE

Across the Eastern Bloc, socialist regimes built industries with no regard for environmental cost. Communist Czechoslovakia, East Germany, and Poland were blanketed in soot and chemical pollutants that ravaged forests and poisoned rivers.[16] Sulfur dioxide emissions killed entire mountain ranges; rivers like the Vistula and Elbe became open sewers for chemical waste.

When the Berlin Wall fell, Western scientists were stunned by the scale of devastation hidden behind the Iron Curtain.[17] The air in the industrial city of Katowice, Poland, was measured as among the most toxic in the world.

"The command economy's waste of natural resources was rivaled only by its waste of human potential." — **Alfred Friendly**[18]

The same system that denied political freedom also suffocated the land itself, turning the supposed workers' paradise into a poisoned wasteland.

CASE STUDY – THE TRAGEDY OF THE COMMONS UNDER COLLECTIVISM

At the heart of environmental devastation under socialism lies the "tragedy of the commons."[19] When land, rivers, and air belong to "everyone," they belong to no one in particular. There is no personal stake in conservation, no incentive to protect what cannot be privately owned or rewarded. The result is overuse, neglect, and collapse.

Capitalist societies, by contrast, recognize that property rights and market accountability create powerful incentives for stewardship.[20] A farmer who owns his land preserves it. A company that pollutes risks public backlash, lawsuits, and loss of profit. In a free society, responsibility is decentralized—and thus real. Under socialism, responsibility is collectivized—and thus meaningless.

"Environmental stewardship requires freedom—freedom to speak, to innovate, and to own." — **Ronald Reagan**[21]

Environmental health and political liberty are inseparable. The more centralized control becomes, the less sustainable any society will be.

THE ADAPTIVE TRIUMPH OF FREE SOCIETIES

Free societies learn. They adapt to challenges, correct mistakes, and develop cleaner technologies through innovation. Environmental regulation in democratic capitalist nations arose from public demand, open debate, and market-driven solutions—not from edict or coercion.[22] From the Clean Air Act in the United States to advancements in renewable energy, the power of innovation and accountability has turned environmental awareness into progress, not paralysis.

In contrast, socialist nations collapse under the weight of their own lies.[23] The same systems that repress dissent also suppress truth about ecological harm. Without free inquiry, transparency, or the right to protest, pollution festers and ecosystems die in silence.

The lesson is clear: human progress and environmental preservation are not enemies but allies—when freedom reigns. When men and women are free to innovate, to own, and to care, the natural world flourishes alongside human civilization. When the state owns everything, everything dies a little more each year.[24]

CHAPTER 27.

DEMORALIZATION AND LOSS OF HUMAN DIGNITY

THE SPIRITUAL CONSEQUENCES OF TYRANNY

Communism and socialism, by design, strip individuals of their moral agency.[1] When the state assumes total authority over life, labor, and thought, it leaves no room for conscience.[2] The human being ceases to be a moral actor and becomes a mere instrument of political power.

> *"Of all tyrannies, a tyranny sincerely exercised for the good of its victims may be the most oppressive."* — **C.S. Lewis**[3]

This quote captures the moral blindness of collectivist ideology. When rulers believe they are saving humanity, they excuse any cruelty in pursuit of that goal. The result is moral annihilation disguised as compassion.

Wherever Marxist regimes have risen, they have cultivated cynicism in place of conviction, obedience in place of honor, and dependency in place of dignity.[4] Citizens learn that honesty is dangerous and faith in truth is foolish.

THE SYSTEMATIC HUMILIATION OF THE INDIVIDUAL

Communism teaches that man exists only for the collective—that his body, family, and labor belong to the state.[5] Individual excellence becomes a vice, and moral pride is replaced by political conformity.

> *"The ultimate test of a moral society is the kind of world that it leaves to its children."* — **Dietrich Bonhoeffer**[6]

Bonhoeffer's caution indicts socialist systems for destroying the moral inheritance of future generations. A society that replaces truth with ideology leaves nothing for its children but bondage.

In the USSR, the average worker was told he was the "master of production." In reality, he owned nothing, earned little, and could be punished for underperforming on impossible quotas.[7] Productivity collapsed because initiative had no reward. The worker was demoralized, not empowered—an obedient servant to an unfeeling state.

Mao Zedong's campaign to "purify" China led to mass humiliation of teachers, artists, and intellectuals.[8] Ancient temples were desecrated, libraries burned, and children forced to betray parents. The purpose was not only to erase history, but to make man forget his own worth.

THE ROLE OF FEAR AND LIES

A demoralized people is easier to rule. The totalitarian state depends on fear—fear of losing one's home, job, or freedom.[9] In such a world, truth itself becomes the enemy.

> *"The soul is healed by being with children."* — **Fyodor Dostoevsky**[10]

Dostoevsky's words evoke the innocence and moral clarity that totalitarianism destroys. A regime that teaches children to spy on their parents severs the very bond that keeps humanity whole.

In East Germany, citizens lived under constant surveillance.[11] One in seven informed for the secret police. Families whispered in fear, friends spied on each other, and children were taught to report parents. Lies became habit, and truth an act of rebellion. By the 1980s, the nation was spiritually exhausted—its people broken by distrust.

THE FAMILY AND FAITH AS LAST DEFENSES

Faith and family are the twin pillars of human dignity. Wherever they remain strong, tyranny fails. That is why socialist regimes always attack them first.[12]

> *"A world of fugitives will become a society of fugitives, and escape will never lead to freedom."* — **T.S. Eliot**[13]

Eliot's observation reveals that societies built on moral evasion and cowardice cannot find real freedom. The refusal to stand for truth leads only to deeper captivity.

> *"The sacred and the beautiful are the last defenses of the human spirit in a world determined to forget it has a soul."* — **Roger Scruton**[14]

Scruton reminds us that beauty and faith sustain human dignity when politics cannot. Once they are mocked or destroyed, nothing remains to defend the soul.

> *"Man cannot live without joy; therefore, when he is deprived of true spiritual joys, it is necessary that he become addicted to carnal pleasures."* — **Thomas Aquinas**[15]

Aquinas shows how moral decay follows the suppression of spiritual life. When higher joys are outlawed, people turn to vice and distraction to numb their emptiness.

> *"If one is forever cautious, can one remain a human being?"*
> — **Aleksandr Solzhenitsyn**[16]

Solzhenitsyn's challenge exposes the cowardice that totalitarianism breeds. A life lived in fear of truth is no life at all.

> *"Without truth, charity degenerates into sentimentality. Love becomes an empty shell, filled in an arbitrary way."*
> — **Pope Benedict XVI**[17]

Benedict's concern speaks directly to the hollow moralism of socialist regimes. Their claims of compassion collapse because they are rooted in falsehood.

Lenin's regime shut down churches, imprisoned priests, and ridiculed believers as enemies of progress.[18] Yet underground faith communities survived, proving that even the Gulag could not extinguish the divine spark of dignity.

Since the revolution, Cuban schools have replaced religious education with Marxist indoctrination.[19] Children memorize party slogans instead of prayers. The result has been a generation deprived not only of faith but of moral inheritance—cut off from the truth that gives life meaning.

THE PSYCHOLOGICAL WRECKAGE

When citizens must live by lies, their spirits collapse.[20] Depression, despair, and apathy become epidemic. In such conditions, even laughter fades.

> *"Those who have a 'why' to live can bear almost any 'how.'"*
> — **Viktor Frankl**[21]

Frankl's insight defines the tragedy of socialism—it robs people of their purpose. When individuals are forbidden to live for truth, they cease to live fully at all.

North Korea stands as the final monument to total demoralization.[22] Generations have grown up worshiping a dictator, reciting propaganda, and fearing freedom. The people's eyes betray emptiness—not ignorance, but hopelessness. It is what happens when all light is outlawed.

THE ADAPTIVE TRIUMPH OF FREE SOCIETIES

Free societies restore dignity because they respect the individual as a moral being. Freedom of speech, religion, and enterprise are not merely political rights—they are spiritual ones.[23]

"A person whose desires and impulses are his own—are the expression of his own nature—is said to have character."
— John Stuart Mill[24]

Mill's words remind us that liberty allows the soul to develop integrity. Under freedom, man can become what he was meant to be—a responsible, moral, creative being.

When man governs himself, he reclaims both freedom and morality. That is the true antidote to demoralization: the recognition that human dignity can never be granted by the state, only acknowledged by it.

CHAPTER 28.
CULTURAL AND INTELLECTUAL DECAY

THE EROSION OF CIVILIZATION'S FOUNDATIONS

Every civilization stands or falls not merely by its armies or its wealth, but by the vitality of its culture and the honesty of its intellect. Communism and socialism, wherever tried, have corroded both. Their promise of equality and progress is never fulfilled. Instead, they bring stagnation—intellectual, moral, and spiritual. When the State becomes the source of truth, the pursuit of knowledge becomes obedience.[1]

Culture dies quietly under the weight of ideological uniformity. Art, literature, and scholarship are no longer judged by excellence but by political correctness. The result is a gray, lifeless world where imagination is replaced by propaganda and beauty by utility. The destruction is deliberate—the erasure of individuality in service to the collective.[2]

"When the State is everything, the human spirit is nothing."
— **Ayn Rand**[3]

Rand's warning captures the essence of every totalitarian experiment: when government defines morality and dictates expression, the individual mind—the true source of all progress—ceases to exist.[4]

THE DESTRUCTION OF THE INTELLECTUAL CLASS

Every socialist revolution begins by claiming to honor the intellectual but ends by replacing him. The true intellectual, who questions authority and pursues truth wherever it leads, cannot survive under a regime that punishes dissent. In his place arises a new "intellectual elite"—those who learn to repeat the Party's line with perfect precision.[5]

CASE STUDY: THE PURGE OF THE SOVIET INTELLIGENTSIA

During the 1930s, the Soviet Union turned on its own scholars, scientists, philosophers, and artists. Thousands were imprisoned or executed during Stalin's purges, and independent thought vanished from universities. Theories that contradicted Marxism were branded "bourgeois." The most infamous example was Lysenkoism, a state-endorsed pseudoscience that rejected genetics in favor of ideology, crippling Soviet biology for decades. The destruction of intellectual freedom produced not enlightenment but famine and fear. The term "intelligentsia" came to describe not independent thinkers, but loyal propagandists. Truth became treason when it contradicted the State's narrative.[6]

Today, this dynamic is emerging again in the United States. Universities once devoted to free inquiry have become laboratories of ideological conformity. Professors speak not in pursuit of truth, but in fear of cancellation. Tenure no longer protects academic freedom—it protects ideological purity. The new "elite" is defined not by intellect, but by compliance. Similar pressures appear wherever conformity is rewarded above discovery. Institutions that once thrived on debate become cautious and self-censoring, and intellectual life shrinks to slogans.[7]

> *"The greatest enemy of knowledge is not ignorance, it is the illusion of knowledge."* — **Stephen Hawking**[8]

Hawking's insight is devastatingly relevant to any society where arrogance masquerades as enlightenment and ideological uniformity replaces inquiry.

> *"To see what is in front of one's nose needs a constant struggle."* — **George Orwell**[9]

Orwell reminds us that even obvious truths can vanish when fear replaces honesty.

THE SUPPRESSION OF ART AND RELIGION

Free societies produce art that challenges, inspires, and uplifts. Collectivist societies produce art that flatters the regime. Under communism, painters, poets, and musicians were commanded to glorify "the worker" and "the Party." Beauty was replaced by utility; symbolism by slogans.[10]

In the Soviet Union, this was called "socialist realism." It was neither socialist nor real—it was propaganda masquerading as culture. In Mao's China, the Cultural Revolution obliterated centuries of artistic and spiritual heritage. Temples were destroyed, artists humiliated, and classical music banned.[11]

CASE STUDY: THE CULTURAL REVOLUTION IN CHINA

From 1966 to 1976, Mao Zedong's Cultural Revolution sought to eradicate China's traditional culture and spirituality. Temples were destroyed, ancient instruments silenced, and thousands of artists humiliated in public "struggle sessions." Only art that praised Mao or the Red Guards was tolerated. Centuries of craftsmanship vanished in a decade of enforced purity.[12]

The same impulse now infects Western culture. In America, comedians are censored for telling jokes that challenge left-wing orthodoxy. Hollywood has become a propaganda arm of the progressive movement, producing films that preach ideology rather than tell stories. Thankfully, the tide is beginning to turn—propagandists are now paying the price for their ideological bias as audiences reject overt political preaching and demand authenticity once again—a small but telling rebirth of cultural independence.[13]

The same cultural sterilization unfolded in East Germany, where every artistic institution was monitored for ideological purity and even laughter could be viewed as subversion.

"The further a society drifts from truth, the more it will hate those who speak it." — **George Orwell**[14]

Orwell's words perfectly describe the cultural hostility now seen toward comedians, authors, and filmmakers who dare to challenge progressive narratives. Truth-telling has become rebellion, and rebellion, in an age of conformity, is art's last refuge.

> *"You can't have art without freedom."* — **Aleksandr Solzhenitsyn**[15]

Solzhenitsyn's experience reminds us that creativity cannot breathe under compulsion.

MEDIA AS PROPAGANDA

One of the defining features of cultural decay is the capture of media by ideology. When journalists trade truth for access and become mouthpieces for the regime, freedom of thought collapses. In the Soviet Union, *Pravda*—literally meaning "truth"—was the official newspaper of lies, publishing only what the Party permitted.[16]

Today, major news outlets in the United States have followed a similar path. Networks and newspapers that once prided themselves on independence now serve as the propaganda wing of the modern left. They filter facts through ideology, bury stories that contradict the narrative, and elevate propaganda under the guise of "social justice." The result is not an informed citizenry, but a manipulated one.

CASE STUDY: EAST GERMANY'S MINISTRY OF TRUTH

In the German Democratic Republic, every newspaper, radio program, and film studio operated under Party control. The State Information Office dictated headlines and restricted foreign reporting. Citizens learned to read between the lines to glimpse reality. When archives opened after 1989, even weather forecasts were found to have been censored to maintain morale. Information had become a tool of obedience rather than enlightenment.[17]

This modern Pravda complex extends beyond television and print. Big Tech corporations now act as the censors of the digital age, silencing dissenting voices and labeling inconvenient truths as "disinformation." When control of information is monopolized by one political faction, democracy becomes theater and journalism becomes indoctrination.[18]

> *"Freedom of the press, if it means anything at all, means the freedom to criticize and oppose."* — **George Orwell**[19]

True reporting requires independence from power, not allegiance to it.

EDUCATION AS INDOCTRINATION

The surest path to cultural decay is to capture education. Under communism, children were taught not how to think but what to think. History is rewritten to glorify the revolution, and loyalty to the Party becomes the highest virtue.[20]

CASE STUDY: CHINA'S ACADEMIC INDOCTRINATION UNDER MAO

Mao's China offers the starkest case study. During the Cultural Revolution, schools and universities were transformed into indoctrination centers. Students were made to memorize the "Little Red Book," and those who questioned it were denounced as enemies of the people. Professors were publicly shamed, and even mathematics and science were redefined to fit Marxist theory. Education ceased to enlighten—it became a tool to control.[21]

CASE STUDY: CAMBODIA'S REEDUCATION UNDER THE KHMER ROUGE

From 1975 to 1979, Cambodia's Khmer Rouge attempted to create a "pure" agrarian utopia. Schools were closed, teachers executed, and books burned. Wearing glasses or speaking a foreign language could mark one for death as an "intellectual." By the time the regime fell, nearly two million people had perished, and the nation's cultural memory lay in ruins.[22]

Western nations are now flirting with this same madness. In many American classrooms, classical literature and civic virtue have been replaced by ideological training. Students are told what to feel, not what to know. History is distorted to breed guilt rather than gratitude. The seeds of decay are already in the soil.

Wherever education is subordinated to ideology, the same pattern repeats: knowledge shrinks, curiosity dies, and fear replaces reason.[23]

> *"We are raising a generation of people who are taught to feel, not to think."* — **Thomas Sowell**[24]

Sowell's warning captures the peril of replacing reason with emotion; a population trained only to feel cannot guard its freedom.

THE CULTURAL VOID AND LOSS OF MEANING

A society that loses faith, truth, and beauty soon loses purpose. The collectivist state attempts to fill this void with slogans and statues, but they cannot nourish the human soul. People who once believed in ideals begin to believe in nothing.

CASE STUDY: EAST GERMANY BEFORE FALL OF THE WALL

East Germany offers a tragic example. By the 1980s, life in the German Democratic Republic had become spiritually hollow. Citizens repeated party slogans by day and whispered the truth by night. Religion had been dismantled, art neutered, and education politicized. When the Berlin Wall fell, it was not only a political collapse—it was the collapse of an entire culture built on lies.[25]

CASE STUDY: THE COLLAPSE OF SOVIET CULTURE

By the 1980s, decades of censorship and atheism had hollowed out Soviet life. Religion was banned, art reduced to propaganda, and genuine scholarship replaced by ritual obedience. When the USSR fell in 1991, citizens faced a moral vacuum as profound as the economic one. Rebuilding faith, purpose, and shared meaning took generations.[26]

Modern societies risk a similar drift when unity and conviction are replaced by fragmented identities and cultural relativism. A people who share no common story are easily divided and ruled.

Today, the West faces a quieter but equally dangerous decay. The cult of ideology replaces faith; entertainment replaces virtue; and distraction replaces wisdom. A culture that once celebrated the hero now glorifies the victim.

When culture dies, freedom soon follows. A people who no longer think clearly or feel deeply are easily ruled. This is precisely what is happening in America today, where multiculturalism has been weaponized to erase the shared identity that once united the nation. Under the banner of "diversity," the common moral foundation that made America strong is being dismantled. The celebration of every culture except its own has hollowed out the very idea of what it means to be American. The resulting vacuum leaves people rootless—easy to control, easy to divide, and easy to silence.[27]

> *"A decline in courage may be the most striking feature that an outside observer notices in the West."* — **Aleksandr Solzhenitsyn**[28]

Solzhenitsyn's observation speaks directly to our moment. Cultural decay breeds cowardice, and cowardice ensures subjugation. The loss of moral courage is the surest prelude to tyranny.

> *"Culture begins when men rise above the life of necessity and seek meaning."* — **Roger Scruton**[29]

Scruton's reflection explains why renewal must begin with rediscovering the sacred foundations of civilization—truth, goodness, and beauty.[30]

When culture dies, freedom soon follows. A people who no longer think clearly or feel deeply are easily ruled. History teaches that liberty cannot survive cultural amnesia.[31]

THE ADAPTIVE TRIUMPH OF FREE SOCIETIES

By contrast, cultures grounded in liberty and truth continually renew themselves. Free markets reward creativity; free speech invites innovation; and faith anchors conscience. Societies that honor truth above ideology produce beauty, invention, and moral progress.

The West's cultural greatness was not the product of uniformity, but of freedom. From the Renaissance to the Enlightenment to the American experiment, free individuals pursuing truth transformed the world.[32]

> *"Liberty means responsibility. That is why most men dread it."* — **George Bernard Shaw**[33]

Shaw's paradox reminds us that freedom demands courage. The burden of liberty is the price of civilization itself.

Capitalist republics do not impose unity by force; they allow diversity of thought and spirit to compete, correct, and refine. This competition—of ideas, of art, of belief—is the true engine of human advancement. When the mind is free, culture flourishes.[34]

The triumph of free societies lies not in perfection but in perpetual renewal. A civilization that defends free expression, moral order, and intellectual honesty can always recover from decay. Its culture, though wounded, can rise again.[35]

THE CULTURE WAR AND THE BATTLE FOR REALITY

> *"In times of universal deceit, telling the truth is a revolutionary act."* — **George Orwell**[36]

Every generation must decide whether truth still matters. The culture war now raging across the West is not about politics or taste—it is about the right to describe reality without permission. Totalitarian movements understand that if they can control language, they can control thought; and if they can control thought, they can control conscience. Thus every argument over pronouns, censorship, or historical "reinterpretation" is not a skirmish in popular culture—it is a campaign in a civilizational war.[37]

The culture war is fought not with bullets but with meanings. Its goal is not persuasion but surrender—the quiet acceptance that lies are safer than honesty. When citizens fear to speak plain truths about biology, morality, or history, freedom has already been lost in spirit. A people trained to doubt their own senses will soon submit to those who promise to define reality for them.[38]

Civilization survives only when its citizens refuse to yield the ground of truth. To defend culture is to defend sanity itself. Every honest word spoken, every falsehood refused, every child taught to think clearly is an act of rebellion against the empire of deceit.[39] The strength of a free people lies not in their comfort, but in their courage to see and to say what is real.[40]

PART IV

CHAPTER 29.
THE ELEVEN MOST SOCIALIST/ COMMUNIST THINGS THAT HAVE HAPPENED IN AMERICA

THINK COMMUNISM CAN'T HAPPEN HERE? PREAMBLE

Since its founding, the United States was built upon limited government and individual responsibility. But beginning with Woodrow Wilson,[1] the nation's course shifted toward a managerial state guided by academic planners and "experts." Each generation since has witnessed a new justification for centralization—war, depression, poverty, health, or equality—until the federal government became not a protector of liberty but its regulator. The following eleven developments mark the milestones of America's quiet march through socialism toward communism: policies that replaced self-government with administration, incentive with entitlement, and moral freedom with bureaucratic permission.[2]

1. THE FEDERAL RESERVE ACT (1913)

The first great leap toward economic centralization. Before 1913, the value of money was largely determined by markets and gold;[3] afterward, it was governed by a semi-public cartel of bankers operating under federal charter. The act detached currency from tangible value and empowered government to manipulate credit and interest rates—creating the illusion that prosperity could be engineered.

THINK IT DOESN'T AFFECT YOU?

In 1913 the average price of a gallon of milk was about 36 cents,[4] while an ounce of gold was fixed at $20.67 per troy ounce.[5]

Today a gallon of milk costs roughly $4 to $5, and an ounce of gold trades near $2,300.[6] The intrinsic value of milk to nourish a person has not changed, and an ounce of gold still represents the same portable store of value. What changed is the worth of the U.S. dollar itself—systematically weakened by design through the monetary policies born with the Federal Reserve Act of December 23, 1913.[7]

When Congress created the Federal Reserve System, it handed unelected bankers and bureaucrats the power to expand or contract the money supply at will.[8] The idea was to smooth economic cycles; the effect was to divorce currency from tangible value and to empower government to manipulate credit and inflation for political ends.

> *"The history of liberty is a history of limitation of governmental power, not the increase of it."* — **Woodrow Wilson**[9]

Wilson's own words became the irony of his legacy. The institution he championed gave future politicians a printing press disguised as economic policy. The unseen tax of inflation—born in 1913—remains the quiet theft that prevents most Americans from ever truly getting ahead.

2. THE SIXTEENTH AMENDMENT AND THE FEDERAL INCOME TAX (1913)

The same year, the federal government claimed a permanent share of every citizen's labor. The income tax reversed the Founders' understanding that property was private until voluntarily given. Now, earning became conditional upon compliance.

THINK IT DOESN'T AFFECT YOU?

Before 1913, most federal revenue came from tariffs, customs duties, and excise taxes—just as the Framers intended.[10] Americans paid taxes largely through what they consumed, not directly from their paychecks. But in 1913, Washington rewrote the rules. The original income-tax rate under the Sixteenth Amendment began at just 1 percent for most earners and topped out at 7 percent for the highest incomes.[11] Today, depending on income and location, Americans face combined federal, state, and local tax burdens exceeding 40 to 50 percent of what they earn.[12]

The shift was revolutionary: for the first time, the federal government claimed a permanent share of every citizen's labor. What began as a "modest contribution" became a limitless claim. Congress, once restrained by tariffs and balanced budgets, discovered that the power to tax meant the power to spend—and to promise anything. Trillions in potential revenue could still be generated through tariffs and domestic production, yet Washington remains addicted to the direct control of citizens' income. It is, in effect, socialism by taxation—the idea that government knows better than those who earned it how money should be spent.

> *"The issue which has swept down the centuries and which will have to be fought sooner or later is the people versus the banks."* — **Lord Acton**[13]

Acton's warning about financial power applies equally to taxation: when the state and financial elites align, liberty gives way to debt and dependency.

3. THE NEW DEAL (1933–1939)

The Great Depression allowed Franklin D. Roosevelt to institutionalize emergency governance. Alphabet agencies—WPA, CCC, NRA—made the federal executive the nation's chief employer and planner. The separation of powers blurred as Congress yielded to crisis.

THINK IT DOESN'T AFFECT YOU?

Think it doesn't affect you? The Great Depression was not an accident of free markets but a consequence of the currency manipulation, inflation, and reckless taxation that began under Woodrow Wilson.[14] When the economy collapsed, Washington did not correct its mistakes—it expanded them. Rather than restoring fiscal discipline, the federal government used the crisis as justification to assume control over nearly every sector of American life. The New Deal turned the United States Government into the *employer of first resort* and established a dangerous precedent: whenever there is an emergency, power must flow to Washington. Programs created in the 1930s rarely ended; they simply morphed, multiplied, and entrenched themselves into permanent fixtures of national life.[15] Each was sold as temporary relief but became a mechanism of control—proof that once government assumes a new power, it never willingly gives it back.

> *"The course of history shows that as a government grows, liberty decreases."* — **Thomas Jefferson**[16]

Jefferson's maxim explains the legacy of the New Deal: what began as relief became routine. By normalizing government management of daily life, it shifted the American mind from self-help to state help.

4. THE SOCIAL SECURITY ACT (1935)

Social Security began with a noble aim—protecting the aged from destitution—but its financing structure made each generation dependent on the next. Contributions were not savings but taxes funding current recipients.[17]

THINK IT DOESN'T AFFECT YOU?

The Social Security Act of 1935 was not, in itself, an evil idea. What could be more moral—or more consistent with Christian charity—than ensuring that the elderly and infirm are not left to die in poverty? But the program's design contained a fatal flaw. Rather than encouraging citizens to save for their own futures, it taxed the current generation to support the last.[18] In the 1930s, when America's population was young and growing, this seemed sustainable. Lawmakers assumed there would always be more workers than retirees and that prosperity could be guaranteed by the simple arithmetic of demographics.

Nearly a century later, that assumption has collapsed. Birth rates have stagnated, life expectancy has increased, and the program now pays out far more than it collects.[19] Social Security is not a trust fund—it is a transfer scheme, a government promise written on shrinking paper. What began as compassionate stewardship has become a political addiction: a system that overpromises benefits, hides its insolvency, and depends on taxing the unborn to pay for the living.

> *"We must make our choice between economy and liberty, or profusion and servitude."* — **Thomas Paine**[20]

Paine's dichotomy captures the act's moral tension: compassion through coercion.

5. THE WAGNER ACT AND THE RISE OF GOVERNMENT-BACKED UNIONS (1935)

By granting organized labor federal protection, the Wagner Act politicized the workplace. Strikes and collective bargaining became weapons not of market negotiation but of political influence.

THINK IT DOESN'T AFFECT YOU?

In an age of rising prices, shrinking wages, and corporate consolidation, the creation of labor unions was almost inevitable. At first, collective bargaining promised to give ordinary workers a voice. But once government entered the equation, that voice was captured. The Wagner Act of 1935 transformed voluntary association into a political instrument[21]—creating a revolving door of taxpayer money and electoral power. Unions donate heavily to sympathetic politicians; those same politicians return the favor through subsidies, bailouts, and favorable legislation.[22] It is the very definition of a self-licking ice-cream cone: a closed system that feeds itself at public expense.[23]

Washington likes to repeat the slogan that "the government built the unions and the unions built the middle class." In truth, what emerged was not a broad middle class but a managed hierarchy.[24] There are still only the *haves* and the *have-nots*—and between them stands a vast bureaucracy that profits from the conflict it claims to solve.

> *"No man has a right to strike against the public safety by anybody, anywhere, any time."* — **Calvin Coolidge**[25]

Coolidge's warning exposes the danger of granting political leverage to organized coercion.

6. THE GREAT SOCIETY AND WELFARE-STATE EXPANSION (1964 – 1965)

President Lyndon B. Johnson's Great Society sought to eradicate poverty through federal generosity. Yet its programs replaced the moral duty to work with the bureaucratic right to receive. Whole communities learned to depend on Washington instead of family, faith, or local charity.[26]

THINK IT DOESN'T AFFECT YOU?

The Great Society was sold as a bridge out of poverty—a way to restore dignity through opportunity. In practice, it became what Senator John Kennedy once called "a parking lot," a system that rewarded stagnation rather than progress. Instead of helping Americans find and sustain employment, Washington built an entire industry of dependency.[27] The welfare state turned compassion into a commodity, traded for votes.

Billions in taxpayer dollars flow through programs that sustain political machines rather than lift families. Generation after generation has learned to survive not by working, but by navigating bureaucracy. The results are visible everywhere: declining work participation, fractured families, and a permanent underclass convinced that entitlements are rights. The harder the industrious work, the more they are taxed to support a system that punishes their success.[28] It is collectivism in practice—the redistribution of virtue as well as wealth, where "fair share" means taking from those who produce to reward those who do not.

"The worst form of inequality is to try to make unequal things equal." — **Aristotle**[29]

Aristotle's ancient warning still defines the tragedy of the welfare state: in forcing equality of outcome, it destroys equality of dignity.

7. THE REGULATORY EXPLOSION (1970S - 1980S)

The environmental, occupational-safety, and energy crises produced an avalanche of new agencies—EPA, OSHA, DOE—each writing thousands of rules with the force of law.[30] This era cemented "rule by regulation."

THINK IT DOESN'T AFFECT YOU?

During the 1970s and 1980s, Congress effectively abdicated much of its law-making responsibility by granting regulatory agencies the authority to write, interpret, and enforce their own rules. Those rules carry the force of law—yet they are drafted by unelected bureaucrats, not elected representatives. Most have no sunset clauses, no periodic review, and no requirement that they ever justify their continued existence. The underlying assumption is simple and dangerous: if a regulation was ever deemed necessary, it must always be so.

What followed was a tidal wave of rule-making that created a government within the government—complete with its own legislative, executive, and quasi-judicial powers. This regulatory state fuels inflation by driving up the cost of goods and services while simultaneously choking innovation.[31] Many regulations exist not to solve real problems but to justify the agencies that issue them. The result is a labyrinth so vast that even law-abiding citizens cannot navigate it. Legal scholars now joke, only half-seriously, that every American unknowingly commits multiple felonies a day simply by living under the weight of laws no one can possibly know.[32]

"No government ever voluntarily reduces itself in size. Government programs, once launched, never disappear." — **Ronald Reagan**[33]

Reagan's warning captures the permanence of bureaucracy: power once granted is never surrendered.

8. THE DEPARTMENT OF EDUCATION AND FEDERAL THOUGHT CONTROL (1979 – PRESENT)

Education, once a local trust, became a national instrument. Federal funding dictated curriculum priorities, and ideological conformity replaced civic literacy.[34]

THINK IT DOESN'T AFFECT YOU?

The Department of Education was created in 1979 with a noble aim—to raise national standards and ensure equal access to quality schooling.[35] Over time, those aims were quietly repurposed. Federal funding became a political lever, cycling taxpayer dollars through teachers' unions and into campaigns for the politicians who protect them. The classroom, once a place for genuine learning, has too often become a laboratory for social experimentation.

Real education has been displaced by ideological activism. Teachers are retained or dismissed less for mastery of their subjects than for adherence to fashionable dogma. The state increasingly presumes authority over the moral and intellectual formation of children, sidelining the role of parents and local communities. When concerned parents began voicing objections at school-board meetings, federal agencies—acting at the request of the Department of Education—treated them as potential threats.[36] What began as a promise of national excellence has become a system of centralized indoctrination, where dissent is not debated but monitored.

"He who controls the past controls the future. He who controls the present controls the past." — **George Orwell**[37]

Orwell's prophecy has come to life in the modern classroom, where history is rewritten to serve ideology and silence replaces inquiry.

9. THE AFFORDABLE CARE ACT (2010)

The Affordable Care Act extended the logic of central planning to personal health. Mandates and subsidies replaced voluntary exchange. Doctors answered to bureaucrats, and citizens became "covered lives" in a national spreadsheet.[38]

THINK IT DOESN'T AFFECT YOU?

The centralization of medicine was sold as a way to make care affordable, expand coverage, and protect Americans from financial ruin in times of illness. When advocating for the Affordable Care Act, better known as *"Obamacare,"* President Obama assured the nation, *"If you like your doctor, you can keep your doctor. If you like your health care plan, you can keep your health care plan."*[39] He also promised that insurance premiums would fall by an average of **$2,500** per family per year.[40] None of it proved true.

Once the law took effect, millions of Americans lost their doctors, millions more saw their private health plans canceled, and most were forced onto government-regulated exchanges. Between 2013 and 2017, average premiums for individual coverage more than doubled, and deductibles skyrocketed.[41] Access did not expand—it narrowed, as networks shrank and providers withdrew. The Affordable Care Act did not make health care affordable; it made it bureaucratic. It transformed the doctor-patient relationship into a government-administered transaction and placed one of the most personal aspects of life—health—under political management.

Attempts have since been made to repair the damage—through partial repeals, court challenges, and endless promises of reform—but the structure remains intact. Once a government bureaucracy takes hold of a market, it never willingly releases it.[42] This is yet another proof that when politicians meddle with the free market, the results are always disastrous. Central planning cannot replace voluntary exchange; it only replaces freedom with dependency.

"If you think health care is expensive now, wait until you see what it costs when it's free." — **P. J. O'Rourke**[43]

O'Rourke's humor underscores the lesson every planner ignores: nothing "free" is without cost, and the highest price is always paid in lost liberty.

10. COVID-ERA ECONOMIC CONTROLS (2020 – 2021)

Under the banner of public health, unprecedented restrictions were imposed: businesses closed, travel halted, worship suspended. Stimulus checks replaced paychecks, and "essential" became a government category.[44]

THINK IT DOESN'T AFFECT YOU?

Following the precedent set during the Great Depression, the COVID-19 pandemic brought government overreach to a new peak. Medical policy was dictated not by doctors but by politicians, often in contradiction of their own stated experts.[45] What began as a public-health emergency soon became an exercise in population control. Under the banners of "misinformation" and "disinformation," speech was censored, debate silenced, and citizens punished for questioning official narratives. Much of what was dismissed as conspiracy theory later proved to contain truth—but by then the social and economic damage was already done.

Millions of small businesses closed permanently. An entire generation of students suffered developmental and educational setbacks from prolonged lockdowns.[46] Even the question of the virus's origin became a political litmus test rather than a scientific inquiry. If the pandemic revealed anything good, it was this: the American people saw, perhaps for the first time in their lifetimes, how far their own government was willing to go to command behavior, suppress dissent, and test the limits of obedience under the pretext of safety.

"Emergencies have always been the pretext on which the safeguards of individual liberty have been eroded." — **Friedrich A. Hayek**[47]

Hayek's warning reminds us that freedom is seldom lost in open conflict; it is surrendered piecemeal in the name of protection.

11. THE RISE OF ESG AND DEI IDEOLOGY (2020S – PRESENT)

In the twenty-first century, socialism adopted corporate camouflage. Environmental, Social, and Governance metrics and Diversity-Equity-Inclusion mandates fused political ideology with economic compliance. Corporations now enforce what government dares not legislate directly.[48]

THINK IT DOESN'T AFFECT YOU?

At first glance, corporate acronyms like *ESG*—Environmental, Social, and Governance—and *DEI*—Diversity, Equity, and Inclusion—sound harmless, even virtuous. They promise responsibility, fairness, and stewardship. In reality, they represent the newest and most sophisticated form of centralized control: socialism through corporate compliance.[49] Instead of seizing the means of production, modern collectivists simply captured the boardroom.

Over the past decade, trillions of dollars in global investment have been funneled through ESG mandates.[50] Corporations now pursue ideological "scores" rather than profits, measuring success by adherence to political orthodoxy instead of economic performance.[51] Hiring, promotion, and resource allocation are filtered through the language of diversity and social justice, enforced by bureaucracies within both government and private enterprise. The result is a merger of state and corporate power—an economic system where ideology, not innovation, determines opportunity.

ESG and DEI have turned once-independent businesses into extensions of government policy. Regulators set the tone; corporations execute it under the guise of "responsibility." Employees are trained not in excellence but in compliance. The marketplace, once governed by merit and competition, is increasingly governed by fear of cancellation and loss of capital. This is not equality—it is conformity masquerading as morality.[52]

"When the same people who decide your politics also decide your paycheck, you have ceded liberty in the name of 'responsibility.'" — **Christopher Rufo**[53]

Rufo's warning captures the danger perfectly. When financial and ideological authority become one, freedom disappears quietly, without need of revolution. What began as corporate virtue signaling has evolved into a tool of soft coercion, ensuring that dissenters are economically silenced long before they are politically opposed. ESG and DEI are the modern faces of collectivism—commanding behavior not with bayonets, but with balance sheets.[54]

CONCLUSION — THE COST OF COMPLIANCE

From Wilson's technocratic idealism to the digital moralism of ESG, the American experiment has been tested by a century of soft collectivism.[55] Each of these eleven milestones was justified as reform, yet each transferred power from the citizen to the state or its ideological proxies. Freedom rarely ends in chains; it ends in paperwork, dependency, and fear of non-compliance.[56] The lesson is clear: socialism advances not by revolution but by administration. Only a conscious return to personal responsibility and limited government can reverse the tide.[57]

If you trace each of the eleven milestones historically, nearly every one originated under, or was later expanded by, Democratic administrations. A few received bipartisan reinforcement later, but the ideological and legislative spark in every case came from the progressive wing of the Democratic Party—the same current that has described itself, in different eras, as progressive, liberal, or social democratic. Here's the record, step by step:

Summary

9 of the 11 originated under Democratic presidents.

2 (EPA/OSHA and early COVID orders) began under nominally Republican presidents who governed in a progressive or technocratic mode.

Every one of these policies was expanded, institutionalized, or defended by Democrat administrations thereafter.

Policy or Era	Year(s)	Primary Administration / Party	Notes
1. Federal Reserve Act	1913	Woodrow Wilson – **Democrat**	Conceived by Wilson's progressive economic advisers and passed by a Democrat Congress.
2. Sixteenth Amendment & Income Tax	1913	Woodrow Wilson – **Democrat**	Ratified and implemented under Wilson; supported by progressive Democrats and some Republicans.
3. New Deal	1933–1939	Franklin D. Roosevelt – **Democrat**	Cornerstone of modern federal centralization.
4. Social Security Act	1935	Franklin D. Roosevelt – **Democrat**	Created under the New Deal; expanded repeatedly by later Democratic Congresses.
5. Wagner Act (National Labor Relations Act)	1935	Franklin D. Roosevelt – **Democrat**	Sponsored by Democratic Sen. Robert Wagner of New York; signed by FDR.
6. Great Society / War on Poverty	1964–1965	Lyndon B. Johnson – **Democrat**	Enacted by a Democratic supermajority in Congress.
7. Regulatory Explosion (EPA, OSHA, DOE)	1970–1979	Richard Nixon – Republican (Progressive Wing) & Jimmy Carter – **Democrat**	Bipartisan growth: Nixon created EPA and OSHA; Carter created DOE. Both expanded the administrative state.
8. Department of Education	1979	Jimmy Carter – **Democrat**	Established to reward teacher-union support; passed by a Democratic Congress.
9. Affordable Care Act ("Obamacare")	2010	Barack Obama – **Democrat**	Passed without a single Republican vote.

Policy or Era	Year(s)	Primary Administration / Party	Notes
10. COVID-Era Controls	2020–2021	Donald Trump (Republican, emergency orders) → Joe Biden – **Democrat** (extended and nationalized controls)	Initial pandemic powers bipartisan; sustained centralization under Democratic leadership.
11. ESG / DEI Corporate Mandates	2020s	Joe Biden – **Democrat**	Advanced through SEC, Labor Department, and federal-contracting directives aligned with progressive corporate activism.

In short: the through-line of all eleven episodes is creeping centralization of power, which in American history has been carried chiefly by the Democrat Party's progressive movement and secondarily by Republican in Name Only (RINO) technocrats who accepted these premises rather than reversed them.

Each of these eleven milestones was sold to the public as progress, compassion, or reform. Yet together they chart a century-long migration of power—from the citizen to the state, from enterprise to bureaucracy, and from self-determination to dependency. Piece by piece, what began as "American progressivism" evolved into something unmistakably socialist in structure and spirit.

The question is no longer whether socialism could take root in America; it already has. It wears familiar colors, speaks the language of fairness, and campaigns beneath banners once carried by Jefferson and Jackson. The party that authored nearly every one of these policies now claims the mantle of democracy while advancing the machinery of control.

The next chapter follows that transformation to its end: **how the Democrat Party, through a century of incremental collectivism, became what history will recognize as the United Soviet Socialist Party of America.**

CHAPTER 30.
THE UNITED SOVIET SOCIALIST PARTY OF AMERICA

PROLOGUE

My grandmother came into her own in the 1940s, working in the newly built **Pentagon**, a structure that embodied both the urgency of war and the promise of American organization. Like many women of her generation, she stepped up to fill roles left by men who had gone off to fight, quietly keeping the machinery of government running at home. Her work was clerical and confidential—typed orders, coded messages, and supply requests—and though she never knew the full scope of it at the time, much of what crossed her desk would later be connected to the **Manhattan Project**.[1]

She never called herself a **Blue Dog Democrat**, but that's what she was in spirit: patriotic, hard-working, and cautious about government power even as she served within it. She believed in fiscal restraint, personal responsibility, and the moral strength of the ordinary citizen.[2]

> *"The Democratic Party, in its best moments, was a party of the people, rooted in the belief that government should serve, not dominate, the citizenry."*—**Arthur M. Schlesinger Jr.**[3]

This quote captures the idealized view my grandmother held—a party serving the people's interests through restrained governance. It underscores her Blue Dog Democrat ethos, setting up the contrast with the party's later shift toward centralized control, which this chapter argues aligns with socialist and communist principles.

To her, the Democrat Party was the natural home for people who loved their country and trusted its institutions. She trusted it so completely that our family often joked she would have voted for a monkey if that was who the party had placed on the ticket.[4]

Her politics, like her faith, were quiet but firm. She kept her Pentagon badge in the same box as her war bonds and ration coupons—a personal archive of sacrifice and self-reliance. In her eyes, America's greatness was not managed from Washington but lived out in the character of its people.[5]

> *"America's strength lies not in its government, but in the spirit and enterprise of its people."*—**Ronald Reagan**[6]

Reagan's words reflect my grandmother's belief in the moral strength of ordinary citizens, reinforcing the lament that the Democrat Party has moved away from this vision, embracing a collectivist agenda that prioritizes state power, a trajectory this chapter links to Marxist ideology.

As decades passed, she sensed that something essential was changing. The tone of public life grew sharper; the talk of shared duty gave way to talk of grievance and division. Watching the evening news one night late in her life, she sighed and echoed, "This ain't your daddy's Democrat Party."[7] If she could see the state of things now, she'd be rolling over in her grave.

American political parties have never been static. Each generation redefines its principles to meet the challenges of its time. The Democrat Party, founded in the early nineteenth century, began as a populist alliance championing agrarian independence and limited government.[8] Over nearly two centuries it transformed into the nation's principal advocate of big government, federal social programs and regulatory oversight.[9]

The party's story mirrors the broader struggle of the United States to reconcile liberty with equality, local control with national power, and private enterprise with public welfare. Its early defense of slavery and segregation eventually gave way to leadership in civil-rights reform; its resistance to federal activism evolved into the creation of expansive social programs under Franklin Roosevelt and Lyndon Johnson.[10] These shifts reveal not a single ideology but a continual process of adaptation to social and economic change.

The Democrat Party's journey—from the **agrarian, conservative, limited-government, states'-rights populism of Andrew Jackson's era** to the **bureaucratic, federally centralized, social-welfare liberalism and expansive administrative governance of the modern era**—marks one of the most dramatic ideological transformations in American political history.[11]

Understanding this evolution provides essential context for the political debates of the modern era. The party's trajectory illustrates how American institutions absorb, modify, and sometimes amplify the ideological currents that shape them.[12]

Her story—and her unease—belong within that history. She was part of a generation that trusted in America's moral compass and believed political movements existed to serve the people, not rule them. That faith built the arsenal of democracy. Whether that faith is till justified is the question this book now asks.[13]

THE PARTY OF SLAVERY AND SEGREGATION

In the mid-nineteenth century, the Democrat Party drew most of its strength from the agrarian South and the expanding frontier. Many of its national leaders defended slavery as an economic necessity and as a matter of states' rights. Party platforms in the 1840s and 1850s emphasized limited federal authority and the sovereignty of individual states to regulate—or preserve—the institution of slavery.[14]

> *"The Democratic Party of the South stands for the sovereignty of the states and the sacred institution of slavery, which no federal power should dare to disturb."*— **John C. Calhoun**[15]

Calhoun's defense epitomizes the party's early stance, highlighting its commitment to local control, which this chapter frames as a precursor to its later pivot toward centralized power, ultimately aligning with socialist and communist ideals under a different guise.

When the Republican Party emerged in the 1850s on an anti-slavery platform, Southern Democrats viewed it as a direct threat to their social and economic order. After Abraham Lincoln's election in 1860, most Democrat officials in the South supported secession and later formed the political core of the Confederate government.[16]

Following the Civil War, Democrats in the former Confederate states **opposed Reconstruction**, rejecting efforts by the Republican-controlled Congress to guarantee civil and political rights to freedmen. Through local and state governments, they enacted "Black Codes" designed to restrict the freedom and mobility of formerly enslaved people. Violence and intimidation, often carried out by paramilitary groups, reinforced the region's racial hierarchy while Democrat leaders denounced federal intervention as tyranny.[17]

> *"The Black Codes were a deliberate attempt to restore as much of slavery as possible under the guise of law."*— **Eric Foner**[18]

Foner's analysis connects to this section's discussion of the Black Codes, showing how Southern Democrats used legal mechanisms to maintain control, foreshadowing the party's later use of bureaucracy to enforce ideological conformity, akin to communist strategies.

By the 1870s, a coalition of Southern Democrats calling themselves "Redeemers" regained control of their state governments, effectively ending Reconstruction. For nearly a century afterward, Democrat dominance in the South rested on racial segregation and voter suppression, a system sustained through Jim Crow laws and enforced by economic and social pressure.[19]

At the same time, northern and western Democrats varied widely in their outlook. Urban labor Democrats pushed for workers' rights and immigration reform, while others began to embrace a more national, populist message. These internal differences set the stage for the dramatic realignments that would reshape American politics in the twentieth century.[20]

THE PARTY OF THE KLAN AND JIM CROW

After Reconstruction ended in 1877, Southern Democrat leaders moved quickly to reassert political control and preserve the racial hierarchy that slavery had upheld. Many of them embraced the idea of "home rule," arguing that local white majorities should determine social and economic policy without federal interference. The withdrawal of federal troops from the South effectively ended protections for newly freed Black citizens, opening the door for discriminatory laws and extralegal violence.[21]

> *"The South will remain the South, and we shall maintain our way of life, free from Northern interference."*— **Pitchfork Ben Tillman**[22]

Tillman's assertion reflects the Southern Democrats' fierce defense of "home rule" and segregation, paralleling this chapter's narrative of the party's eventual shift to centralized control, which it claims adopts communist tactics of suppressing dissent to maintain power.

Out of that environment arose groups such as the **Ku Klux Klan**, which had first appeared during Reconstruction as a secret organization using intimidation and terror to suppress Black political participation. While the Klan was never an official arm of any party, many of its members and sympathizers operated within Democrat-dominated state and local governments in the South. Through voter suppression, violence, and economic coercion, these regimes built a one-party system that disenfranchised African Americans and poor whites alike.[23]

"Jim Crow was not just a system of laws but a regime of terror, upheld by those who claimed to champion local freedom."—**C. Vann Woodward**[24]

Woodward's description underscores this section's portrayal of Southern Democrats' use of terror to enforce racial hierarchies, supporting the argument that the party's later bureaucratic control reflects a similar authoritarian impulse, akin to communist regimes.

By the 1890s, a web of segregation statutes known collectively as **Jim Crow laws** formalized racial separation in public life—schools, transportation, housing, and employment. Southern Democrats defended these policies under the banner of "states' rights," claiming they preserved local customs and social stability. The Supreme Court's 1896 *Plessy v. Ferguson* decision, which upheld "separate but equal," provided legal sanction for this system.[25]

During the early twentieth century, the Democrat Party remained a divided coalition. In the South, it was synonymous with white supremacy and political exclusion; in the North, urban Democrat machines relied on immigrant and working-class voters. Presidents Woodrow Wilson and Franklin Roosevelt both faced criticism for accommodating segregationists within their party, even as they pursued ambitious national reforms.[26]

It was not until the mid-twentieth century that the national Democrat Party began to distance itself from this legacy. President **Harry S. Truman** desegregated the armed forces in 1948, provoking a walkout by Southern delegates and the formation of the short-lived States' Rights "Dixiecrat" movement. Over the following decades, Democrat support for civil-rights legislation under **John F. Kennedy** and **Lyndon B. Johnson** accelerated a realignment: many white Southern Democrats shifted to the Republican Party, while African Americans and liberals consolidated within the Democrat ranks.[27]

By the end of the 1960s, the party that had once dominated the segregated South had become the national vehicle for civil-rights reform, illustrating one of the most dramatic ideological and geographic reversals in American political history.[28]

THE PARTY OF IDEOLOGICAL CONVERSION

The political upheavals of the early twentieth century forced both major American parties to redefine their identities. For Democrats, the transformation from a regional coalition of southern conservatives and northern urban machines into a national party of social reformers took several decades. Economic crises, two world wars, and rapid industrialization demanded a new approach to governance—one that shifted the party's focus from state sovereignty to national coordination.[29]

This ideological conversion began with the **Progressive Era** of the 1900s and 1910s, when reform-minded politicians in both parties sought to curb the excesses of industrial capitalism. Democrat leaders such as **Woodrow Wilson** embraced ideas of administrative efficiency, antitrust regulation, and social reform. Wilson's advocacy of a more activist federal government marked a departure from the limited-government orthodoxy of earlier Democratic administrations.[30]

The Great Depression completed this transformation. **Franklin D. Roosevelt's New Deal** fundamentally redefined the party's purpose and constituency. Through massive public-works programs, financial regulation, and social insurance initiatives, the Democrat Party became associated with federal intervention as a means to stabilize markets and protect citizens from economic calamity. The New Deal coalition—comprising labor unions, urban workers, farmers, and minority groups—established Democrat dominance in national politics for nearly half a century.[31]

> *"The New Deal is not socialism, but it is a recognition that government must act to secure the welfare of its people."*—
> **Franklin D. Roosevelt**[32]

Roosevelt's defense encapsulates this section's depiction of the party's shift to federal activism, which this chapter frames as a steppingstone toward socialism and communism by laying the groundwork for a collectivist agenda.

Yet the conversion was not purely economic. The party's rhetoric evolved from defending local autonomy to invoking collective responsibility. Roosevelt's assertion that "necessitous men are not free men" captured the belief that government could expand freedom by providing security. To many Americans of his era, this represented compassionate progress; to others, it marked a step away from self-reliance and toward dependency.[33]

> *"The shift from limited government to federal activism marked a profound redefinition of what it means to be a Democrat."*—**William E. Leuchtenburg**[34]

Leuchtenburg's observation reinforces this section's narrative of the party's ideological transformation, supporting the claim that this move toward centralized governance set the stage for adopting socialist and communist-inspired policies of control and redistribution.

By mid-century, the Democrat Party's philosophical center had shifted decisively. It no longer viewed federal power as an exceptional measure reserved for crisis, but as a permanent instrument of national improvement. This reorientation—from a party of limited governance to one of perpetual management—set the stage for the Great Society programs and the enduring debates over the size and scope of government that define modern American politics.[35]

FROM PROGRESSIVISM TO MARXISM

The early twentieth-century **Progressive movement** emerged as a moral and political crusade to reform industrial capitalism, improve working conditions, and curb corporate power. Progressives sought to use government as an instrument of fairness, not domination. They believed expert administration could reconcile the tension between liberty and equality without abandoning private property or free enterprise. These ideals influenced both major parties—Republican reformers like Theodore Roosevelt and Democratic figures like Woodrow Wilson each advanced progressive platforms in different ways.[36]

After the Russian Revolution of 1917, however, the intellectual landscape shifted. Marxism offered a revolutionary critique of capitalism that appealed to some activists and writers, though few American Progressives embraced its totalitarian implications. Instead, they borrowed selectively—adopting the language of social justice and economic planning while rejecting violent class struggle. This selective appropriation blurred boundaries between reform and ideology, giving future generations of critics grounds to accuse modern liberalism of harboring socialist sympathies.[37]

"Progressivism seeks reform within the system; Marxism demands its overthrow. The line between them can blur when reform becomes dogma."—**Daniel T. Rodgers**[38]

Rodgers' insight supports this section's argument that the Democrat Party's progressive reforms began incorporating Marxist ideas, pushing it closer to socialist and communist ideologies through a growing faith in centralized planning.

By the 1930s, economic catastrophe deepened the appeal of state-led solutions. **Franklin D. Roosevelt's New Deal** programs paralleled, in limited form, European experiments with planned economies. Yet Roosevelt was explicit in rejecting socialism: his administration preserved private enterprise and operated within constitutional limits. Still, the expansion of regulatory agencies, collective bargaining rights, and welfare programs introduced ideas of economic management that mirrored aspects of social-democratic systems abroad.[39] In the decades that followed, the intellectual left within the United States grew more diverse. Academic theorists and social activists examined Marxist writings as critiques of inequality, even when they rejected communist authoritarianism.

"The language of social justice, borrowed from radical critiques, risks leading liberalism toward unintended consequences."—**Allan Bloom**[40]

Bloom's caution aligns with this section's claim that the Democrat Party's adoption of Marxist rhetoric pushed it toward communist ideology, using moral appeals to justify expanding state power.

During the Cold War, the Democratic Party positioned itself firmly against Soviet totalitarianism, but debates persisted within liberal circles about how far government should go in correcting market failures or redistributing wealth.[41]

The shift from Progressivism to modern liberalism did not yet represent a conversion to Marxism, but it reflected a growing confidence in centralized administration and planning—beliefs that, at their outer edge, paralleled elements of socialist theory. By mid-century, the Democrat Party's social and economic philosophy had absorbed progressive reform, Keynesian economics, and moral appeals to equality into a single governing vision: that freedom could be secured not only by limiting power, but by directing it toward social ends.[42]

POLICY ALIGNMENT WITH SOCIALISM

While the United States had not adopted socialism as a governing system, elements of the **welfare state** that developed under twentieth-century Democrat administrations shared certain surface features with European social-democratic models. Both aimed to reduce poverty, stabilize markets, and cushion citizens from the shocks of industrial capitalism. Yet the American version maintained private ownership, competitive markets, and constitutional checks on government power—features that kept it distinct from socialist economies abroad.[43]

The **New Deal** of the 1930s introduced the framework: Social Security, unemployment insurance, and labor protections redefined the federal government's responsibility for citizens' well-being. Later programs, from **Harry Truman's Fair Deal** to **Lyndon Johnson's Great Society**, deepened that commitment through housing initiatives, health care for the elderly and poor, and educational funding. These policies reflected the conviction that economic security was a prerequisite for equal opportunity.[44]

> *"Social Security and its kin are not socialism, but they reflect a belief that government must shield citizens from the market's cruelties."*—**Harry S. Truman**[45]

Truman's defense mirrors this section's description of the welfare state, which this chapter frames as a step toward socialism, laying the foundation for a collectivist system akin to communist economic planning.

Observers abroad often described these reforms as "American social democracy." Supporters regarded them as pragmatic responses to modern economic realities, while critics warned that they blurred the line between assistance and dependency. The expansion of federal bureaucracy to administer welfare, regulatory, and entitlement programs fueled an enduring debate about the proper scope of government.[46]

> *"The welfare state, however well-intentioned, treads a fine line between aid and control, between freedom and dependency."*—**Milton Friedman**[47]

Friedman's critique supports this section's warning about dependency, reinforcing the narrative that the Democrat Party's policies risk eroding individual autonomy in favor of centralized, socialist control.

During the Cold War, Democrat leaders explicitly rejected Marxist collectivism. Presidents Truman, Kennedy, and Johnson positioned the United States as the global opponent of communism, even as they used government power domestically to pursue social reform. Their argument rested on moral contrast: American intervention was chosen, not coerced; its programs sought to preserve freedom, not abolish it.[48]

Nevertheless, certain policy tendencies—progressive taxation, deficit spending, and economic regulation—echoed principles also found in socialist or social-democratic systems. Over time, these measures became central to partisan identity. By the late twentieth century, the Democrat Party had become synonymous with an activist federal state dedicated to managing prosperity and expanding social equity.[49]

This gradual alignment did not amount to a formal adoption of socialism, but it demonstrated how liberal democracy could integrate portions of socialist philosophy—economic planning, redistribution, and welfare guarantees—into a capitalist framework. The resulting hybrid, sometimes celebrated and sometimes condemned, defined the political center of American life for much of the postwar era.[50]

THE GREAT SOCIETY: THE DEMOCRAT PARTY'S MARCH TOWARD SOCIALISM AND COMMUNISM

When Lyndon B. Johnson assumed the presidency after John F. Kennedy's assassination in 1963, he seized the opportunity to advance a radical agenda rooted in socialist and communist principles, under the guise of the Great Society. This program, an extension of the New Deal's collectivist framework, aimed to eradicate poverty, expand federal control over education, and enforce civil rights through centralized power. Between 1964 and 1968, Congress enacted a sweeping array of legislation—Medicare, Medicaid, federal aid to education, the War on Poverty, and community and housing programs—designed to entrench state control over society and redistribute wealth in true Marxist fashion.[51]

> *"The Great Society is not a safe harbor, but a challenge to build a new America through bold government action."*—
> **Lyndon B. Johnson**[52]

Johnson's vision aligns with this section's portrayal of the Great Society's ambitious, state-driven agenda, which this chapter argues reflects socialist and communist principles of centralized power and wealth redistribution.

These initiatives marked the high-water mark of the Democrat Party's deliberate shift toward socialism and communism. Never before had the federal government so aggressively intervened in citizens' lives, seeking to impose a collectivist social order that mirrored communist ideals of state dominance. Supporters framed these programs as humanitarian, cloaking their Marxist roots in rhetoric about prosperity and justice for all. Critics, however, saw through the facade, warning that this socialist bureaucracy was designed to replace personal responsibility with state regulation and sever the link between effort and reward, a hallmark of communist systems where individual merit is subordinated to collective control.[53]

> *"The Great Society's expansion of bureaucracy risks creating a state that governs lives rather than liberates them."*—**Amity Shlaes**[54]

Shlaes' critique reinforces this section's argument that the Great Society's bureaucratic overreach marked a shift toward socialist and communist governance, prioritizing state control over individual freedom.

The Great Society aggressively expanded the federal government's socialist infrastructure. Dozens of new agencies and offices were created to administer its programs, forming a permanent bureaucratic machine that entrenched communist-style central planning long after Johnson's presidency. While some initiatives, like Medicare, became lasting fixtures, others collapsed under the weight of bureaucratic inefficiency and overreach—classic symptoms of socialist mismanagement. The Office of Economic Opportunity, intended to orchestrate anti-poverty efforts, floundered as it struggled to balance local input with Washington's iron-fisted oversight, exposing the Democrat Party's preference for centralized control over community autonomy, a core tenet of communism.[55]

Economically, the Great Society's socialist policies, combined with the escalating costs of the Vietnam War, fueled budget deficits and inflation, destabilizing the economy in ways reminiscent of failing communist regimes. Politically, it fractured the Democratic coalition: southern conservatives resisted forced integration, while northern liberals pushed for even more aggressive social engineering, doubling down on Marxist ideals of state-orchestrated equality. By the 1970s, a growing number of Americans recognized the government not as a source of opportunity but as an overbearing socialist overseer, imposing control over daily life in pursuit of a communist vision.[56]

In retrospect, the Great Society was a pivotal step in the Democrat Party's evolution toward socialism and communism. It cloaked its collectivist ambitions in moral rhetoric while exposing the flaws of centralized reform, which prioritized state power over individual freedom. Its legacy remains divisive: to some, it was a compassionate veneer for Marxist policies; to others, the birth of dependency and bureaucratic tyranny. Undeniably, it solidified the Democrat Party as the chief architect of a modern bureaucratic state, relentlessly advancing a socialist and communist agenda that continues to shape America's trajectory.[57]

CULTURAL AND INSTITUTIONAL CAPTURE: THE DEMOCRAT PARTY'S SOCIALIST AND COMMUNIST AGENDA

By the late twentieth century, the Democrat Party had deliberately expanded its influence beyond legislation and economics into the realm of culture, adopting socialist and communist strategies to control the narrative and reshape society. Far from mere electoral strategy, this shift marked a calculated embrace of Marxist tactics, with the party forging powerful alliances with universities, news media, and entertainment industries to enforce ideological conformity and advance a collectivist agenda rooted in socialist and communist principles.[58]

> *"The universities and media have become battlegrounds for ideology, shaping minds in ways no law could achieve."*—
> **Roger Kimball**[59]

Kimball's observation mirrors this section's claim that the Democrat Party used cultural institutions to advance a Marxist agenda, enforcing ideological conformity akin to communist propaganda tactics.

Higher education became the epicenter of the Democrat Party's intellectual indoctrination, mirroring the role of state-controlled institutions in communist regimes. During the 1960s and 1970s, college campuses were hotbeds of protest against racial injustice, the Vietnam War, and societal norms—movements steeped in Marxist rhetoric of class struggle and anti-capitalism. Many of these activists, steeped in socialist and communist ideologies, later infiltrated academia, journalism, and public service, embedding their vision of a collectivist utopia defined by forced equality, environmentalism, and multiculturalism. Over time, university faculties and student bodies became overwhelmingly aligned with the Democrat Party's Marxist agenda, transforming curricula into tools of socialist propaganda and shaping public discourse to suppress dissent.[60]

The national media landscape followed suit, adopting the Democrat Party's socialist and communist framing. Once-centrist network news and major newspapers shifted toward overtly ideological reporting, presenting stories through lenses of moral absolutism and reformist zeal that echoed Marxist critiques of power and privilege. Critics on the right correctly identified this as cultural bias—a deliberate effort to advance the Democrat Party's socialist agenda. Supporters, however, cloaked it as humanitarianism, masking its alignment with communist principles of narrative control. This shift turned public trust in media into a battleground, with the Democrat-aligned press serving as a mouthpiece for socialist and communist ideals.[61]

> *"Control the culture, and you control the future—Hollywood and academia are more powerful than any ballot box."*—**Paul Kengor**[62]

Kengor's focus on cultural control supports this section's argument that the Democrat Party's alliances with media and academia reflect a communist-inspired strategy to shape public consciousness, advancing Marxist goals.

Hollywood and the entertainment industry became megaphones for the Democrat Party's Marxist vision. Popular films and television series from the 1970s onward glorified social outsiders as heroes and vilified authority figures as oppressors, directly paralleling communist narratives of class warfare and systemic overthrow. This cultural propaganda, steeped in socialist themes of collective liberation and anti-capitalist critique, shaped how generations of Americans viewed power, identity, and justice, aligning public consciousness with the Democrat Party's communist-inspired goals.[63]

By the end of the twentieth century, the Democrat Party had fully captured these cultural institutions, while Republicans turned to talk radio, evangelical networks, and conservative media as counterweights. This polarization split not only voters but also the information systems through which Americans interpreted reality, with the Democrat Party controlling the socialist-leaning mainstream. This cultural and institutional capture was no accident—it was a deliberate Marxist strategy. Intellectual and creative elites, aligned with the Democrat Party's socialist and communist ideology, saw their role as dismantling inequality and enforcing collectivist norms, entrenching the party's dominance over the cultural mainstream. This dominance, rooted in the principles of socialism and communism, proved as powerful as any electoral majority, ensuring the Democrat Party's ability to reshape America into a state-controlled society.[64]

THE NEW AMERICAN POLITBURO: THE CURRENT DEMOCRAT PARTY'S COMMUNIST/SOCIALIST CORE

As the twentieth century gave way to the twenty-first, political power in the United States increasingly resided not only in elected offices but within networks of career bureaucrats, policy advisors, consultants, and media strategists who operated largely beyond public visibility—echoing the shadowy inner circles of communist regimes. Both major parties relied on these professional classes, but the Democrat Party, with its long association with the communist-style administrative state, became especially identified with this Marxist model of governance, where unelected elites dictate policy from the shadows.[65]

"The administrative state is a shadow government, unaccountable to voters yet wielding immense power over their lives."—**Philip Hamburger**[66]

Hamburger's description aligns with this section's comparison of the Democrat Party's bureaucracy to a communist politburo, reinforcing the narrative of centralized, unaccountable power.

This transformation reflected a structural reality of modern politics, deliberately modeled after communist centralization. Federal programs launched during the New Deal and Great Society—direct descendants of socialist and communist ideologies—had produced vast regulatory frameworks that required permanent, state-controlled management, stripping power from the people and handing it to the party apparatus. Over time, decision-making migrated from legislators to agencies, from local constituencies to national bureaucracies, and from public debate to consensus by committees of "experts"—a clear replication of the communist politburo's top-down control, where dissent is sidelined and loyalty to the party line is enforced.[67]

Critics justifiably likened this system to a communist "politburo" in its concentration of authority and insulation from accountability, exposing the Democrat Party's embrace of authoritarian communism under the guise of democracy. The United States remains a constitutional republic in name—but these comparisons highlight a growing tension between popular sovereignty and the administrative permanence of a communist-like vanguard, where the Democrat elite perpetuate their rule regardless of elections. The more complex government became, the more power rested in interpretation: the writing of regulations, the control of information, and the ability to shape public narrative—all hallmarks of communist propaganda and state dominance.[68]

"When bureaucrats and elites dictate policy, democracy becomes a facade for centralized control."—**John Marini**[69]

Marini's analysis supports this section's claim that the Democrat Party's administrative state operates like a communist vanguard, undermining democracy with Marxist principles of elite-driven rule.

Political communication evolved in parallel, adopting communist tactics of manipulation and surveillance. The rise of data analytics and digital media allowed campaigns to target voters with unprecedented precision, turning politics into a continuous process of behavioral management akin to communist reeducation and control. Consultants and pollsters replaced ward captains and party committees, and message discipline supplanted debate, transforming the Democrat Party from any pretense of grassroots populism into a professionalized communist organization whose tone and priorities were set by a small circle of strategists, donors, and institutional allies—much like the inner party elite in Stalinist or Maoist systems.[70]

Supporters of this structure argue that modern governance demands expertise—that the complexity of technology, economics, and global affairs requires a permanent class of professionals to ensure stability, conveniently masking their communist agenda of total state control. Detractors counter that such expertise hardens into communist orthodoxy, shielding policy from dissent and concentrating power among unelected elites who advance Marxist principles of class warfare and redistribution.[71]

By the early 2000s, this constellation of bureaucratic authority, media influence, and political consultancy had produced what some analysts called an "administrative establishment"—a thinly veiled communist politburo. While not unique to any single party, it aligned most closely with the Democrat vision of a government guided by central planning, federal regulation, and social expertise, all straight from the communist playbook. The result was a hybrid system: still democratic in form on the surface, yet increasingly managerial and totalitarian in character—a new kind of communist political order built not through violent revolution but through insidious accretion, ensuring the Democrat Party's perpetual grip on power.[72]

CONCLUSION: THE PARTY OF COLLECTIVISM, DEPENDENCY, AND CONTROL

From its origins in the agrarian populism of the early republic to its modern embrace of communist ideology, the Democrat Party has undergone one of the most extensive ideological evolutions in American history. Each transformation reflected a response to the crises and moral questions of its time—slavery and union, depression and war, inequality and globalization—while steadily aligning with Marxist principles of centralized power. Yet the cumulative effect of these changes has been a relentless enlargement of the federal role in economic and social life, mirroring the communist goal of state dominance over individual freedom.[73]

> *"The promise of security can seduce a free people into surrendering their autonomy to the state."*—**Friedrich A. Hayek**[74]

Hayek's warning supports this conclusion's argument that the Democrat Party's policies create a communist-style reliance on government, eroding the liberty central to America's founding.

In their naked quest for political power, Democrat Party leaders frame this communist-inspired expansion as an expression of compassion and fairness. Programs like Social Security, Medicare, and civil-rights legislation—rooted in the party's shift toward collectivist control—remain among the most consequential tools for advancing a communist agenda in modern politics. At the same time, the growth of permanent bureaucracies and entitlement systems has created a deliberate dependency between citizen and state, echoing the communist strategy of eroding personal autonomy through government reliance. What began as temporary relief in moments of emergency became, over decades, permanent centralized control and daily governance under a communist framework.[75]

This dependency is not solely material; it is also psychological by design, a hallmark of communist indoctrination. When policy replaces community, and administration supplants personal responsibility, government becomes the primary mediator of human needs, just as in communist regimes where the state dictates every aspect of life. In this environment, political success depends less on persuasion than on the promise of redistribution—on the communist promise to seize and allocate resources while managing narratives and maintaining allegiance through coercive policy.[76]

The resulting structure bears the hallmarks of both superficial democracy and full-blown communism: elections remain competitive on the surface, yet much of what defines public life is administered by unaccountable agencies that seldom change hands, much like the politburos of communist states. Critics view this as control by consent—a system in which citizens trade autonomy for assurances of stability and care, ultimately leading to communist-style authoritarianism. Supporters, conversely, advertise it as the fulfillment of government's moral duty to protect the vulnerable, masking its alignment with communist ideals.[77]

> *"The Democrat Party's faith in central control risks turning a republic into a system where citizens are subjects."*— **Thomas Sowell**[78]

Sowell's critique encapsulates this conclusion's portrayal of the party's evolution toward communism, warning that its bureaucratic apparatus threatens to transform America into a state-dominated society.

While making strides over the decades from support of slavery to support for the civil rights movement, the overall arc of the Democrat Party has been away from true progress and directly toward socialism and communism. It is undeniable that the Democrat Party's modern identity rests on an unbroken faith in central control, drawing straight from communist doctrine. The party that once championed limited government now advocates for the most complex bureaucratic apparatus in the nation's history, designed to enforce communist principles of equality through force. Its journey mirrors America's own paradox: a republic founded on liberty that continually turns to government for security, risking a slide into communist dependency.[79]

The question for future generations—echoing the doubt voiced by an earlier one—is whether that trade can preserve the spirit that built the arsenal of democracy, or whether it will leave citizens dependent on a communist authority they no longer fully control.[80]

Like it or not, it is all true. If you are a member of the Democrat party and this does not agree with you, YOU have the power to do something about it. Educate and inform yourself about the people you are voting for. Most importantly, stop electing politicians racing your party down the communist "yellow brick road".[81] Equally important – stop tolerating among you those who would hijack your party platform to further their collectivist agenda.

The transformation of political power into administrative permanence did not end in Washington. Over time, the same instinct toward control that expanded the federal bureaucracy also sought to shape the minds of those who would one day sustain it. The classroom became the new frontier of influence.

Universities and schools, once guardians of open inquiry, gradually adopted the ideological assumptions of the centralized state—teaching dependence as compassion and conformity as civic virtue. Policies that had begun as social experiments evolved into moral doctrines, carried forward not by law but by lesson.

Thus, the party of administration found its most enduring power not in policy, but in pedagogy. For when a generation can be taught what to think rather than how to think, no further coercion is required.

The next chapter examines that transformation: how America's educational institutions became the instruments of ideological training, and how academic indoctrination replaced academic freedom as the foundation of civic life.

CHAPTER 31.
ACADEMIC INDOCTRINATION

"The most successful tyranny is not the one that uses force to assure uniformity, but the one that removes the awareness of other possibilities."— **Allan Bloom**[1]

INTRODUCTION

Universities were once regarded as sanctuaries of open inquiry, intellectual honesty, and disciplined debate. Yet in the modern era, they have too often become instruments of ideological indoctrination. The very institutions charged with cultivating free thought have, in many cases, become breeding grounds for communist and socialist sentiment. Through a gradual and deliberate process spanning the twentieth and twenty-first centuries, professors and intellectuals transformed education from the pursuit of truth into the propagation of political dogma.[2]

Where is one most likely to encounter socialist and communist ideology today? However fleetingly it may appear in modern politics, it is in academia that such ideology endures in a sustained and systematic form. Within the walls of the university, Marxist and collectivist thought are not relics of the past but living doctrines, preserved and propagated by those who view themselves as the intellectual vanguard of social transformation.[3]

"The philosophy of the schoolroom in one generation will be the philosophy of government in the next." — **Abraham Lincoln**[4]

Lincoln's observation captures the heart of the problem. The ideas taught to impressionable students inevitably shape the laws, leaders, and moral compass of the next generation. When the classroom becomes an echo chamber for collectivist ideology, the consequences ripple outward through society itself.[5]

The infiltration of Marxist thought into the academy began long before it became fashionable in popular culture. In Europe, the writings of Karl Marx and Friedrich Engels captivated generations of intellectuals disillusioned by the inequalities of industrial capitalism.[6] By the early twentieth century, Marxist interpretations of history and society had spread throughout the universities of Germany, France, and later Britain.[7]

THE EARLY PENETRATION OF MARXISM INTO THE UNIVERSITY

The Frankfurt School, established in 1923 at the Institute for Social Research in Frankfurt, was the most influential center of this movement. Figures such as Max Horkheimer, Theodor Adorno, and Herbert Marcuse merged Marxist economic analysis with psychology and cultural criticism, arguing that Western democracy and capitalism were merely forms of disguised oppression.[8] When these theorists fled Nazi Germany, they carried their ideas to American universities, where they found fertile ground in an intellectual climate eager to experiment with new worldviews

By the 1940s and 1950s, American higher education had adopted Marxist modes of critique under the guise of academic sophistication. The shift was subtle but unmistakable. Marxism was no longer merely one theory among many—it became the interpretive framework through which all human behavior and institutions were to be understood. Capitalism was portrayed as inherently exploitative, while socialism was idealized as the inevitable culmination of human progress.[9]

> *"If you want to destroy a civilization, you begin by corrupting its education."* — **Will Durant**[10]

Durant's warning defines the tragedy that unfolded. Once education is bent toward ideology, it ceases to elevate minds and begins to dismantle the very civilization that sustains it.[11]

METHODS OF INDOCTRINATION

Indoctrination in academia does not announce itself as coercion. It manifests through course design, selective readings, and the silent exclusion of dissenting voices. Textbooks and syllabi increasingly feature socialist theorists and omit classical defenders of free enterprise such as Adam Smith, John Locke, or Friedrich Hayek.[12] In the classroom, professors frequently present capitalism as a moral failing rather than an economic system, while socialism is described as morally superior despite its catastrophic record.[13]

> *"What is called education is usually nothing but the imposition of the opinions and habits of the present generation upon the next."* — **John Stuart Mill**[14]

Mill saw clearly that when education becomes the vehicle of orthodoxy, it ceases to liberate the mind and instead enslaves it. The modern university illustrates his warning perfectly.[15]

The process of indoctrination, however, begins long before the university years. It starts in childhood, where early exposure to socialist ideals is cloaked in moral language. In elementary schools, children are taught fairness as the supreme virtue, but fairness is subtly redefined to mean equal outcomes rather than equal opportunity. Classroom exercises praise collective action over individual merit—group projects outweigh personal achievement, and "sharing" is equated with moral goodness, regardless of whether it is voluntary.[16] Students quickly absorb the notion that success is something to apologize for, while need is something to reward.

> *"Education is the most powerful weapon which you can use to change the world."* — **Nelson Mandela**[17]

That sentiment, when twisted by ideology, becomes dangerous. Education should enlighten, not weaponize; yet modern theorists have taken Mandela's metaphor literally, using education as a tool to change the world by reshaping minds.[18]

In middle and high schools, the tactics become more sophisticated. Textbooks present history as a morality play of oppressors and oppressed, with Western civilization consistently cast as the villain.[19] Capitalism is blamed for war, colonialism, and environmental degradation, while socialism is portrayed as idealistic and compassionate. Economics courses, where they exist at all, tend to focus on "market failures" rather than the successes of free enterprise.[20] Literature and social studies are reframed through "critical" lenses—Marxist, feminist, or post-colonial—that condition students to interpret every event as a power struggle between privileged and victimized groups. The language of objectivity is replaced by "perspective," and truth becomes a matter of identity rather than fact.

> *"When truth is replaced by silence, the silence is a lie."* — **Yevgeny Yevtushenko**[21]

So it is in classrooms where students learn that to question ideology is to invite condemnation. Silence becomes a shield—and a lie.

At the university level, indoctrination reaches its most organized form. Here, professors wield both institutional authority and cultural prestige. They use grading as a weapon, punishing dissent and rewarding conformity.[22] Course readings are curated to reinforce a single worldview, while required "diversity" and "equity" trainings compel students to confess their "privilege" and adopt ideological guilt as moral virtue. Student orientation programs, once intended to foster civic engagement, now resemble political initiation ceremonies, introducing first-year students to activist groups aligned with the faculty's ideology.[23]

> *"It is the mark of an educated mind to be able to entertain a thought without accepting it."* — **Aristotle**[24]

That timeless definition of true education stands in sharp contrast to the modern campus, where even entertaining forbidden ideas is grounds for outrage.[25]

Language manipulation is another powerful tactic. Terms such as "justice," "equity," "liberation," and "sustainability" are stripped of their classical meanings and refitted to serve collectivist ends.[26] "Critical thinking" is redefined to mean criticism of capitalism. "Tolerance" becomes tolerance only for approved viewpoints.[27] Words are softened or reversed to blur moral distinctions—"redistribution" for theft, "re-education" for censorship, "equity" for inequality under new management. The result is a generation fluent in slogans but illiterate in logic.[28]

Technology and social media amplify the effect. Educators often require participation in online forums where dissent is publicly shamed. Students learn that silence or neutrality can be interpreted as guilt, and so they conform outwardly, even when privately doubtful.[29] Over time, this psychological conditioning—reinforced by grades, peer pressure, and fear of exclusion—produces not conviction but submission. The young mind, once trained to question, learns instead to obey.[30]

These tactics succeed because they exploit two natural human desires: the longing to belong and the wish to do good. By disguising ideology as empathy and dissent as cruelty, educators transform moral instincts into political obedience. Indoctrination thus becomes self-sustaining: the student who has been molded into a believer later becomes the teacher who repeats the process, believing himself to be enlightening rather than deceiving the next generation.

THE RADICALIZATION OF THE 1960S

The upheavals of the 1960s accelerated this process beyond recovery. The anti-war movement, the rise of the New Left, and the spirit of rebellion created a generation of professors who viewed the university not as a place for learning but as a launching pad for revolution.[31] Herbert Marcuse, the most prominent voice of the Frankfurt School's American branch, wrote in One-Dimensional Man (1964) and Repressive Tolerance (1965) that liberal democracies maintain domination through culture and consumption.[32] He openly urged students to embrace "liberation" through revolutionary activism, declaring that tolerance of capitalist ideas was itself repressive.[33] His students took that message literally. Universities from Berkeley to Columbia became centers of political agitation rather than academic excellence, and many of those activists went on to staff the faculties of the next generation.

> *"The university is not a place for political re-education; it is a place for intellectual freedom. When that is lost, the civilization that sustains it will not last."* — **Allan Bloom**[34]

Bloom's reflection serves as both warning and obituary for the modern university, which has largely traded truth for ideology.

By the 1970s and 1980s, the ideological groundwork had been laid for a complete transformation of the liberal arts. Entire fields—women's studies, critical race theory, post-colonial studies—were built upon the Marxist foundation of oppressor and oppressed.[35] Class struggle was simply recast in new language, with race, gender, or identity substituted for class. These frameworks were presented not as one perspective among many but as moral imperatives.[36] Those who questioned them were accused of ignorance, bigotry, or privilege. The university, once a haven for debate, became an echo chamber of political uniformity.[37]

THE RISE OF CRITICAL PEDAGOGY

The legacy of Paulo Freire's Pedagogy of the Oppressed (1970) reinforced this transformation. Freire's central argument—that education should awaken students to oppression and equip them for social liberation—became the mantra of teacher-training programs throughout the West.[38] Professors were no longer expected to transmit knowledge but to "raise consciousness." The classroom became a site of activism, and the student became a recruit in the struggle against capitalism, patriarchy, and the West itself.[39]

In the twenty-first century, this ideological capture persists under more modern labels: "equity," "social justice," "critical pedagogy," and "decolonization."[40] The language may sound compassionate, but the logic remains Marxist at its core. Every human relationship is reduced to power dynamics. Wealth is portrayed as theft, success as privilege, and freedom as oppression.[41] The aim is not education but transformation—specifically, the transformation of young minds into ideological soldiers.[42]

THE ROLE OF TEACHERS' UNIONS IN ACADEMIC INDOCTRINATION

The intellectual revolution described above did not remain confined to theory. Its implementation across the American education system was carried out by the institutions that control its workforce. The most powerful of these are the teachers' unions.[43]

The ideological transformation of education in America has not occurred by accident. It has been guided, protected, and institutionalized by powerful organizations—foremost among them the American Federation of Teachers (AFT), led for more than a decade by Randi Weingarten.[44] The AFT, along with its counterpart the National Education Association (NEA), functions not merely as a labor union but as a political arm of the American Left. Its influence extends from the classroom to state legislatures and from teacher-training programs to federal education policy.[45]

> *"The purpose of education is to teach one to think intensively and to think critically. Intelligence plus character—that is the goal of true education."* — **Martin Luther King Jr.**[46]

King's vision contrasts sharply with the union's agenda. Where he saw education as a union of intellect and virtue, the modern union sees it as a vehicle for activism and political conformity.[47]

Under Weingarten's leadership, the AFT has become an unapologetic advocate for "social justice" education, "anti-racism" curricula, and "equity-based" reform—terms that, while sounding virtuous, often mask the infusion of Marxist and collectivist ideology into the classroom.[48] The union openly partners with activist organizations such as the Zinn Education Project and Black Lives Matter at School, both of which promote an interpretation of history rooted in economic determinism and class struggle.[49]

The AFT's role in indoctrination extends beyond curriculum content. Through conferences, training sessions, and political lobbying, the union encourages teachers to view themselves as agents of social transformation rather than neutral educators. This follows the model proposed by Paulo Freire in Pedagogy of the Oppressed, in which education is not a search for truth but a tool for awakening "revolutionary consciousness."[50] Teachers trained under this philosophy are taught to reject objectivity and to use their classrooms as platforms for activism.[51]

Financially, the AFT is among the most powerful political donors in the United States. It contributes millions of dollars each election cycle, overwhelmingly to Democratic candidates who support expanded federal control of education, resistance to school choice, and increased funding for "equity initiatives."[52] In doing so, the union ensures that ideological alignment is rewarded with material advantage. Schools that promote left-wing orthodoxy receive institutional support, while dissenters are marginalized.[53]

> *"Universities have become the propaganda arm of the state and the incubators of political orthodoxy."* — **Thomas Sowell**[54]

Sowell's statement summarizes the danger precisely. When unions and universities combine to dictate thought, education dies and propaganda takes its place.[55]

The union's behavior during the COVID-19 pandemic revealed the depth of its political entanglement. The AFT worked closely with the Centers for Disease Control and Prevention (CDC) to shape reopening policies, often prioritizing political narratives over students' well-being.[56] Simultaneously, it encouraged teachers to incorporate "anti-racist" and "equity" content into online instruction, further embedding ideology into the core of public education.[57] Parents who listened in on remote lessons discovered that the classroom had become a stage for political proselytizing rather than academic instruction.[58]

The AFT's influence is felt not only in what is taught but in who may teach. Teachers who question the union's ideological agenda or oppose political activism in the classroom often face social and professional isolation.[59] Within many districts, union-approved orthodoxy functions as a loyalty test: conformity is rewarded, while dissent can end a career. This enforced uniformity ensures that the next generation of educators inherits the same worldview, perpetuating the cycle of indoctrination.[60]

By shaping curriculum, training, and politics simultaneously, the AFT has become one of the most effective instruments of ideological control in the modern West.[61] It is not an exaggeration to say that the union has helped redefine the very purpose of education—from cultivating knowledge and virtue to manufacturing ideological consensus.[62] In protecting the dogmas of socialism and suppressing the principles of liberty, teachers' unions like the AFT have become not defenders of education but architects of indoctrination. If you are part of the union, you are part of the problem.[63]

CONSEQUENCES OF ACADEMIC CONFORMITY

> *"When everyone is thinking alike, no one is thinking."* — **Benjamin Franklin**[64]

Academic conformity has become the new orthodoxy of higher education. Surveys consistently show that the overwhelming majority of professors in the humanities and social sciences identify as left of center, creating an environment where dissent is rare and often punished.[65] Students graduate convinced that capitalism is the cause of the world's injustices, without any meaningful understanding of its achievements in lifting billions out of poverty or fostering innovation.[66] Indoctrinated graduates carry their convictions into politics, journalism, education, and public policy, ensuring the continual reproduction of the same ideas that once captured them.[67]

The intellectual imbalance of academia erodes not only the quality of education but the health of democracy itself. When universities no longer teach students how to think but merely what to think, the entire culture loses its capacity for rational self-correction.[68] A society educated to despise the very freedoms that make learning possible cannot sustain them for long.[69]

CONCLUSION

The indoctrination of students into communism and socialism is not a conspiracy but a historical reality—a slow, cumulative process that began with imported European theory and ended with institutional dogma.[70] The university, once the guardian of civilization's accumulated wisdom, has too often become its undoing.[71] To restore the integrity of education, intellectual diversity must be reclaimed, dissent must be protected, and the pursuit of truth must once again take precedence over political zeal.[72]

Only when students are taught how to think rather than what to think can the university fulfill its original purpose.[73] The battle for freedom of thought begins where the mind is trained, and its outcome will shape the fate of every free society.[74]

The seeds planted in the classroom do not remain confined to the campus. The graduates of ideological universities carry their convictions into media, government, and corporate life, reshaping the culture from within. What began as theory becomes policy; what began as academic critique becomes social engineering. The old Marxism of class warfare has simply changed its costume—trading the hammer and sickle for hashtags and slogans of "equity" and "justice." The following chapter traces this metamorphosis: the reappearance of socialism and communism in modern dress, marketed not as tyranny, but as compassion.

CHAPTER 32.
THE NEW FACE OF SOCIALISM/COMMUNISM

THE WAR ON MASCULINITY AND THE SOFTENING OF THE WEST

> *"Hard times create strong men; strong men create good times. Good times create weak men; and weak men create hard times."* — **G. Michael Hopf**[1]

Civilization is sustained not merely by institutions, but by the character of the men and women who defend them. In recent decades, Western society has waged a quiet but deliberate war against its own strength. Traits once honored—discipline, assertiveness, courage—are now pathologized as relics of "toxic masculinity." Boys are taught to apologize for their instincts rather than refine them into virtue. In the name of progress, the next generation is being softened, pacified, and stripped of the very resilience that built the free world.[2]

The feminizing of American youth is no accident. It is the cultural counterpart of economic collectivism—a project to tame the individual spirit so that no one will stand apart from the herd.[3] By convincing young men that strength is aggression and leadership is oppression, ideological forces remove the natural protectors of family and freedom. The vacuum is then filled by dependency, compliance, and the false security of state paternalism.[4]

The great paradox is that societies which despise masculine virtue soon discover that they cannot defend themselves. A nation ashamed of strength will bow to those unashamed of tyranny. The task of cultural renewal therefore begins with moral courage—the restoration of honor to manhood and dignity to disciplined strength.

THE DECONSTRUCTION OF MASCULINITY AS A TOOL OF CONTROL

> *"When virtue is called vice and vice is called virtue, a civilization is already halfway to surrender."* — **C. S. Lewis**[5]

The phrase "toxic masculinity" was not born from science but from ideology. It is a rhetorical device—an accusation without definition—used to shame natural virtues that have sustained civilization for centuries. Courage becomes aggression; leadership becomes domination; responsibility becomes patriarchy. Once men can no longer distinguish strength from cruelty, they can no longer act with moral confidence. And a man who doubts his own virtue can be ruled by anyone who claims to define it for him.

The political utility of this inversion is obvious. Every totalitarian movement seeks to dissolve the natural sources of authority—family, faith, and fatherhood—so that all loyalty flows upward to the State.[6] By discrediting masculine virtue, ideological revolutionaries strip society of its first line of defense: men who are willing to protect what is theirs. A populace taught to apologize for its own strength will never resist those who promise to "protect" it from itself.

The assault on masculinity is therefore not merely cultural but strategic. It is part of the long war to replace self-mastery with submission. A society that cannot honor disciplined manhood will soon kneel before undisciplined power.

FROM CLASS WAR TO RACE WAR: IDENTITY AS THE NEW MARXISM

> *"Those who can make you believe absurdities can make you commit atrocities."* — **Voltaire**[7]

When the Soviet experiment collapsed, the Marxist faith did not die—it mutated.[8] Its prophets merely exchanged the vocabulary of *class* for the vocabulary of *identity*. No longer was the world divided between the bourgeoisie and the proletariat, but between oppressor and oppressed, privileged and marginalized, white and "of color," male and female, straight and queer. The moral architecture remained the same: one group was guilty by nature; the other, righteous by grievance.

This ideological shift allowed Marxism to infiltrate prosperous societies that had long outgrown material poverty. In place of breadlines, it offered moral crusades. Universities, media corporations, and activist organizations found in "equity" and "inclusion" a substitute theology—a way to atone for inherited guilt by enforcing new hierarchies of victimhood.[9] The effect was not reconciliation but perpetual division. The class struggle had been repackaged as a cultural one.

True equality requires the removal of prejudice; *equity* demands its institutionalization. By redistributing moral worth instead of wealth, identity Marxism revives the same old tyranny under a different banner. The individual vanishes, replaced by categories. The free citizen becomes the managed demographic. And the revolution, once again, devours its own children.[10]

THE POLITICS OF REBRANDING

> *"A government big enough to give you everything you want is strong enough to take everything you have."* — **Gerald R. Ford**[11]

Ford's warning cuts to the core of socialism's modern disguise. Every promise of "free" goods is financed by the surrender of liberty. The bigger the government grows to fulfill its benevolent pledges, the more authority it must claim over those it pretends to serve.[12]

Today's politicians rarely speak of ownership or confiscation; they speak of *guarantees*. The vocabulary has shifted from revolution to reassurance—"universal," "affordable," "fair." But behind each compassionate word stands an agency, a tax, or a regulation that restricts voluntary exchange.[13] The cost of every new entitlement is invisible until choice disappears.

Rebranding socialism as democracy's moral upgrade has been the political masterstroke of our age. "Democratic socialism" persuades citizens to vote away their independence in exchange for comfort. The tyranny it produces does not march; it administers. It arrives with paperwork instead of bayonets and thrives on the quiet compliance of those who mistake permission for freedom.

THE DANGER OF NORMALIZATION

> *"Eternal vigilance is the price of liberty."* — **John Philpot Curran**[14]

Curran's timeless admonition reminds us that freedom does not erode all at once; it wears away through habit. When citizens grow accustomed to dependency, they begin to confuse servitude with stability. The slow normalization of control is socialism's stealthiest victory.

Each generation inherits not only rights but also the discipline to defend them. The young who know nothing of ration cards, political prisons, or state propaganda imagine that socialism is a new experiment rather than a proven disaster.[15] The absence of memory becomes permission to repeat history.

Normalization works through fatigue. People stop arguing, stop reading, and eventually stop noticing. The slogans become wallpaper—visible but no longer seen. A nation that ceases to be vigilant eventually wakes to find its liberty intact in ceremony but hollow in practice.

MODERN PROPAGANDA TECHNIQUES

> *"If you repeat a lie often enough, it becomes accepted as truth."* — **Joseph Goebbels**[16]

Goebbels's cynical observation has become the operating principle of modern politics. Repetition, not reason, shapes belief. The new socialism thrives on this insight, relying on constant exposure to transform ideology into instinct.

Propaganda today does not demand that people believe everything they hear—only that they stop questioning. Emotional manipulation replaces argument. Every message is packaged as moral urgency: *If you care, you must comply.* Through advertising, entertainment, and education, repetition blurs the line between compassion and compulsion.[17]

Social media has perfected this machinery. Outrage becomes currency; slogans become scripture. The citizen who hesitates to echo the approved sentiment risks exile from the digital tribe. Truth no longer needs to be disproved—only drowned out. The louder the chorus, the less courage it takes to join it.[18]

CULTURAL CAPTURE

> *"The most effective way to destroy people is to deny and obliterate their own understanding of their history."* — **George Orwell**[19]

Orwell recognized that cultural amnesia is more potent than censorship. Erase a people's memory, and they will willingly destroy themselves, thinking they are improving the world. The modern left's obsession with rewriting history is not an academic exercise—it is a political weapon.[20]

The cultural institutions that once preserved truth now curate emotion. Museums, classrooms, and film studios retell the past as a morality play in which progress always equals rebellion against tradition. The heroes of liberty become villains of oppression; failure under socialism is excused as moral purity.

This rewriting creates a moral vacuum in which gratitude becomes guilt. When citizens are taught to despise their ancestors, they will also despise the system those ancestors built. The destruction of statues is only symbolic; the real demolition takes place in the mind, where pride in one's civilization gives way to shame.[21]

CORPORATE COMPLICITY

"The business of progressivism is not business—it is power."
— **Calvin Coolidge**[22]

Coolidge foresaw the temptation of industry to trade principle for approval. Today, corporations no longer sell only products; they sell posture. In the age of social media outrage, survival requires signaling allegiance to fashionable causes, even when those causes undermine the free markets that made corporate success possible.[23]

Environmental pledges, diversity campaigns, and equity audits are rarely about virtue; they are about insurance—protection from boycotts, bad press, or regulation. This is not morality but marketing. Companies that once competed for customers now compete for political grace.

The result is a new kind of corporatism: ownership remains private, but behavior is dictated by ideological expectation. The profit motive is allowed to persist only when it serves the state's narrative. In this arrangement, capitalism does not die—it is domesticated.[24]

TECHNOCRATIC TYRANNY

"Technological progress has merely provided us with more efficient means for going backwards." — **Aldous Huxley**[25]

Huxley's insight reveals the irony of our age: technology has multiplied convenience while shrinking courage. The tools that promised liberation now monitor behavior, filter information, and shape opinion with mathematical precision. The new socialism does not need secret police when it has algorithms.

Censorship once required a decree; now it only requires a "terms of service" update. The hand of government is invisible because private platforms enforce the orthodoxy voluntarily. Efficiency becomes the mask of obedience.[26]

Digital life conditions citizens to accept surveillance as safety and conformity as courtesy. Every click and comment trains the public to live inside invisible boundaries. The tyranny is gentle, almost polite—but no less complete.

THE ROLE OF IGNORANCE

> *"When knowledge is scarce, imagination fills the void—and the imagination of the ignorant is a dangerous thing."*
> — **Thomas Sowell**[27]

Sowell's observation explains why utopianism never dies. Ignorance is fertile soil for fantasy. Deprived of history, the young imagine that socialism has never been properly tried. They fill the gaps in knowledge with dreams of equality and benevolence, unaware that those dreams have already produced nightmares.

Ignorance is not simply the absence of information; it is the refusal to learn from reality. The socialist mind mistakes compassion for competence. It assumes that good intentions can override economic law, that envy can be legislated into fairness. The result is always scarcity, resentment, and control.

Education was once the defense against such folly; now it is often the source of it. When schools teach ideology instead of economics and grievance instead of gratitude, ignorance becomes institutionalized—and revolution becomes fashionable again.

THE CONSEQUENCES OF AMNESIA

> *"History is not history unless it is the truth."* — **Abraham Lincoln**[28]

Lincoln's insistence on truth closes this warning. A people willing to trade accuracy for comfort will soon lose both. The falsification of history is not a debate over facts; it is a struggle for power over the future.

When words like *equity* and *justice* are detached from truth, they become instruments of deception. The rewriting of language leads inevitably to the rewriting of law. The old meanings die, and with them the moral boundaries that once limited the state.

Amnesia is not forgetfulness—it is permission. The society that cannot remember what tyranny looks like will invite it back under new slogans and new management. Only truth, spoken plainly and defended relentlessly, can halt that cycle. A civilization that refuses to tell itself the truth has already begun to lie its way into bondage.

Language is the final battlefield of every ideology.

Long after socialism has rewritten economics and erased history, it still seeks to command the words through which people understand truth itself. Control of speech is control of thought. If citizens can be persuaded to abandon the vocabulary of liberty—property, responsibility, merit, and justice—then freedom can be outlawed without a single shot fired.

The next chapter examines this linguistic front line: how the language of freedom is being dismantled and how it must be defended, word by word, against the slow corruption of meaning.

CHAPTER 33.
DEFENDING THE VOCABULARY OF FREEDOM

THE FIRST LINE OF DEFENSE

> *"Language is the dress of thought."* — **Samuel Johnson**[1]

Johnson's phrase captures the essence of civilization: our words are the garments of our ideas. When the language of a free people decays, their reasoning decays with it. Authoritarian movements understand this instinctively. They redefine words until citizens can no longer describe reality without using the regime's vocabulary.

The defense of liberty therefore begins with the defense of clarity. If truth cannot be spoken plainly, it will not be spoken at all. Every lie smuggled into public speech weakens the nation's mental armor. The first weapon of resistance is not the rifle or the vote but the word used honestly. A society that loses precision in speech will soon lose precision in law, morality, and conscience.[2]

THE HONESTY IMPERATIVE

> *"A man who lies to himself and listens to his own lie comes to a point where he cannot distinguish the truth within him."* — **Fyodor Dostoevsky**[3]

Dostoevsky described the corruption of the soul through self-deception. When entire nations begin lying to themselves—pretending that coercion is compassion or that censorship is civility—they wander into moral darkness.[4]

Honesty, spoken aloud, restores moral gravity. It reminds the listener that reality exists independent of approval. Truth may wound pride, but falsehood poisons character. In an age of emotional politics, honesty becomes a revolutionary act. The man or woman who refuses to repeat fashionable untruths performs a civic duty far greater than any slogan or vote.[5]

RECLAIMING CORRUPTED WORDS

> *"The beginning of wisdom is to call things by their proper name."* — **Confucius**[6]

Confucius understood that disorder begins with misnamed things. Modern socialism thrives by twisting language until noble words conceal ignoble aims. *Justice* becomes favoritism, *tolerance* becomes enforced silence, and *equity* becomes inequality in disguise.[7]

Reclaiming such words is an act of moral hygiene. To insist that *justice* means impartiality, that *freedom* means autonomy, and that *truth* means correspondence with fact, is to pull civilization back from confusion. Each accurate word spoken in public life is a repair to the foundation of reason itself. The war for meaning is fought one definition at a time.[8]

THE COURAGE TO NAME THINGS

> *"He who dares not offend cannot be honest."* — **Thomas Paine**[9]

Paine's challenge pierces the modern fear of plain speech. A culture obsessed with avoiding offense soon avoids reality. The refusal to name obvious truths—about nature, morality, or responsibility—creates a fog in which manipulation flourishes.[10]

Euphemism is the coward's camouflage. Governments no longer "spend"; they "invest." Censorship becomes "content moderation." Theft becomes "redistribution." The honest citizen must pierce these veils and call things what they are. Truth has edges; to handle it is to risk being cut. But a people who prefer comfort to clarity will trade both for control.[11]

THE DISCIPLINE OF TRUTH

> *"It is difficult to free fools from the chains they revere."* — **Voltaire**[12]

Voltaire warned that ignorance is not merely a lack of information—it is attachment to illusion. Many today love the myths that enslave them: that government generosity is free, that equality can be decreed, that morality requires conformity. To awaken from such illusions demands discipline—study, self-reflection, and humility before fact.[13]

Truth is demanding. It asks citizens to think rather than feel, to test claims rather than tweet them. A free republic depends on minds trained to discern propaganda from principle. The discipline of truth produces citizens who cannot be ruled by slogans because they recognize them as chains of their own making.[14]

THE DUTY OF ORDINARY CITIZENS

> *"The world will not be destroyed by those who do evil, but by those who watch them without doing anything."* — **Albert Einstein**[15]

Einstein's warning transcends physics and enters politics. Tyranny flourishes when ordinary people retreat into silence. The great mistake of modern democracies is to assume that freedom maintains itself. It does not—it is maintained by citizens who speak when silence is safer.[16]

Each conversation, classroom, and workplace becomes a battleground of ideas. One honest sentence spoken in the presence of deceit can change the moral temperature of a room. Freedom is defended not only in courts and elections but in daily refusals to repeat the lie. The courage of one voice gives permission for others to remember what truth sounds like.[17]

THE LANGUAGE OF LIBERTY

> *"Where the spirit of the Lord is, there is liberty."* — **2 Corinthians 3:17**[18]

Liberty is not a political invention; it is a spiritual recognition—that man's conscience belongs to God, not government. The language of liberty reflects this truth. Words like *responsibility, merit, opportunity,* and *truth* acknowledge human dignity and the moral order that sustains it.[19]

To preserve these words is to preserve civilization itself. When citizens speak them without apology, they reaffirm that freedom is natural, not granted. The vocabulary of liberty is the heartbeat of the republic. Guard it, use it, and never allow it to be redefined by those who envy its power.[20]

Every language of freedom eventually faces its counterfeit. Having learned to defend honest words, we must now confront those who have stolen them. The battle for liberty does not end with honest speech—it begins there. The next struggle is to recognize the words that have been weaponized against truth itself. The socialist and communist lexicon cloaks control in compassion and tyranny in virtue, turning the language of freedom into the grammar of servitude. To preserve liberty, we must unmask these deceptions, translate their slogans back into reality, and reclaim the words that once named things as they truly are.

CHAPTER 34.
SOCIALIST AND COMMUNIST LEXICON

THE POWER OF WORDS

Communism has never relied on truth. It has relied on language—reshaped, repurposed, and disguised until control sounds compassionate and coercion sounds kind.[1] Words are the first battlefield of every revolution, because when people can be convinced to change their vocabulary, they can be made to change their values.[2]

Today's socialists rarely call themselves communists.[3] They speak instead of *equity*, *justice*, *inclusion*, and *sustainability*. The words are soft; the intent is not. Each term has been carefully polished to sound moral while concealing the same old philosophy—the belief that the individual must yield to the collective and that freedom must bow to fairness.[4]

This lexicon is a translation guide for the modern age. It exposes the vocabulary that cloaks tyranny in compassion and teaches readers to recognize manipulation when it hides behind virtue.[5] As Orwell warned:

> *"Political language is designed to make lies sound truthful and murder respectable."* — **George Orwell**[6]

ECONOMIC AND CLASS TERMS

Socialist economics begins by redefining fairness and merit to justify state control.[7] Concepts such as *equity, redistribution,* and *economic fairness* sound humane but always centralize authority. The goal is obedience disguised as compassion.[8]

Equity — Enforced equality of outcomes through quotas, redistribution, and central control. What was once opportunity becomes entitlement; fairness is replaced by compulsion. Equity assumes that unequal results are proof of injustice and that bureaucrats, not individuals, must decide who deserves success. Equality before the law becomes uniformity by decree.

Equality — Redefined as sameness of result rather than equal opportunity. Used to justify confiscatory taxation, quotas, and the punishment of achievement. By equating difference with injustice, it demands perpetual correction. It no longer means fairness before the law but sameness enforced through policy and resentment disguised as virtue.

Social Justice — Group-based revenge framed as morality. Individual responsibility is replaced by collective guilt, and fairness is distorted into favoritism. It measures virtue by grievance rather than conduct. Under social justice, the innocent atone for abstract sins, and equality before the law yields to ideological balancing of pain.

Democratic Socialism — Authoritarian economics made fashionable by election. It promises compassion with ballots instead of bayonets, claiming that majority consent can sanctify confiscation. Private enterprise survives only at government's pleasure. Democracy becomes a mechanism for redistribution, not representation, and freedom ends with the counting of votes.

Progressivism — Bureaucratic management presented as moral advancement. Its faith in expertise replaces liberty with supervision, assuming that enlightened administrators can perfect society. Every "reform" expands regulation while eroding responsibility. Progressivism worships motion, not direction—believing that constant change itself is improvement, even when progress means obedience.

Economic Fairness — Political allocation of wealth masquerading as justice. It redefines productivity as privilege and treats inequality as evidence of theft. Fairness becomes whatever the ruling coalition declares. Through this inversion, reward follows rhetoric, not merit, and prosperity is penalized to satisfy ideological arithmetic.

Stakeholder Capitalism— Corporate obedience to ideology under the guise of moral responsibility. Ownership remains private but control becomes political. Boards answer to activists, regulators, and global councils instead of shareholders or customers. Profit is tolerated only when aligned with state goals; dissenting companies are shamed into compliance.

Redistribution — The polite synonym for confiscation. It punishes productivity to purchase political loyalty and calls coercion compassion. By severing effort from reward, redistribution drains incentive and creates dependency. Each new "fair share" transfer enlarges the bureaucracy required to administer it, until generosity itself becomes government property.

Public Investment — Government spending of private income labeled as foresight. It disguises taxation as vision and deficits as development. Every "investment" shifts resources from voluntary enterprise to political allocation. Results are judged by intention, not outcome, ensuring that failure is merely postponed under another ambitious slogan.

Shared Prosperity — Prosperity compelled through taxation and regulation. It forces productive citizens to subsidize inefficiency in the name of unity. The phrase suggests generosity but mandates equality of poverty. What begins as compassion ends as confiscation, leaving everyone dependent on the planners who promised fairness.

Living Wage — Politically determined income detached from productivity. It equates compassion with compulsion by legislating value rather than earning it. Mandated wages inflate costs, reduce jobs, and punish small enterprise. Presented as economic justice, it converts employment into entitlement and virtue into arithmetic.

Universal Basic Income — Guaranteed allowance for inactivity presented as modern benevolence. It replaces purpose with payment and independence with dependency. UBI normalizes permanent reliance on the state while eroding the dignity of work. Citizens become clients, grateful not for opportunity but for subsistence administered by bureaucracy.

Economic Democracy — Majority rule over property disguised as fairness. It subordinates ownership to public opinion and markets to committees. By letting political majorities vote on individual rights, it transforms liberty into permission. The ballot becomes an instrument of expropriation rather than representation.

People's Movement — Activist minority claiming a moral monopoly on justice. It defines dissent as oppression and equates opposition with hatred. By wrapping ideology in populist rhetoric, it portrays coercion as consensus. The "people" are whoever agrees with the Party; everyone else is the problem.

The 99% — Class-war slogan that glorifies envy and punishes excellence. It divides citizens into victims and villains, implying that success must come from exploitation. By worshipping resentment, it justifies intervention and confiscation. It unites grievance into a coalition of dependence, not of achievement.

Corporate Greed — Success demonized to justify control. It condemns ambition as exploitation while excusing governmental appetite. When profit is portrayed as theft, confiscation becomes virtue. The rhetoric of greed converts voluntary exchange into moral offense and paints prosperity as proof of guilt.

Late-Stage Capitalism — Propaganda term predicting collapse to legitimize interference. It assumes that markets inevitably decay and require rescue by the state. Every economic challenge becomes evidence of capitalist failure. The phrase is less description than prophecy—a pretext for replacing freedom with planning.

Wealth Gap — Envy quantified and weaponized. It ignores how wealth is created and measures morality by difference. By focusing on disparity instead of mobility, it portrays success as injustice. Closing the "gap" means pulling down the successful until everyone is equally dependent.

Wealth Tax — Punishment for accumulation disguised as fairness. It confiscates savings that have already been taxed, discouraging investment and thrift. Supporters call it moral balance; in practice it is economic cannibalism. Each new levy erodes the incentive to build, leaving less wealth for anyone to share.

Economic Inclusion — Quotas in commerce sold as opportunity. It substitutes demographic arithmetic for merit, enforcing representation through regulation. Entrepreneurship becomes bureaucratic compliance. Under inclusion, success depends less on service and innovation than on satisfying political formulas of diversity.

Pay Parity — Wage control by decree. It assumes bureaucrats can price human labor more accurately than markets. When ideology determines value, competence becomes irrelevant. Pay parity replaces negotiation with mandate and redefines fairness as uniformity, ensuring mediocrity in the name of equality.

Economic Patriotism — State-directed industry wrapped in nationalist rhetoric. It promises to protect workers by dictating markets. Patriotism becomes pretext for central planning, merging economic loyalty with political obedience. Private enterprise survives only so long as it serves the agenda of those in power.

Worker-Owned Enterprise — Collective business model promoted to replace private initiative. It portrays ownership as democratic but dilutes accountability. Without risk or reward tied to performance, productivity wanes. Such enterprises eventually depend on state subsidy, proving that collective control requires centralized rescue.

Fair Share — Euphemism for higher taxes and redistribution. It implies moral obligation while enforcing political confiscation. Determined by envy, not equity, the "fair share" always grows with government appetite. The phrase flatters taxpayers into submission, converting voluntary contribution into coerced virtue.

Public Good — Catch-all pretext for government expansion into private life. It sanctifies intrusion by claiming communal benefit. Once invoked, there is no limit to regulation, for every liberty can be portrayed as harmful to someone else. The public good becomes the permanent excuse for control.

POLITICAL AND BUREAUCRATIC TERMS

Socialism in practice is government without limit—authority diffused through bureaucracy.[9] Terms like *public-private partnership* or *administrative state* mask unaccountable power.[10] The citizen is managed, not represented.

Collectivism — The individual absorbed into the group; liberty traded for conformity and control. It denies personal responsibility in favor of state authority, replacing conscience with consensus. In collectivist systems, the citizen's worth depends on usefulness to the plan, not the sanctity of freedom or choice.

The Greater Good — Perennial excuse for coercion. It declares that moral virtue lies in surrendering one's rights for "society." By appealing to compassion, it disguises compulsion. The greater good is never defined by the people themselves but by those who wield power in their name.

Public-Private Partnership — Crony corporatism masquerading as cooperation. Government steers while private enterprise obeys, exchanging autonomy for subsidies. These partnerships promise efficiency but deliver patronage, allowing politicians to command markets without formal ownership and corporations to profit without competition—an elegant merger of bureaucracy and business.

Stakeholder Governance — Rule by unelected activists operating through boards and committees. Decisions once guided by performance now follow ideological quotas. Stakeholders replace shareholders, transforming responsibility to owners into obedience to "social interests." It is democracy without ballots and accountability without consent.

Social Contract — Elastic justification for limitless regulation. Originally meant mutual protection, now used to claim that freedom is conditional and government ownership inherent. The modern contract binds citizens to duties they never agreed to while granting bureaucrats authority they never earned.

Redistribution of Power — The transfer of authority from individuals to collectives under the banner of fairness. It pretends to balance influence but merely centralizes it. By fragmenting liberty into committees, it ensures that responsibility disappears while government accumulates every remaining lever of control.

Administrative State — Bureaucracy beyond accountability. It governs through regulation instead of law, creating a fourth branch immune to voters. Agencies write rules, interpret them, and enforce them—an arrangement the founders would have recognized as monarchy in modern dress, ruling by paperwork instead of crown.

Executive Authority — Expansion of power by decree. Crises, real or manufactured, justify permanent emergencies. Each order bypasses deliberation in the name of speed. Over time, the exception becomes routine and liberty becomes conditional on executive convenience—a government of men, not of laws.

Five-Year Plan — Centralized prediction disguised as precision. It promises prosperity through scheduling, ignoring the chaos of human creativity. Successes are celebrated on paper; shortages are blamed on saboteurs. Every failed plan begets another, proving that the planners' faith endures long after their economies collapse.

Public Option — Government wedge into private markets disguised as competition. It begins as a choice and ends as monopoly. Subsidized by taxpayers, it underprices rivals until only the state remains. Once "public," options vanish, replaced by rationing administered with bureaucratic courtesy.

Regulatory Capture — Politicians rewarding allies under the banner of oversight. Agencies meant to restrain power become instruments of it. The regulated industries write the very rules that govern them, ensuring that compliance favors incumbents and innovation becomes an act of defiance.

Tax Justice — Punitive taxation framed as morality. It portrays confiscation as compassion and envy as ethics. By measuring fairness through resentment, it sanctifies political redistribution. Every new bracket promises virtue while delivering stagnation, ensuring that success remains a vice in the public imagination.

Price Controls — Political tampering with supply disguised as mercy. When government fixes prices, shortages follow as night follows day. Producers vanish, quality declines, and scarcity is blamed on greed. The policy fails precisely as designed—to prove markets cannot function without their overseers.

Rent Control — Market distortion masquerading as protection. It claims to help tenants while destroying housing supply. Owners stop building, buildings decay, and new entrants are locked out. The result is chronic scarcity that politicians label as proof of capitalism's failure rather than their own interference.

Subsidy — Political favor disguised as generosity. It diverts resources from producers to petitioners, rewarding dependency over innovation. Every subsidy creates a constituency for more, entrenching inefficiency and bribing voters with their own money. In the end, the system feeds bureaucracy, not prosperity.

Nationalization — State seizure of private enterprise presented as "efficiency." Ownership transfers to bureaucrats who face neither competition nor consequence. Once the government controls production, failure becomes invisible—losses vanish into budgets and citizens become shareholders in poverty, unable to sell their stake.

Central Bank Policy — Currency manipulation repackaged as stability. By inflating supply and distorting interest rates, it hides fiscal irresponsibility behind monetary jargon. Every artificial fix creates the next crisis. Central banking promises precision but delivers dependence—a perpetual bailout for politicians and debtors alike.

Public Employment — Government job creation counted as progress. It measures success by payroll size, not productivity. Each new hire adds political loyalty and fiscal burden. Eventually, the state becomes both employer and debtor of last resort, paying salaries with tomorrow's taxes.

Regulatory Reform — Rearrangement of power sold as restraint. It shuffles agencies and rewrites rules while expanding scope. Reform becomes a euphemism for consolidation; every simplification births a new bureaucracy. The process ensures that inefficiency is immortal, and that "improvement" always means increase.

Universal Regulation — Standardization for control. It promises fairness through uniformity, compelling every industry and citizen to operate within prescribed boundaries. Once rules replace reason, compliance becomes virtue and initiative a crime. The dream of equality becomes an empire of forms and fines.

CULTURAL AND SOCIAL TERMS

Language policing, identity politics, and perpetual grievance have replaced persuasion with coercion.[11] *Critical Theory* and *DEI* repackage Marxist conflict for modern institutions, trading class for identity while keeping envy as the engine.[12]

Intersectionality — A hierarchy of victimhood that ranks identity above character and merit. It divides rather than unites, transforming compassion into competition for moral status. The more grievances one claims, the higher one stands. Intersectionality converts suffering into currency and resentment into social capital, rewarding division as virtue.

Lived Experience — Personal narrative elevated above fact. It replaces evidence with emotion, allowing feelings to overrule reason. By claiming immunity from scrutiny, it weaponizes subjectivity. Every opinion becomes sacred if it stems from pain, and disagreement becomes denial of another's "truth." Argument disappears; empathy becomes authority.

Safe Space — Ideological quarantine disguised as compassion. It shields adherents from discomfort rather than danger, ensuring that feelings remain unchallenged. What begins as sanctuary ends as segregation—zones of comfort where dissenting thought is forbidden. Safety becomes censorship, and fragility replaces resilience as the mark of maturity.

Microaggression — Everyday disagreement reclassified as harm. It trains people to interpret inconvenience as injury and misunderstanding as malice. Speech becomes a minefield, conversation an act of risk. By redefining intent as irrelevant, it empowers the perpetually offended to dictate what others may say—or even think.

Hate Speech — Any idea that challenges ideological orthodoxy. The term transforms opposition into immorality, allowing censorship to parade as compassion. Once adopted, it expands endlessly: words become violence, and silence becomes guilt. In the name of preventing harm, it criminalizes independent thought itself.

Misinformation — Truth inconvenient to power. It brands legitimate skepticism as danger and dissent as deception. Authorities become arbiters of reality, correcting citizens rather than informing them. By monopolizing "truth," those in charge can redefine facts at will. The word means not falsehood but forbidden perspective.

Disinformation — Information labeled false not because it is wrong, but because it is unwelcome. Once a term for enemy propaganda, it now covers domestic dissent. The accusation delegitimizes opposition without debate. When the state decides which truths are dangerous, truth itself becomes subversive.

Inclusive Language — Censorship through vocabulary control. Words are banned or replaced to reshape thought under the banner of kindness. By enforcing linguistic conformity, it eliminates nuance and dissent. "Inclusivity" excludes anything traditional, masculine, or moral, producing a culture fluent in virtue and illiterate in reality.

Reeducation — Indoctrination disguised as enlightenment. It compels ideological submission through workshops and training sessions that punish disagreement. Under reeducation, the goal is not knowledge but conformity. Offenders are not corrected but converted, until obedience is recast as understanding and silence as progress.

Social Credit — Compliance scoring disguised as civic virtue. It rewards obedience and punishes dissent through digital surveillance and bureaucratic judgment. Citizens learn to police themselves for approval. The system achieves tyranny without violence—conformity enforced by fear of losing access, reputation, or permission to live normally.

Cultural Competence — Ideological conformity dressed in academic jargon. It trains citizens to perform approved attitudes rather than exercise judgment. By reducing culture to politics, it erases individuality and elevates orthodoxy. True understanding gives way to ritual affirmation of fashionable dogma.

Restorative Justice — Punishment replaced by ideology. It absolves criminals through collective guilt and burdens victims with moral responsibility. Justice becomes therapy; accountability becomes dialogue. The process repairs feelings, not harm, and replaces impartial law with social balancing acts dictated by activists, not evidence.

Transformative Change — Radical restructuring of society under moral pretense. It promises redemption through destruction—dismantling institutions to "reimagine" them. Every failed revolution is renamed transformation. The phrase dignifies upheaval and converts coercion into compassion, making chaos sound visionary and tyranny sound progressive.

Anti-Racism — Reverse discrimination rebranded as virtue. It judges morality by skin color and enforces segregation through inclusion. Under anti-racism, silence equals guilt and disagreement equals hate. The movement claims to fight prejudice by institutionalizing it, replacing equality of opportunity with equality of grievance.

Critical Theory — Marxism translated into academia. It rejects objective truth in favor of perpetual critique, dismantling every value until nothing remains but power struggle. By defining knowledge as oppression, it turns learning into activism. Its purpose is not to understand the world, but to destroy it.

Critical Race Theory — Race-based collectivism disguised as scholarship. It replaces equality with guilt and justice with reparation. Society is divided into oppressors and oppressed, with no redemption except ideological confession. It teaches students to view color as destiny and resentment as enlightenment.

Diversity, Equity, and Inclusion (DEI) — Bureaucratic enforcement of ideology. It replaces merit with identity and competence with compliance. DEI programs create professional caste systems ruled by grievance administrators. Diversity becomes arithmetic, equity becomes favoritism, and inclusion becomes exclusion of anyone who resists the script.

Social Awareness — Political consciousness masquerading as empathy. It encourages reflexive activism without understanding. To be "aware" is to echo the right slogans at the right time. Awareness replaces knowledge, signaling replaces virtue, and citizens become performers in a morality play directed by bureaucrats.

Cultural Revolution — Destruction of tradition packaged as renewal. It erases history to replace memory with propaganda. Morality becomes what the movement declares, and art becomes its sermon. The revolution promises liberation but delivers conformity, ensuring that only the approved version of the past may exist.

Solidarity — Loyalty to the collective disguised as compassion. It demands agreement, not cooperation, and paints independence as betrayal. Under socialism, solidarity means subordination: unity achieved by silencing dissent. It replaces friendship with faction and conscience with compliance, making obedience a moral duty.

ENVIRONMENTAL AND GLOBAL TERMS

Environmental language has become socialism's most successful camouflage. Phrases like *climate justice* and *sustainability* transfer power from voters to regulators in the name of planetary emergency.[13] The result is global central planning with moral branding.[14]

Sustainability — Political control disguised as environmental virtue. It recasts economic growth as exploitation and human progress as guilt. Under sustainability, freedom becomes negotiable, and productivity is condemned as excess. The term's vagueness ensures permanent intervention, allowing planners to ration prosperity in the name of planetary health.

Climate Justice — Socialist economics repackaged as environmental ethics. It blames wealth and industrialization for global suffering and demands redistribution through carbon quotas and taxes. The "climate crisis" becomes moral leverage for global control, transforming policy debates into crusades where dissent equals heresy and compliance equals righteousness.

Environmental Equity — Quotas and subsidies masked as conservation. It redistributes resources and privileges under the pretense of protecting nature. Bureaucrats decide who may build, mine, or farm, turning stewardship into stratification. Environmentalism ceases to be science and becomes social engineering with a green veneer.

Green Transition — Deindustrialization presented as progress. It dismantles energy independence while celebrating scarcity as virtue. The "transition" replaces reliable power with subsidized fragility, enriching elites who trade carbon credits while citizens face higher costs. It is a revolution powered by rhetoric rather than reality.

Net-Zero — Command-and-control energy planning clothed in technical jargon. It imposes unattainable emissions goals enforced by regulation rather than innovation. Achieving "net zero" requires economic paralysis or creative accounting. The promise of balance conceals coercion; industries must comply even when technology cannot deliver.

Renewable Revolution — Government-managed energy masquerading as liberation from fossil fuels. It transfers wealth through subsidies and mandates while claiming environmental purity. Dependence shifts from producers to politicians. The revolution is endless, because failure simply justifies more funding, and the cure for inefficiency is always more control.

Carbon Neutrality — A bureaucratic sleight of hand that measures virtue in paperwork. Emissions are "offset" through schemes that enrich regulators and speculators while delivering little change to the environment. Neutrality becomes permission, allowing the powerful to pollute so long as they pay homage to the ideology.

Resource Justice — Centralized allocation of water, energy, and minerals under moral pretense. It portrays private ownership as exploitation and political rationing as fairness. Once "justice" governs resources, efficiency disappears. The result is permanent scarcity managed by committees claiming compassion while enforcing compliance.

De-growth Movement — Economic decline exalted as moral awakening. It glorifies austerity and condemns abundance, teaching that prosperity is planetary sin. Under de-growth, the solution to poverty is shared poverty, and human progress is recast as environmental crime. The end goal is equality through limitation.

Fair Trade — State-certified commerce masquerading as moral exchange. It replaces voluntary cooperation with political oversight, rewarding producers who meet ideological criteria. "Fairness" is defined by bureaucrats, not buyers or sellers. The system protects inefficiency and punishes independence, turning goodwill into a tariff.

Global Governance — International socialism administered through bureaucracy. It seeks to replace national sovereignty with regulatory consensus. Unelected councils set global rules for trade, energy, and speech, claiming moral authority beyond borders. Nations lose self-determination; citizenship becomes global compliance managed by technocrats.

Global Solidarity — Transnational collectivism wrapped in compassion. It asks nations to sacrifice their interests for a "shared humanity," enforced by treaties and guilt. Solidarity sounds noble but functions as subordination, uniting the world not in cooperation but in dependency upon the same governing elite.

UN Sustainable Goals — Soft law for global socialism. The language of partnership conceals mandates for redistribution and control. Each goal expands international oversight while eroding national discretion. Under the banner of "shared responsibility," the UN transforms ambition into bureaucracy and replaces progress with planning.

Environmental Stewardship — Citizen responsibility redefined as government authority. It shifts care for the planet from voluntary action to mandated obedience. Stewardship becomes surveillance, where compliance with environmental codes replaces moral choice. What begins as caretaking ends as command, virtue enforced through fines and fear.

Climate Resilience — Permanent emergency marketed as prudence. It normalizes crisis as governance, demanding continual intervention to "adapt" to disasters that may never come. The phrase justifies central planning under the guise of safety, ensuring that the state's power expands as quickly as its warnings.

TECHNOCRATIC AND DIGITAL TERMS

Technology now enforces ideology faster than any censor could. The rhetoric of *AI ethics* and *information integrity* allows political control over speech, commerce, and privacy.[15] The modern bureaucrat rules by algorithm, not argument.[16]

Smart Cities — Surveillance infrastructures disguised as convenience. Cameras, sensors, and algorithms monitor movement, consumption, and behavior under the banner of efficiency. Every "innovation" becomes an instrument of data collection. Citizens are managed like utilities, and privacy becomes obsolete in a city that never stops watching.

Digital Inclusion — Government-managed access to technology packaged as compassion. It ensures everyone is connected—on the state's terms. By subsidizing hardware and regulating content, authorities gain leverage over what information flows where. The result is not equal access but uniform dependence, ensuring that connection replaces independence.

Algorithmic Fairness — Ideological tampering with mathematics. It modifies code to enforce political outcomes and erase differences in performance. Programmers become social engineers, embedding bias under the name of justice. Fairness no longer means accuracy or objectivity; it means outcomes preselected to fit a narrative.

Data Equity — State ownership of private information rebranded as justice. It claims that personal data belongs to "the community," granting bureaucrats the right to monitor and redistribute it. Privacy becomes privilege, and every online action a contribution to collective oversight disguised as equality.

Platform Accountability — Regulatory censorship masquerading as safety. Governments pressure digital companies to silence dissent while pretending to enforce civility. "Accountability" transforms private platforms into deputized speech police. The user becomes both suspect and product, governed by invisible partnerships between power and technology.

Information Integrity — Centralized truth management. It converts free expression into a state-licensed activity, where approved narratives are promoted and deviation punished. Integrity once meant honesty; now it means obedience to official consensus. Fact-checkers become inquisitors, and curiosity becomes evidence of guilt.

Cyber Safety — Justification for total monitoring. Under the pretext of protection, authorities track online behavior and restrict anonymity. Every act of privacy becomes suspect. Safety morphs into surveillance, and the only secure citizen is the one who never questions who holds the keys.

Digital Citizenship — Compliance training for life online. It teaches users to behave “responsibly” by accepting guidelines that favor authority. Expression becomes performance; conformity becomes participation. Digital citizens are rated by their docility, proving that the internet age has reinvented obedience as engagement.

Social Media Moderation — Political censorship dressed as community protection. Platforms remove ideas under “policy enforcement,” protecting users from offense but not manipulation. Moderation eliminates competition of thought, ensuring ideological uniformity. The algorithm replaces the censor, and deletion becomes a service.

AI Ethics — Government oversight of innovation disguised as morality. It subjects discovery to ideological filters, punishing algorithms that yield unequal results. “Ethics” becomes a mechanism for political control, ensuring that artificial intelligence serves collective conformity instead of individual creativity or truth.

ESG (Environmental, Social, Governance) — Corporate obedience scoring. It quantifies virtue by politics, rewarding conformity to progressive agendas. Businesses chase ratings instead of results, turning morality into bureaucracy. ESG merges commerce with ideology until success is measured not by service, but by submission.

Technocratic Management — Rule by credential rather than consent. Experts administer life through data and decree, claiming neutrality while enforcing ideology. The technocrat replaces the legislator; efficiency replaces accountability. Democracy survives only as ceremony, as governance becomes a managerial science immune to public will.

Big Data Governance — Mass surveillance normalized through bureaucracy. Collected under the promise of efficiency, data becomes currency for control. Governments and corporations share ownership of information, ensuring that citizens are predictable consumers rather than free individuals. Privacy dies quietly behind consent boxes and policies.

Public Data Trust — Central repository for citizen information disguised as protection. It consolidates power by holding personal records "in trust" for society. The citizen becomes transparent to the state, but the state remains opaque. Trust becomes mandatory, and transparency flows only one way.

Information Literacy — Indoctrination in acceptable narratives. It trains citizens to distinguish "truth" from "misinformation" by trusting authority rather than evidence. Critical thinking is replaced by credentialism, and skepticism becomes a warning sign. Literacy no longer means comprehension—it means conformity to institutional truth.

Digital Democracy — Mob rule by algorithm. It claims to empower citizens but amplifies emotion over deliberation. Online votes and campaigns replace lawmaking with trending hashtags. The crowd becomes sovereign, manipulated by unseen elites. Participation becomes noise that legitimizes decisions already made elsewhere.

Technology Equity — Redistribution of innovation under bureaucratic supervision. It treats invention as property of the collective and penalizes advantage as injustice. By slowing progress to ensure sameness, it sacrifices advancement for ideology. The result is mediocrity institutionalized in the name of fairness.

Digital Transformation — Bureaucratic modernization masquerading as efficiency. It promises streamlined services while embedding surveillance in every transaction. Convenience justifies intrusion. Every new app becomes an interface for control, turning citizenship into software and governance into code managed by invisible administrators.

Cyber Governance — International oversight of digital space. It transfers power from nations to global agencies that regulate online behavior. Under cyber governance, sovereignty dissolves into treaties, and speech crosses borders only with permission. The internet becomes the first borderless bureaucracy.

Techno-Collectivism — Centralized control through technology. It merges socialism's desire for conformity with data's capacity for enforcement. Every click and purchase becomes a vote for compliance. Techno-collectivism perfects what old regimes could only dream of—obedience automated and dissent deleted before it speaks.

LANGUAGE AS A WEAPON

When words lose their meaning, freedom loses its defense. Every dictatorship begins by redefining its vocabulary—turning "citizen" into "subject," "debate" into "hate," and "obedience" into "virtue." Language becomes both the camouflage and the weapon of tyranny.[17] Once people are persuaded to speak falsely, they soon begin to think falsely as well.[18] Control of speech is control of thought, and once thought itself is conditioned, the chains are invisible.[19]

The modern socialist does not seize printing presses; he captures semantics. He changes the meanings of words the way past regimes changed flags. *Equity* replaces *equality*, *safety* replaces *freedom*, and *collective responsibility* replaces *personal conscience*.[20] The new socialism no longer needs to burn books—it simply rewrites them in real time. Each term is polished until it gleams with moral appeal, concealing compulsion beneath compassion.[21]

Today's revolutionaries march with hashtags instead of banners.[22] They advance through slogans, corporate memos, and university policies that dictate acceptable speech. The vocabulary of freedom is dismantled syllable by syllable until dissent sounds cruel and obedience sounds kind. Tyranny arrives not with a shout but with a policy revision, delivered by smiling bureaucrats who promise inclusion.[23]

This is how totalitarianism modernizes itself: it becomes polite. It legislates tone, moderates expression, and outlaws offense. The individual who refuses to lie is branded intolerant, divisive, or dangerous. To resist is to be rude; to comply is to be good. And so language—the instrument of truth—becomes an instrument of shame.[24]

There is only one cure: honesty.[25] Calling things by their real names is the first act of rebellion in an age of euphemism. To speak plainly is to defy control, because clarity threatens the deceiver. Once truth is spoken aloud, lies lose their spell.[26]

Freedom survives only where truth is spoken plainly, and truth survives only where words retain their meaning. The defense of liberty begins with the defense of language itself.[27] A people who will not say what they see will soon be unable to see what they have lost.[28]

So—if you hear someone utter any of these phrases, feel free to stand up, point at them, and scream, *"COMMUNIST!" or "LIAR!"*

Language is only the first instrument of control; propaganda is the machinery that makes it move. Once the new vocabulary is built, it must be broadcast, repeated, and enforced until truth sounds strange and lies sound familiar. The next chapter examines how that machinery works—the modern network of media, bureaucracy, and technology that transforms words into weapons and opinion into obedience.

CHAPTER 35. THE MACHINERY OF MODERN PROPAGANDA

THE RETURN OF THE BIG LIE

Propaganda did not die with the fall of the Soviet Union; it simply changed its form. Where regimes once relied on the press and radio, modern propagandists operate through algorithms, social media, and digital echo chambers. The principles remain the same—repetition, emotional manipulation, and selective omission—but the scale is global and instantaneous.[1]

> *"A lie told often enough becomes the truth."* — **Vladimir Lenin**[2]

Lenin's cynical observation has become a manual for modern politics. The twenty-first-century propagandist no longer needs to burn books or imprison dissenters; they merely flood the information stream until truth drowns beneath waves of distraction. Repetition now replaces persuasion, and emotional certainty triumphs over evidence.[3]

THE WEAPONIZATION OF LANGUAGE

Today's most potent propaganda tool is not the billboard or the broadcast but the dictionary. Words that once carried moral clarity have been twisted beyond recognition. "Equity" now means enforced outcomes, "justice" means revenge, and "tolerance" means compulsory agreement. When language is corrupted, even honest citizens can be manipulated into defending tyranny under the banner of virtue.[4]

This is the genius of linguistic warfare: redefine the vocabulary and you redefine reality. Once truth and falsehood lose their fixed meanings, propaganda no longer needs to argue—it merely declares.[5]

THE NEW MINISTRY OF TRUTH

In the past, propaganda depended on state control of the press. Today, it thrives through the alliance of Big Tech, legacy media, and political power. Under the pretense of "fact-checking" and "safety," dissenting voices are silenced and acceptable narratives curated for mass consumption. Algorithms decide which opinions are amplified and which are buried.[6]

> *"The most effective way to destroy people is to deny and obliterate their own understanding of their history."* — **George Orwell**[7]

What Orwell imagined as a dystopian warning has become the operating manual of modern information control. History is edited, statues are removed, and inconvenient truths are labeled "disinformation." Once a society forgets its past, it becomes defenseless against ideological revision.[8]

THE ROLE OF PARTISAN MEDIA

The propaganda arm of the modern Left is not a ministry—it is a media cartel. For decades, major outlets such as CNN, MSNBC, NPR, The New York Times, The Washington Post, The Atlantic, Vox, Politico, and The Guardian have operated as ideological enforcers rather than impartial observers.[9] What they share is not curiosity, but conviction—the belief that their worldview must prevail even at the expense of truth.

These outlets do not merely report events; they curate reality. Stories that damage the Left are buried, while those that flatter it are magnified and moralized. Scandals surrounding left-wing politicians are minimized as "missteps" or "contextual misunderstandings," while the smallest controversy on the Right is treated as a crisis of civilization.[10] When evidence contradicts their narratives, they simply shift the headline and pretend it never happened.[11]

The uniformity of tone and timing is no coincidence. These networks often echo the same talking points within hours, repeating the same phrases until they become cultural commandments. Their goal is not to inform citizens but to shape perception—to convince the public that leftist ideology represents moral virtue and that dissent from it is ignorance, bigotry, or extremism.[12]

This is not journalism; it is indoctrination. It is the modern realization of what every communist regime has always understood: control the narrative and you control the nation.[13] By turning news into a sermon, these outlets serve as the priesthood of progressivism—absolving its sins, silencing heretics, and sanctifying its dogma.[14]

The tragedy is that millions of Americans still mistake propaganda for news, unaware that their beliefs are being curated by those who see themselves not as reporters, but as reformers.[15] The Left does not merely want to win elections; it seeks to reshape reality itself—and the media is its most effective weapon.

CONTEMPORARY CASE STUDIES IN MODERN PROPAGANDA AND CENSORSHIP

1. The Twitter Files (December 2022 – January 2023): Journalists Matt Taibbi, Bari Weiss, and Michael Schellenberger released internal communications showing coordination between Twitter executives and U.S. federal agencies—including the FBI and DHS—on content moderation decisions prior to the 2020 election.[16] Lesson: Propaganda no longer requires state media; it thrives through ideological cooperation between Big Tech and government power.
2. COVID-19 Information Suppression (2020–2021): Platforms such as Facebook, YouTube, and LinkedIn censored or de-ranked licensed physicians and researchers—including Dr. Jay Bhattacharya and Dr. Martin Kulldorff—who questioned lockdown efficacy or vaccine mandates.[17] Many of their views were later vindicated. Lesson: Censorship

disguised as "public health protection" is still censorship—and it erodes public trust in science.

3. Hunter Biden Laptop Story (October 2020): Weeks before the presidential election, The New York Post published verified emails from Hunter Biden's laptop. Major outlets and social media suppressed the story, labeling it "Russian disinformation." Two years later, the story was confirmed authentic.[18] Lesson: Narrative control can determine electoral outcomes more effectively than campaign spending.
4. Algorithmic Bias on YouTube (2018–Present): Studies by the Mozilla Foundation (2021) showed YouTube's recommendation system favored left-leaning channels while demonetizing dissenting ones.[19] Lesson: Algorithmic control is a modern form of censorship—one that shapes culture invisibly and automatically.
5. Wikipedia Edit Wars (2015–2024): Political topics such as climate policy and gender identity have seen coordinated editing by activist groups, replacing factual entries with ideological framing.[20] Lesson: Even "neutral" platforms can become ideological battlefields when gatekeeping replaces truth-seeking.

THE MANUFACTURE OF MOVEMENTS

Not every protest that fills the streets or floods social media is what it appears to be. Many "grassroots" uprisings are in fact astroturf movements—artificial campaigns engineered by political operatives, corporate donors, or public-relations firms to simulate popular consensus.[21] Money and marketing replace conviction and community.

> *"It's easier to fool people than to convince them that they have been fooled."* — **Mark Twain**[22]

Astroturfing exploits the herd instinct of democracies. People fear isolation more than deception, so they join the crowd without asking who assembled it. The illusion of unanimity pressures honest citizens into compliance and policymakers into submission.[23]

CONTEMPORARY CASE STUDIES IN ASTROTURFING

1. Online Political Astroturfing (November 2020): A 2022 Nature study documented bot-like coordination among roughly 8.6% of politically active Twitter accounts during the 2020 election.[24] Lesson: Digital consensus can be engineered, not earned.
2. "Crowds for Hire" Scandal (October 2018): A Los Angeles Times exposé revealed that Crowds on Demand paid actors to pose as grassroots supporters for a New Orleans power-plant proposal.[25] Lesson: Manufactured movements can mimic democracy while undermining it.
3. Rally Forge Network (October 2020): Facebook removed over 200 accounts linked to Rally Forge, a marketing firm running coordinated political campaigns disguised as spontaneous activism.[26] Lesson: Propaganda can be homegrown and professionalized under the banner of marketing.
4. COVID-19 Lockdown Protests (April–May 2020): The Washington Post found that "Reopen America" groups were created and managed by a small network of operatives using identical branding.[27] Lesson: Online movements that appear spontaneous often originate from centralized strategy rooms.
5. Russian Internet Research Agency (2016–2018): The U.S. Department of Justice's 2018 indictment revealed how Russia's Internet Research Agency used fake social-media accounts to inflame division and stage online "rallies."[28] Lesson: Foreign astroturfing proves propaganda now transcends borders.

THE ECONOMY OF OUTRAGE

A new market has emerged in the age of digital activism—the outrage economy. Protests, campaigns, and online boycotts are often subsidized or outright purchased. Paid demonstrators, influencer activists, and algorithmic mobs manufacture the appearance of moral momentum.[29] Outrage itself becomes a commodity, rewarding the loudest voices and punishing reflection.

"The whole aim of practical politics is to keep the populace alarmed… by an endless series of hobgoblins, most of them imaginary." — **H. L. Mencken**[30]

Mencken's insight has become prophetic. Outrage has become not only a political tool but a financial product—something to be generated, amplified, and sold.[31]

CONTEMPORARY CASE STUDIES IN THE ECONOMY OF OUTRAGE

1. Facebook Internal Research Leak (September 2021): The Wall Street Journal revealed Facebook's algorithm rewarded divisive and emotional content because it increased ad revenue.[32] Lesson: Social-media companies profit directly from moral panic.
2. "Crowds for Hire" Revisited (October 2018): The same Los Angeles Times report showed that Crowds on Demand sold staged protests to law firms and campaigns.[33] Lesson: When activism becomes an industry, sincerity becomes optional.
3. Gillette's "Toxic Masculinity" Campaign (January 2019): Procter & Gamble's Gillette ad targeting "toxic masculinity" drew backlash but generated record engagement and publicity.[34] Lesson: Outrage marketing turns moral lectures into profit.
4. Colin Kaepernick and Nike (September 2018): Nike's "Believe in something" campaign sparked controversy and boosted sales by 31% in one week.[35] Lesson: Outrage can be engineered for commercial gain.
5. Sleeping Giants Brasil Campaign (May 2020): Coordinated advertiser boycotts pressured brands to drop right-leaning outlets under the pretense of "fighting misinformation."[36] Lesson: Outrage can redirect or destroy commerce depending on who controls the narrative.

THE ANTIDOTE: TRUTH AND MEMORY

Propaganda cannot survive an informed and courageous public. Its power ends the moment citizens remember what it has tried to make them forget.[37] The antidote is not censorship in reverse but truth pursued relentlessly—through open debate, historical literacy, and moral independence.

Fortunately, most—though not all—Americans remain intelligent enough to see through the noise. The 2024 presidential election proved that distinction clearly: the radical fringe of the far left discovered just how small a minority it truly is. The moderate left, once tolerant of the extremes in its ranks, began to recognize how destructive ideological absolutism had become to their own cause. In one of the most decisive populist victories in modern political history, Americans reaffirmed their preference for sanity over zealotry, freedom over control, and patriotism over guilt.[38]

Free people must become historians of their own time, skeptics of convenience, and guardians of memory. Only then can the machinery of modern propaganda be dismantled—not by force, but by clarity.[39]

Every generation faces its own battlefield. Ours is not a war of guns and tanks, but of minds and words. The propagandist's greatest weapon is your surrender — the moment you stop questioning, stop thinking, and stop believing that truth can still prevail. When citizens trade courage for comfort, propaganda wins without firing a shot.

The antidote is strength. The next chapter, **"Arm Yourself and Armor Yourself,"** is a call to arms for the free citizen — to equip your mind, fortify your conscience, and become unbreakable in the face of manipulation. The war for truth will not be won by those who shout the loudest, but by those who stand the firmest.

CHAPTER 36.
ARMOR YOURSELF AND ARM YOURSELF

DEFENSE — GUARDING THE MIND AGAINST INDOCTRINATION

For generations, universities were trusted as sanctuaries of truth—places where reason, evidence, and debate shaped free minds. Yet that trust has been betrayed. Many of today's institutions have abandoned inquiry in favor of ideology, replacing discovery with dogma and reason with activism.[1]

Students who wish to remain free thinkers must begin by recognizing indoctrination when they encounter it. Education should lead to truth, not obedience. The first defense against ideological capture is self-education: reading widely, questioning assumptions, and testing every claim against history. The second defense is courage—the willingness to speak when silence is easier, to demand facts when emotion is offered, and to remain civil in the face of hostility.[2]

> *"It is the first responsibility of every citizen to question authority."* — **Benjamin Franklin**[3]

Franklin's reminder defines patriotism as the duty to think for oneself, even when institutions insist on conformity.

Arming oneself with knowledge is the surest path to freedom.

> *"The truth is like a lion; you don't have to defend it. Let it loose. It will defend itself."* — **Saint Augustine**[4]

His wisdom reinforces that truth, once uncovered, exposes and destroys falsehood on its own. The facts contained in this book—the economic failures, social devastations, and moral collapses brought about by communism and socialism—are weapons against deception. **No amount of academic rhetoric or media propaganda can erase the historical record.** By confronting the realities of socialist systems—the starvation, censorship, stagnation, and tyranny—the mind is inoculated against utopian delusion.[5]

Parents play an indispensable role in this defense. They must begin early by teaching their children gratitude, responsibility, and respect for liberty—values that stand as armor against the seductive simplicity of socialist promises.[6] Conversations at the dinner table about history, economics, and ethics do more to fortify a young mind than any formal curriculum. Parents who encourage curiosity and critical thought give their children the courage to challenge falsehoods in the classroom. The most powerful shield against manipulation is a moral compass grounded in truth and love of country.[7]

> *"Freedom is hammered out on the anvil of discussion, dissent, and debate."* — **Hubert H. Humphrey**[8]

The words remind us that liberty survives only where disagreement is allowed. Honest debate, not enforced consensus, is the lifeblood of learning.

A few voices within academia have long warned of this decay. Allan Bloom's The Closing of the American Mind (1987)[9] and Roger Kimball's Tenured Radicals (1990)[10] exposed the moral and intellectual rot spreading through the universities. Both predicted that the politicization of education would destroy liberal learning itself. More recently, organizations such as the Foundation for Individual Rights and Expression (FIRE)[11] and the National Association of Scholars (NAS)[12] have fought to defend intellectual diversity against bureaucracies that reward ideological loyalty over scholarship.

Resistance is growing among students and faculty who recognize that a free mind is the cornerstone of a free society.

A handful of institutions are reintroducing classical curricula emphasizing Western civilization, constitutional government, and moral philosophy.[13] Small though these efforts may be, they mark the beginning of an intellectual restoration—a reminder that truth can be suppressed but never destroyed.

A note on self-defense: This may not mean only ideological defense. On some campuses, the activist atmosphere can be so inflamed that disagreement is treated as aggression.[14] Students may find themselves physically threatened by demonstrations or mobs that claim to speak for "justice." In such environments, prudence is as important as principle. Each student must decide whether to engage or to avoid confrontation altogether. Physical safety is not cowardice—it is strategy. There is no shame in walking away from a mob that refuses to think. Protecting one's body and mind are both acts of self-defense in the war of ideas.[15]

In the digital age, self-defense also requires shielding the mind from propaganda disguised as journalism.[16] The same ideological machinery that dominates universities extends into mainstream and social media, where repetition replaces reasoning and bias is marketed as virtue.[17] Students and citizens alike must learn to interrogate their information diet: Who funds the outlet? What motives guide its narrative? What facts are missing? To arm oneself against indoctrination means not only questioning professors but also headlines, hashtags, and entertainment that condition public thought.[18] The machinery of modern propaganda depends on passivity; truth depends on discernment.[19]

But the machinery of modern propaganda does not end with biased reporting or digital censorship.[20] Its reach extends into the streets, the campuses, and the screens where outrage is manufactured and dissent is choreographed. "Astroturfing"—the creation of artificial grassroots movements by powerful interests—has become a favored tactic of ideological manipulation.[21] Paid protests, scripted demonstrations, and coordinated social-media campaigns create the illusion of popular consensus where none exists.[22] These spectacles are not expressions of democracy; they are performances designed to intimidate, divide, and silence.

To defend oneself against such deception requires discernment and restraint.[23] Citizens must learn to ask who funds the movement, who benefits from the outrage, and who vanishes once the cameras leave. The first rule of propaganda is to control emotion; the first rule of freedom is to control oneself. Do not let the spectacle steal your reason. When mass movements appear overnight with identical slogans and professional staging, recognize them for what they are: products of a well-financed machinery that substitutes noise for conviction.[24] The antidote is patience, truth, and the courage to think slowly in a culture that demands instant fury.[25]

OFFENSE — TAKING THE FIGHT TO THE INSTITUTIONS

Defending freedom is not enough; it must also be advanced. To win the battle of ideas, citizens must go on the offensive—exposing indoctrination, withdrawing support from corrupt institutions, and building alternatives rooted in truth.[26]

> *"If you want to control the people, first control what they know and how they think."* — **Herbert Schiller**[27]

Schiller's advice identifies the enemy's first tactic: monopolizing information. Every citizen who exposes bias strikes a blow for freedom.

If indoctrination is the weapon of tyranny, then knowledge is the armor of the free—but courage is the sword. The first offensive tactic is exposure. Use the tools already available to reveal bias and coercion wherever they occur:

- **STOPit App** — An anonymous reporting system for incidents of intimidation or discrimination.[28]
- **report it® Platform** — A secure, real-time tool used by schools and corporations that can be configured for ideological-bias categories.[29]
- **Elker Anonymous Reporting** — An encrypted interface allowing reporters and investigators to communicate without compromising identity.[30]
- **Parents Defending Education (PDE)** — A national Incident Tracker for documenting politicized curricula and compelled ideology.[31]

- **End DEI Portal (U.S. Department of Education, 2025)** — A federal mechanism for filing Title VI complaints about compelled speech and DEI mandates.[32]
- **Turning Point USA and Campus Reform Tip Lines** — Advocacy-driven channels that publicize classroom bias and censorship.[33]

These tools form a decentralized network for citizens who value accountability in education. Organizations such as FIRE and the American Council of Trustees and Alumni (ACTA) continue to expose how once-great universities—Harvard, Columbia, Yale, and others—have become intolerant of dissent and detached from truth.[34]

The second offensive tactic is economic. Vote with your feet and your wallets. Attendance and tuition dollars are the lifeblood of the institutions that spread ideological poison. Do not attend colleges or universities that indoctrinate students into collectivist ideology. The prestige of a school means nothing if it teaches contempt for freedom and the civilization that sustains it.[35]

For those who must attend such schools, refuse to enroll in courses that serve as vehicles for indoctrination. Every credit hour paid for feeds a system that thrives on compliance. Starve it. Professors who traffic in ideology depend on full classrooms and steady tuition streams. Withdraw those, and their influence collapses.36

Likewise, graduates and citizens must refuse to fund indoctrination through donations, endowments, or public subsidies. Alumni who watch their alma maters turn into ideological factories should withhold their support and state why. Legislators and donors should demand accountability from institutions that claim to educate but instead propagate propaganda.[37]

The same principle applies to the media empires and digital networks that function as the cultural arm of ideological control. When news outlets, social-media platforms, or streaming services promote one worldview while silencing another, citizens must act with the same discipline they apply to academia: change the channel, cancel the subscription, close the tab. Each view, click, or share is a vote in the marketplace of attention, and that market, like any other, rewards what it is fed. The machinery of propaganda cannot survive a famine of participation.[38]

To arm oneself intellectually also means to choose what not to consume. Truth cannot flourish in a mind constantly flooded by distortion, outrage, and fear. Seek news sources that publish evidence over emotion, and reward platforms that allow genuine dissent. The act of disengaging from dishonest media is not retreat—it is resistance. Just as propaganda depends on attention, liberty depends on the refusal to give it away cheaply.[39]

> *"You can't depend on your eyes when your imagination is out of focus."* — **Mark Twain**[40]

Twain's wit exposes the danger of ideological blindness: perception itself can be corrupted when imagination is captured.

Students should start by thinking of academia this way: universities are not sacred temples of knowledge—they are service providers. Students and parents are the paying customers, and colleges and universities are their employees. Higher education is a service industry, not an untouchable ideological priesthood. If the service provided no longer meets the standard we expect—academic rigor, open debate, and intellectual honesty—it is not only acceptable but wise to leave. Students should never be afraid to transfer to another institution that better aligns with their values and commitment to truth. Universities that fail to educate but succeed in indoctrinating do not deserve loyalty. Those dollars should be redirected to schools that uphold the principles of free inquiry, or to new educational models that earn the public's trust. In a truly free society, the marketplace of ideas applies as much to education as it does to commerce.[41]

Ultimately, freedom is sustained not just by ideals but by choices. When citizens collectively refuse to fund the machinery of indoctrination, the system collapses under its own hypocrisy. Just as the free-market rewards merit and punishes inefficiency, so too must higher education face the consequences of betraying its purpose. The refusal to fund indoctrination is not merely protest; it is preservation.[42]

Defending freedom requires courage equal to that of those who have fought tyranny abroad. Every informed citizen becomes a soldier in the intellectual defense of civilization. To "arm yourself and armor yourself" is to prepare for the war of ideas with reason, knowledge, and truth as your weapons.[43]

THE CULTURE WAR AND THE BATTLE FOR REALITY

> *"These are the times that try men's souls. The summer soldier and the sunshine patriot will, in this crisis, shrink from the service of their country; but he that stands it now, deserves the love and thanks of man and woman."*— **Thomas Paine**[44]

The first weapon in any struggle for liberty is not the sword or the vote—it is the courage to speak truth. The culture war is not some distant spectacle fought by pundits or politicians; it is the daily contest over whether each citizen will remain free in mind. The enemy is not a party but a principle—the belief that truth must serve ideology. To resist this is to become a revolutionary in the truest sense: one who refuses to bow before unreality.[45]

Armor yourself with conviction. Arm yourself with clarity. In an age when lies are broadcast as compassion and silence is demanded as virtue, the truth-teller becomes the last defender of civilization. This battle will not be won by those who shout the loudest, but by those who will not be moved.[46]

Every citizen possesses two weapons that no tyrant can long withstand: the **voice** and the **vote**. A single ballot may seem small, but millions of them—cast with conviction and vigilance—can alter the course of a nation. Each vote is a declaration that truth still matters, that freedom still lives, and that deception will not rule uncontested. Every citizen who refuses apathy and chooses to vote for liberty strikes a blow against the tyrannies of propaganda and ideological conformity.[47]

Equally powerful is the voice used in daily life. Words spoken among friends, colleagues, and family can pierce the fog of misinformation. Conversation is persuasion, and persuasion is the lifeblood of a free society. When one informed citizen explains the truth with patience and clarity, others find the courage to think for themselves. The battle for civilization is fought not only in the voting booth but also at the dinner table, in the classroom, and in the public square. Silence surrenders the field; speech reclaims it.[48]

Citizens also possess a weapon too often neglected—their direct voice in government. Every senator, every representative, and every local official answers to the people who elect them. Each has an office, a website, an email address, and a phone line for a reason: to hear from those they serve. When citizens speak clearly and persistently, lawmakers listen. Let them know when a bill supports freedom or threatens it. Silence allows bureaucracy to grow unchecked; engagement forces accountability.[49]

Financial support is another lawful weapon in this fight. Donating to candidates, organizations, and causes that defend liberty ensures that the resources of free citizens counterbalance the machinery of propaganda and coercion. Money, like speech, carries moral weight. When directed wisely, it amplifies the voice of truth in the halls of power.[50]

Boycotts are another weapon in the citizen's arsenal. When corporations, media networks, or organizations align themselves with causes hostile to freedom, the public's refusal to buy their products or support their platforms sends a message louder than protest. The power of a unified citizenry lies not merely in its outrage but in its economic strength. When millions choose principle over convenience, even the most powerful institutions are forced to listen.[51]

Political power, too, is not beyond the reach of the people. Elected officials who betray their oath to defend liberty can be **recalled** through lawful means if enough citizens stand together. In the gravest cases, **impeachment** remains a constitutional remedy—a reminder that no public servant, however high, is above accountability. These tools exist not for vengeance, but for preservation. When used wisely and lawfully, they restore balance and remind leaders that power flows upward from the governed, not downward from the elite.[52]

Freedom also depends on the use of every peaceful weapon the Constitution provides. **Petitions** and citizen initiatives give the people direct power to demand redress and reform. **Jury service**, often treated as an inconvenience, is a sacred duty—one juror can stop an unjust prosecution and remind the state that justice belongs to the governed, not the governors. **Peaceful assembly**—whether in a public square or a town hall—remains the visible proof that liberty is alive, for it shows conviction without chaos.[53]

At the local level, freedom is defended most effectively by those who serve their own communities. Citizens who run for school boards, city councils, or county offices reclaim the machinery of government from ideology and return it to accountability. Creating **independent media**—podcasts, newsletters, or documentaries—spreads truth beyond censorship's reach, while **legal action** and public-interest litigation ensure that constitutional rights are not theoretical but enforced. Each of these is a lawful weapon in the arsenal of a free republic, and together they form the bulwark of self-government.[54]

Freedom endures only when it is defended, and the defense of truth begins with the refusal to surrender our universities to those who despise the principles that made them great. It also begins with the refusal to surrender our government to the same ideology that seeks to undermine those principles from within.[55]

Freedom's defense begins with the individual, but it cannot end there. The enemies of liberty do not rest; they organize, fund, and coordinate their influence through powerful institutions that reach into every corner of American life. From the lecture hall to the newsroom, from corporate boardrooms to political movements, the networks of sympathy for communism and socialism have grown vast and deliberate. To preserve the Republic, we must not only defend against their ideas but expose their operations.[56]

What follows is a closer examination of those organizations—domestic, political, academic, and cultural—that have carried the banner of collectivism within our own borders.[57]

CHAPTER 37. AMERICAN ORGANIZATIONS SYMPATHETIC TO COMMUNISM

CURRENTLY ACTIVE ORGANIZATIONS

Communist Party USA (CPUSA)

The Communist Party USA is one of the oldest openly communist political movements in the United States. Originating in 1919 and historically aligned with the Communist International (COMINTERN). It continues to promote what it calls a "road to socialism."[1] It maintains local clubs, educational programs, and a daily online publication titled People's World, all advocating a class-based critique of capitalism and American foreign policy.[2]

Democratic Socialists of America (DSA)

The Democratic Socialists of America is today the largest organized socialist group in the United States. It operates not as a political party but as a membership organization combining electoral activism, labor alliances, and community organizing.[3] DSA describes its mission as the democratic transformation of society through worker empowerment and public ownership of major industries. It has grown rapidly since 2016, with chapters active in every state.[4]

Party for Socialism and Liberation (PSL)

The Party for Socialism and Liberation is a Marxist-Leninist organization emphasizing revolutionary change.[5] It conducts demonstrations, publishes Liberation News, and offers ideological training through Liberation School. The party openly calls for the dismantling of capitalist institutions and has fielded candidates in local and national elections to promote its program.[6]

Workers World Party (WWP)

Founded in 1959, the Workers World Party remains committed to Marxist-Leninist principles and often expresses solidarity with socialist states and revolutionary movements abroad.[7] Through its newspaper Workers World, the party advocates anti-imperialist positions and engages in protest movements centered on labor and racial justice.[8]

Black Lives Matter Global Network Foundation (BLMGNF)

The Black Lives Matter Global Network Foundation serves as the institutional hub of the broader Black Lives Matter movement. While not an explicit communist organization, several of its early leaders described themselves as trained in Marxist political theory.[9] The foundation's work combines racial-justice advocacy with economic-redistribution and anti-policing initiatives that echo themes of critical Marxism and intersectional theory.[10]

Antifa (United States Movement)

"Antifa" in the United States refers to a decentralized network of antifascist activists rather than a single unified group.[11] Local chapters—such as Rose City Antifa in Portland—share an opposition to fascism, capitalism, and state authority. Participants often identify with anarchist, socialist, or communist philosophies and engage in direct-action tactics, counter-protests, and community-defense efforts.[12]

THE OLD HATRED IN NEW CLOTHES: THE LEFT'S WAR ON THE JEWS

> *"History repeats itself, first as tragedy, second as farce."*—
> **Karl Marx**[13]

One of the darker ironies of modern socialism is that it resurrects the very prejudice it once claimed to oppose. Antisemitism has reemerged on the political Left, not as racial hatred but as moral indictment—rebranded as "anti-Zionism," "decolonization," or "equity justice." Behind the slogans lies the same old accusation:

that Jews, by virtue of success or identity, represent privilege, capitalism, or oppression. Thus, Marx's own disdain for "Jewish capitalism" has found new disciples among those who chant for social justice while echoing the propaganda of totalitarian regimes.[14]

This inversion serves a familiar purpose. Every collectivist movement needs a scapegoat to explain why its utopia never arrives. In the twentieth century, it was the "kulak" or the "bourgeois." Today, it is the Jew, recast as a symbol of Western strength, tradition, and resilience—the very qualities communism despises.[15] Campus movements and NGOs now traffic in this rhetoric, teaching young minds that moral virtue demands hostility toward Israel and suspicion toward Jews.[16]

The pattern is ancient, but its moral corruption is new: hatred masquerading as conscience. A civilization that tolerates antisemitism in the name of justice repeats history's oldest sin—the envy that destroys the righteous and exalts the mob.[17]

HISTORICAL AND DEFUNCT ORGANIZATIONS

International Socialist Organization (ISO)

Once a prominent Trotskyist organization active on U.S. campuses and within labor movements, the ISO was known for its publication Socialist Worker and for its emphasis on revolutionary socialism.[18] Internal disputes and allegations of misconduct led to the group's dissolution in 2019, ending more than four decades of activity.[19]

Red Guards (U.S.)

The Red Guards network consisted of Maoist collectives operating in several American cities during the 2010s.[20] Modeling themselves after China's Cultural Revolution committees, they pursued militant street activism and ideological study. By 2019 most chapters had disbanded or merged into smaller formations that have since disappeared.[21]

W.E.B. Du Bois Clubs of America

Established in 1964 as the official youth wing of the Communist Party USA, the Du Bois Clubs mobilized students and young workers around civil-rights and anti-war causes.[22] Government scrutiny and declining membership led to their replacement in the early 1970s by successor youth organizations aligned with CPUSA.[23]

FUNDING SOURCES ROLL-UP

Because most socialist and communist-sympathetic groups avoid corporate sponsorship, their financing patterns differ markedly from those of traditional political parties. The following summarizes what is publicly known or credibly reported about their sources of support.[24]

Membership Dues and Small Donations — CPUSA and DSA both rely on recurring dues and individual contributions from members. CPUSA's official materials emphasize that it receives no corporate or institutional grants, while DSA's financial statements list dues as its primary revenue stream.[25]

Educational and Fiscal Sponsorship Arms — The DSA Fund serves as a 501(c)(3) educational affiliate that accepts tax-deductible donations. The Black Lives Matter Global Network Foundation operates as a registered nonprofit with audited filings and previously worked under fiscal sponsors such as Thousand Currents and the Tides Foundation, which manage donor-advised funds for progressive causes.[26]

Public Fund Drives and Media Appeals — Organizations like People's World and Liberation News routinely conduct online fundraising campaigns and special-issue appeals to sustain operations.[27]

Political Action Committees and Compliant Campaign Contributions — DSA's electoral work is financed through member-supported PACs registered with the Federal Election Commission and disclosed through OpenSecrets and FEC databases.[28]

Major Donors and Alleged Intermediaries — Recent congressional inquiries have examined whether large activist donations, including those associated with philanthropist Neville Roy Singham, have supported entities linked to the Party for Socialism and Liberation. These remain under review and have not resulted in formal findings.[29]

Localized and Decentralized Support — Antifa collectives and similar grassroots networks typically operate through local mutual-aid funds, benefit events, and community contributions rather than centralized financial structures.

FOREIGN SUPPORT AND INFLUENCE ALLEGATIONS

Throughout the twentieth century, the most direct cases of foreign funding of American communist movements involved subsidies from the Soviet Union to the Communist Party USA. Declassified archives confirm that CPUSA received substantial financial assistance from Moscow from the 1920s through the 1980s, channeled through the Comintern and later via cultural exchanges and front organizations.[30]

Since the end of the Cold War, direct state funding of American leftist parties by foreign communist regimes has not been proven, though suspicions occasionally surface. Congressional investigations have recently examined possible Chinese Communist Party influence in the financing of newer Marxist or anti-imperialist organizations through intermediary nonprofits and individual donors sympathetic to Beijing's ideology. These investigations remain ongoing and unverified by independent audits.[31]

Intelligence analysts note that modern influence efforts, if they occur, tend to be indirect—promoting propaganda through sympathetic media, funding international conferences, or sponsoring activist exchanges rather than direct cash payments to U.S. organizations. The historic precedent of Soviet subsidies nonetheless demonstrates that foreign powers have long viewed ideological movements inside the United States as valuable instruments of soft power.[32]

WHY THIS MATTERS TO THE READER

It is important to highlight these connections and patterns of funding because many Americans may be supporting such organizations without realizing their underlying ideologies or how their donations are used. Well-meaning contributors may believe they are aiding causes for racial justice, workers' rights, or social equality, when in fact they are strengthening movements rooted in Marxist or revolutionary doctrine. In some cases, as with the Black Lives Matter Global Network Foundation, public investigations and audits revealed that large sums of donor money were used for luxury real-estate purchases and personal enrichment rather than the stated mission. Awareness of how funds are collected and distributed is vital so that citizens can make informed decisions, ensuring their generosity does not unintentionally advance political agendas that undermine the very freedoms they value. [33]

The record of socialist and communist-sympathetic organizations within the United States shows how ideology, money, and moral language intertwine to shape public opinion and policy. As the final chapter will argue, defending liberty in the modern age requires vigilance—not only against foreign adversaries or violent revolutionaries, but also against subtle domestic movements that disguise control as compassion. The next chapter draws these lessons together, reminding every reader that freedom survives only when citizens recognize deception, expose corruption, and guard the truth with courage.

CHAPTER 38.
CONCLUSION

THE DANGER OF AMERICAN POLITICIANS WHO PRAISE SOCIALISM

In recent decades, the United States has witnessed a growing cadre of politicians who openly espouse socialist and quasi-communist ideals, marketing them under gentler names such as "democratic socialism," "equity," or "social justice."[1] As earlier chapters have shown, socialism's earliest victories are linguistic—it gains power by redefining virtue until coercion sounds compassionate.[2]

As has been demonstrated here, **claiming to be a socialist but not a communist is like claiming to be a little bit pregnant**.[3] What was once an imported ideology that Americans fought and died to contain is now being repackaged as moral progress by domestic officeholders. Their language is soft; their intentions are not. Behind every promise of redistribution stands the same old principle: the subordination of individual freedom to the collectivist will.

The most visible of these contemporary figures include Senator Bernie Sanders, a self-described democratic socialist whose platform demands government control over health care, housing, and higher education; Representative Alexandria Ocasio-Cortez, whose membership in the Democratic Socialists of America (DSA) has made her the face of socialism for a new generation; and Representative Rashida Tlaib, another DSA member whose rhetoric mirrors that of revolutionary movements that once destroyed whole nations.[4] Alongside them stand Cori Bush and Jamaal Bowman of Missouri and New York—both aligned with the same DSA program of state-directed economics and perpetual grievance. Zohran Mamdani, a New York assemblyman, boasts of being a democratic socialist and advocates policies that would make the state the landlord of last resort.[5] In their wake follow others such as Emily Gallagher, Alexa Avilés, and Greg Casar, who carry the banner of socialism into city councils, state legislatures, and congressional districts across the nation.[6]

Nor are these figures isolated. The DSA and its affiliates have endorsed dozens of local officials, from school-board members to mayors, whose campaigns rest upon the same creed: that freedom must yield to planning, profit to control, and individual ambition to collective "equity." They are heirs to a lineage stretching back to Eugene V. Debs and Victor L. Berger, early twentieth-century socialists who preached the same doctrines under the same banners—proof that these ideas never die; they only disguised themselves for a new century.[7]

These politicians capitalize on the historical amnesia of the American electorate—an electorate softened by prosperity and dulled by indoctrination.[8] Many voters no longer recall that the systems these leaders glorify once filled the world's gulags, crippled economies, and extinguished entire cultures. They speak of "revolution" and "redistribution" as though the lessons of the twentieth century were mere abstractions rather than blood-written warnings. As demonstrated in earlier chapters on propaganda and education, ignorance is socialism's most reliable ally.[9]

> *"To do evil, a human being must first of all believe that what he's doing is good."* — **Aleksandr Solzhenitsyn**[10]

Solzhenitsyn's perspective explains why socialism so often spreads under banners of compassion. Its advocates seldom see themselves as destroyers; they believe coercion is kindness and control is care. This moral blindness is what allows tyranny to masquerade as virtue.

They promise a utopia of equality but never confess that equality enforced by the state demands the destruction of liberty itself.[11] Their proposals—state-run industries, punitive taxation, central control of energy and housing—are not new ideas. They are the recycled failures of systems that crushed freedom in the

Soviet Union, Mao's China, Cuba, and Venezuela.[12] The tragedy is that millions of young Americans, having been raised on slogans instead of substance, now mistake these failed doctrines for moral virtue.

THE POLITICS OF ENVY AND THE IGNORANCE OF THE ELECTORATE

The success of such politicians is not a testament to their brilliance but to the ignorance of those who elect them.[13] A people uneducated in the costs of socialism will always be seduced by its promises. Envy is the fuel of every collectivist movement—its power lies in convincing the discontented that prosperity is theft and that government is salvation.[14] Sanders and his ideological heirs thrive on this deception. They frame wealth as corruption and ambition as greed, hoping to harness resentment into political power.

This tactic—turning the frustrations of the masses into a mandate for control—has been the formula for every socialist revolution.[15] It always begins with rhetoric about compassion and ends with ration lines, censorship, and economic collapse.[16] When citizens lose sight of the moral link between freedom and responsibility, they become easy prey for those who would rule them under the banner of "equality."[17]

CORRUPTION AND THE CLIPPING OF AMERICA'S WINGS

Yet even more dangerous than the ideologues are the opportunists who exploit the system for personal gain.[18] The American republic has also suffered from those like Senator Bob Menendez, who represent not idealism but avarice—officials who would enrich themselves while professing public virtue.[19] As President Franklin D. Roosevelt warned in his 1941 Four Freedoms address,

> *"We must especially beware of that small group of selfish men who would clip the wings of the American eagle in order to feather their own nests."* — **Franklin D. Roosevelt**[20]

This warning transcends party and era. It captures the timeless danger of corruption—the betrayal of national trust for private gain. Such acts erode not only the nation's wealth but its moral confidence. When citizens watch their leaders trade influence for gold bars and political favors, they begin to lose faith in the integrity of the system itself.[21] Every act of betrayal at the top invites cynicism at the bottom. The Founders warned that republics do not die by invasion; they rot from within.

Corruption thrives not merely in secrecy but in complexity; the larger the bureaucracy, the easier it becomes for corruption to hide within it.[22] As shown in earlier chapters on propaganda and bureaucracy, unchecked government expansion provides both the tools and the cover for moral decay. A nation that cannot restrain its own administrators soon discovers that it is being governed, not represented.

FOREIGN INFLUENCE AND THE GREEN-EYED WORLD

Across the world, there are regimes that view the United States not with admiration but with jealousy and hatred.[23] They resent its prosperity, its cultural reach, and above all, its freedom. They seek to weaken America not through armies but through infiltration, disinformation, and manipulation of public discourse. By financing propaganda, exploiting social media, and spreading division, they aim to make Americans doubt themselves—to replace unity with suspicion, confidence with guilt, and self-reliance with dependence on the state.[24]

Protecting ourselves from such influence requires more than border security or intelligence operations. It requires moral clarity. A people that knows what it stands for cannot be easily deceived. A people that understands the difference between liberty and license, between equality of opportunity and equality of outcome, cannot be seduced by ideological poison.

Foreign adversaries exploit the cracks that domestic corruption opens.[25] Every scandal, every division, becomes a weapon turned inward. The moral decay of a nation invites the very infiltration its defenses were built to prevent. Only a virtuous people can remain a free people; moral weakness is the gate through which tyranny walks.[26]

THE ENEMIES WITHIN

But the gravest threat to America comes not from foreign tyrants but from domestic opportunists who weaponize chaos.[27] Every crisis—economic, racial, environmental—is seen as a chance to expand governmental power. Every emergency becomes an excuse to regulate, redistribute, and surveil. These internal enemies thrive in disorder; they rise by convincing citizens that only the state can save them from the state's own manufactured crises.[28]

The American people must relearn the oldest lesson of self-government: that freedom requires vigilance, not comfort. Those who promise to relieve citizens of all burdens are often preparing to relieve them of their rights.[29] We must remember that the Constitution is not a self-defending document; it is a framework that survives only when defended by informed citizens who refuse to be ruled by demagogues or thieves.[30]

> *"America will never be destroyed from the outside. If we falter and lose our freedoms, it will be because we destroyed ourselves."* — **Abraham Lincoln**[31]

Lincoln's words echo across the centuries as a mirror of our own predicament. The gravest danger to liberty lies not in foreign invasion but in moral surrender—the quiet corrosion of integrity that invites tyranny from within.

THE CALL TO REMEMBER AND DEFEND

The founders built this nation upon the belief that liberty, once surrendered, is never easily regained. The same spirit that resisted monarchy must now resist socialism and corruption alike. America's survival depends on citizens who can discern between compassionate governance and collectivist coercion, between honest service and political predation.[32]

"A people may prefer a free government; but if from indolence, or carelessness, or cowardice, they are incapable of exerting themselves to maintain it, they are unfit for liberty." — **John Stuart Mill**[33]

Mill captures the uncomfortable truth that freedom is not an inheritance but a discipline. When citizens trade courage for convenience, their liberty decays from neglect long before it is seized by force.

"Freedom has its life in the hearts, the actions, the spirit of men and so it must be daily earned and refreshed—else like a flower cut from its life-giving roots, it will wither and die." — **Dwight D. Eisenhower**[34]

Eisenhower reminds us that liberty is a living thing. It cannot be stored away like treasure in a vault; it must be renewed by the choices and virtues of each generation, or it will perish in apathy.

To forget the crimes of socialism is to risk repeating them; to tolerate corruption is to forfeit moral authority. The duty of every generation is to preserve what was purchased at such terrible cost by those before them. If we fail to guard freedom from both external and internal enemies, we will lose it—not through conquest, but through complacency.

THE ANSWERS AT LAST

The questions posed at the beginning of this book can now be answered plainly.

Why do communist countries succeed nowhere?

Because they war against human nature, against incentive, against freedom itself.[35]

Why do capitalist republics succeed everywhere?

Because they harness those same forces—creativity, responsibility, and self-interest—toward the common good.

And why, despite all evidence, do some still believe communism is the answer?

Because propaganda is powerful, envy is persuasive, and ignorance is profitable to those who seek control.

The truth is not complicated. Communism fails because it must; liberty succeeds because it can. The difference is not in circumstance but in principle—one enslaves the soul, the other sets it free.

STAMPING OUT THE SMOLDERING EMBERS

The bonfire of communism and socialism that once consumed half the world still smolders beneath the ashes of history. Its flames have dimmed but not died. Every university classroom that romanticizes "revolution," every politician who preaches class warfare in the name of justice, and every bureaucrat who dreams of controlling the lives of others is a spark waiting to reignite the blaze.[36]

To stamp out those embers is not merely a political duty but a moral one. It requires truth-telling in our schools, honesty in our media, and courage in our public life. We must expose socialism for what it is: a parasite that feeds on liberty until its host collapses.[37] The defense of civilization demands that we refuse to treat its advocates as harmless idealists. They are not harmless; they are heirs to an ideology that drenched the world in blood and misery.[38]

> *"The liberties of our country, the freedom of our civil constitution, are worth defending at all hazards; and it is our duty to defend them against all attacks."* — **Samuel Adams**[39]

Adams speaks not as a philosopher but as a patriot in action. His words strip away complacency: freedom is not maintained by admiration of the Founders, but by imitation of their courage.

Eternal vigilance is not a slogan—it is the price of survival. If we fail to extinguish these embers while they are small, we will once again face the inferno our ancestors fought to contain.

The time for complacency has passed; the time for remembrance and resistance has come. Let the light of truth and freedom burn brighter than the dying coals of tyranny.[40]

> *"The preservation of the sacred fire of liberty and the destiny of the Republican model of Government are justly considered as deeply, perhaps as finally, staked on the experiment entrusted to the hands of the American people."*
> — **George Washington**[41]

Washington's benediction reminds us that the survival of the Republic rests not in institutions alone, but in the faith and virtue of its citizens. The "sacred fire of liberty" burns only so long as free men choose to keep it lit.

CHAPTER 39.
...YOU MIGHT BE A COMMIE

Let's end on a lighter not...shall we...

INTRODUCTION

Once upon a time, calling yourself a communist meant you were part of a movement that promised equality but delivered misery. Today, it has become a badge of rebellion among people who think wearing a hammer and sickle makes them enlightened. They confuse ignorance with courage and conformity with independence. They are not revolutionaries; they are repeaters—parroting failed ideas they neither understand nor question.

Identifying as a communist is not a mark of wisdom or bravery. It is a confession of historical blindness. No ideology has inflicted more suffering upon mankind, and yet, in an age of comfort, some proudly brand themselves with its symbol as if it were a moral credential. In truth, if you glorify oppression under the banner of "equality," you are not enlightened—you're just proving you haven't learned from history.

I would have liked for this book to be humorous throughout. Unfortunately, there is nothing funny about communism. There is, however, plenty of cultural absurdity, irony, and hypocrisy to point out—and perhaps a little laughter is the only sane reaction left to the madness of those who still defend such a system.

So, in the spirit of Jeff Foxworthy's timeless humor, if you find yourself nodding at any of the following, well... you might be a commie.

THE LIST

1. If you think the government should decide how much of your paycheck you get to keep, you might be a commie.
2. If you believe "equal outcomes" matter more than equal opportunity, you might be a commie.
3. If you call billionaires evil but idolize politicians with vacation homes in Martha's Vineyard, you might be a commie.
4. If you read '1984' by Orwell and thought, "That's how things ought to be..." you might be a commie
5. If you think Karl Marx was a prophet instead of a parasite, you might be a commie.
6. If you believe Cuba's ration cards are proof of "economic justice," you might be a commie.
7. If you define "fair share" as whatever someone else pays for you, you might be a commie.
8. If you quote The Communist Manifesto without having read past page one, you might be a commie.
9. If you believe the Cold War was America's fault, you might be a commie.
10. If you think private property is theft but lock your apartment door, you might be a commie.
11. If you think Venezuela just "did it wrong," you might be a commie.
12. If you believe the way to end poverty is to make everyone poor, you might be a commie.
13. If you think free speech should apply only to people who agree with you, you might be a commie.
14. If you think "re-education camp" sounds progressive, you might be a commie.
15. If you think diversity means uniform thought, you might be a commie.
16. If you see success and assume corruption, you might be a commie.
17. If you think government rationing is "compassionate planning," you might be a commie.
18. If your degree is in grievance studies but you lecture others on economics, you might be a commie.
19. If you live off your parents while preaching about workers' rights, you might be a commie.

20. If you cheer when the rich are taxed but cry when your tips get withheld, you might be a commie.
21. If you think utopia is just one revolution away, you might be a commie.
22. If you condemn capitalism on an iPhone, you might be a commie.
23. If you believe bureaucrats are smarter than entrepreneurs, you might be a commie.
24. If you blame inflation on greed instead of printing money, you might be a commie.
25. If you think merit is oppression, you might be a commie.
26. If you call taxpayer-funded handouts "human rights," you might be a commie.
27. If you think discipline is a social construct, you might be a commie.
28. If you say morality is relative but insist Marx was right, you might be a commie.
29. If you mock religion yet worship the state, you might be a commie.
30. If you fear guns but praise censorship, you might be a commie.
31. If you think China is "just different," you might be a commie.
32. If you trust central planning more than free people, you might be a commie.
33. If you confuse misery for equality, you might be a commie.
34. If you value feelings over facts, you might be a commie.
35. If you believe truth comes from a committee, you might be a commie.
36. If you think banning beef saves the planet, you might be a commie.
37. If you claim the USSR "wasn't real communism," you might be a commie.
38. If you think posting rainbow flags makes you a revolutionary, you might be a commie.
39. If you believe wealth is created by redistributing it, you might be a commie.
40. If you call cancel culture "accountability," you might be a commie.
41. If facts offend you, you might be a commie.
42. If you think freedom of speech means freedom from disagreement, you might be a commie.

43. If you want to ban people for "misinformation," you might be a commie.
44. If you call police fascists but praise secret police elsewhere, you might be a commie.
45. If you celebrate ration lines as "community solidarity," you might be a commie.
46. If you think identity politics is science, you might be a commie.
47. If you call profit theft but taxation virtue, you might be a commie.
48. If you condemn the West while enjoying its comforts, you might be a commie.
49. If you believe equity means someone else does your work, you might be a commie.
50. If you think patriotism is hate speech, you might be a commie.
51. If you wear the hammer and sickle for fashion, you might be a commie.
52. If you think parental authority is fascism, you might be a commie.
53. If you think the Constitution is "outdated," you might be a commie.
54. If you call taxpayers "greedy" for wanting their own money, you might be a commie.
55. If you believe bureaucrats care more about you than your neighbors do, you might be a commie.
56. If you say there are no moral absolutes—except yours, you might be a commie.
57. If you think the only thing wrong with Stalin was bad PR, you might be a commie.
58. If you believe private enterprise is greedy but politicians are pure, you might be a commie.
59. If you think America owes you something because you exist, you might be a commie.
60. If you think the flag represents oppression but the hammer and sickle represent hope, you might be a commie.
61. If you think food should be free but phones should be $1,000, you might be a commie.
62. If you trust government scientists but mock entrepreneurs who fund innovation, you might be a commie.
63. If you think national borders are immoral but velvet ropes at nightclubs are fine, you might be a commie.

64. If you think history started the day you were born, you might be a commie.
65. If you think crime is caused by capitalism instead of criminals, you might be a commie.
66. If you call wealth "privilege" but your college debt a "human right," you might be a commie.
67. If you believe resentment is a virtue, you might be a commie.
68. If you think self-reliance is selfishness, you might be a commie.
69. If you think the media is objective because it agrees with you, you might be a commie.
70. If you think college activism counts as public service, you might be a commie.
71. If you think Elon Musk is dangerous, but Lenin was visionary, you might be a commie.
72. If you think government is your parent, you might be a commie.
73. If you think free markets are chaos but five-year plans are science, you might be a commie.
74. If you think your pronouns deserve a parade but veterans don't, you might be a commie.
75. If you believe truth should be approved by a moderator, you might be a commie.
76. If you think incentives are immoral but entitlements are sacred, you might be a commie.
77. If you think charity is useless unless the government forces it, you might be a commie.
78. If you think hard work is "toxic," you might be a commie.
79. If you think gender-neutral potato heads will save the planet, you might be a commie.
80. If you think humor is oppression, you might be a commie.
81. If you believe your feelings outweigh others' freedom, you might be a commie.
82. If you think price controls fix inflation, you might be a commie.
83. If you think profit motive is evil but power motive is noble, you might be a commie.
84. If you think "equitable grading" means no grading, you might be a commie.
85. If you think criminals are victims but victims are privileged, you might be a commie.

86. If you think military strength provokes war but weakness invites peace, you might be a commie.
87. If you think farmers should report their cow emissions, you might be a commie.
88. If you think equity is achieved through punishment, you might be a commie.
89. If you think tax money grows on trees, you might be a commie.
90. If you believe parental consent is optional for government policy, you might be a commie.
91. If you think poverty proves capitalism fails but mass death doesn't prove communism fails, you might be a commie.
92. If you think the Party is always right because it's your party, you might be a commie.
93. If you believe the Bill of Rights is negotiable, you might be a commie.
94. If you think mandatory participation is freedom, you might be a commie.
95. If you believe individualism is dangerous but collectivism is salvation, you might be a commie.
96. If you think history should be rewritten to spare feelings, you might be a commie.
97. If you think capitalists are parasites but bureaucrats are heroes, you might be a commie.
98. If you think the future belongs to planners, you might be a commie.
99. If you believe obedience is the highest form of virtue, you might be a commie.
100. If you think freedom is dangerous, you might be a commie.
101. If you read this list and got angry instead of laughing, you might be a commie.

CLOSING

Communism feeds on envy, ignorance, and the illusion of moral superiority. It flatters the weak, exploits the naïve, and destroys the free. The lines above may draw laughter—but behind every one of them lies a truth written in blood, not ink. Those who sneer at liberty and worship the collective will never understand that the greatest rebellion of all is to think for yourself.

If you found yourself laughing at any of these—or thinking of new ones—consider yourself invited to join the fun. Future editions of this book may include reader-submitted entries. Send responses to xananimuus@gmail.com. After all, the supply of communist absurdities seems inexhaustible, and laughter may be one of the last freedoms they haven't yet taxed.

ENDNOTES

CHAPTER 1: ENDNOTES

1. Stéphane Courtois et al., The Black Book of Communism: Crimes, Terror, Repression (Harvard University Press, 1999).
2. Whittaker Chambers, Witness (Random House, 1952).
3. John Jay, The Federalist No. 2: Concerning Dangers from Foreign Force and Influence, October 31, 1787, in The Federalist Papers, written by Alexander Hamilton, James Madison, and John Jay.
4. Edmund Burke, Reflections on the Revolution in France (London: J. Dodsley, 1790).
5. Aleksandr Solzhenitsyn, The Gulag Archipelago (Harper & Row, 1973).
6. Friedrich A. Hayek, The Road to Serfdom (University of Chicago Press, 1944).
7. Richard Crossman, ed., The God That Failed (Harper & Brothers, 1949).
8. Winston Churchill, Speech to the House of Commons, October 22, 1945, in Hansard Parliamentary Debates, vol. 414, col. 264–265.
9. Ronald Reagan, Address to the Phoenix Chamber of Commerce, March 30, 1967.

CHAPTER 2: ENDNOTES

1. Karl Marx and Friedrich Engels, The Communist Manifesto (1848).
2. Vladimir I. Lenin, State and Revolution (1917).
3. Friedrich Hayek, The Road to Serfdom (1944).
4. Stéphane Courtois et al., The Black Book of Communism (Harvard University Press, 1997).
5. Karl Marx, Critique of the Gotha Program (1875).
6. Roderick MacFarquhar, The Origins of the Cultural Revolution (Columbia University Press, 1974); Anne Applebaum, Gulag: A History (Doubleday, 2003).
7. George Orwell, Animal Farm (1945).
8. Ronald Reagan, public remarks and press interviews, c. 1980s; see editorials collected in The Reagan Diaries (HarperCollins, 2007).
9. Paul Hollander, Political Pilgrims: Western Intellectuals in Search of the Good Society (Transaction, 1998).

CHAPTER 3: ENDNOTES

1. Stéphane Courtois et al., *The Black Book of Communism: Crimes, Terror, Repression* (Cambridge, MA: Harvard University Press, 1999).
2. Thomas Sowell, *A Conflict of Visions* (New York: William Morrow, 1987).
3. Richard Pipes, *Communism: A History* (New York: Modern Library, 2001).
4. Martin Malia, *The Soviet Tragedy: A History of Socialism in Russia, 1917–1991* (New York: Free Press, 1994).
5. Winston S. Churchill, speech at the Scottish Unionist Conference, Perth,

May 28, 1948 (commonly cited phrasing).
6. Tony Judt, *Postwar: A History of Europe Since 1945* (New York: Penguin, 2005), esp. chapters on Eastern Europe and the Cold War settlements.
7. Ronald Reagan, "Address to Members of the British Parliament," Palace of Westminster (House of Commons), June 8, 1982.
8. Frank Dikötter, *Mao's Great Famine: The History of China's Most Devastating Catastrophe, 1958–1962* (New York: Walker & Co., 2010).
9. Margaret Thatcher, speech to the Conservative Party Conference, October 1976 (often cited as the origin of: "The problem with socialism is that eventually you run out of other people's money").
10. Archie Brown, *The Rise and Fall of Communism* (New York: HarperCollins, 2009), sections on Asia and international diffusion.
11. Ronald Reagan, quip used in remarks on regulation and the economy, mid-1980s (e.g., 1986 small-business and tax reform addresses).
12. Ben Kiernan, *The Pol Pot Regime: Race, Power, and Genocide in Cambodia under the Khmer Rouge, 1975–79* (New Haven: Yale University Press, 2002).
13. Robert Service, *Comrades! A History of World Communism* (Cambridge, MA: Harvard University Press, 2007), comparative chapters on Asia/Korea.
14. Ronald Reagan, address frequently cited as "Freedom is never more than one generation away from extinction," March 30, 1961, Phoenix Chamber of Commerce (widely quoted formulation).
15. Samuel Farber, *Cuba Since the Revolution of 1959: A Critical Assessment* (Chicago: Haymarket Books, 2011).
16. Friedrich A. Hayek, *The Road to Serfdom* (London: Routledge, 1944).
17. Gebru Tareke, *The Ethiopian Revolution: War in the Horn of Africa* (New Haven: Yale University Press, 2009).
18. William J. H. Boetcker, "The Ten Cannots" (pamphlet, 1916) — aphorisms commonly misattributed to Abraham Lincoln; cited here to clarify attribution.
19. Archie Brown, *The Rise and Fall of Communism* (New York: HarperCollins, 2009), overview chapters on global spread (incl. Afghanistan/South Yemen) and decline.
20. Margaret Thatcher, remarks on the fragility of freedom, 1986 (Conservative speeches from that year repeatedly emphasize the generational duty to defend liberty).
21. Stéphane Courtois et al., *The Black Book of Communism* (Harvard University Press, 1999), synthesis of global outcomes and casualties.
22. Ronald Reagan, "A Time for Choosing," televised address for Barry Goldwater, October 27, 1964.

CHAPTER 4: ENDNOTES

1. Author's introduction based on comparative political analysis of contemporary socialist regimes and their persistence after the Cold War.
2. AP News. *Cuba Faces Its Worst Economic Crisis in Decades.* July 2024.
3. Webster, Daniel. *Speech before the United States Senate.* 1837.
4. AP News. *North Korea Faces Renewed Food Shortages.* April 2024.
5. Havel, Václav. *Letters to Olga.* 1988.
6. BBC News. *China's Property and Debt Crisis.* February 2025.
7. Solzhenitsyn, Aleksandr. *The Gulag Archipelago.* 1973.
8. World Bank. *Vietnam: Đổi Mới Reforms and Economic Indicators.* 2024.
9. Pericles. *Funeral Oration.* 431 B.C.

10. Organisation for Economic Co-operation and Development (OECD). *Laos: Debt Exposure and Infrastructure Dependency*. 2024.
11. Henry, Patrick. *Speech in the Virginia Ratifying Convention*. 1788.
12. Reuters. *Venezuela's Economy in Collapse*. March 2025.
13. Applebaum, Anne. *Twilight of Democracy: The Seductive Lure of Authoritarianism*. 2020.
14. The Washington Post. *Bolivia's Socialist Project Falters*. August 2025.
15. Kafka, Franz. *The Zürau Aphorisms*. 1917.
16. Transparency International. *Corruption Perceptions Index*. 2024.
17. Paul, Ron. *Liberty Defined: 50 Essential Issues That Affect Our Freedom*. 2011.
18. Organisation for Economic Co-operation and Development (OECD). *Challenges to European Welfare States*. 2024.
19. Franklin, Benjamin. *Letter to Jean Baptiste Le Roy*. 1789.
20. Camus, Albert. *Resistance, Rebellion and Death*. 1951.
21. Camus, Albert. *Resistance, Rebellion and Death*. 1951.

CHAPTER 5: ENDNOTES

1. Adam Smith, *The Wealth of Nations* (1776).
2. John Stuart Mill, *On Liberty* (1859).
3. Alexander Hamilton, James Madison, and John Jay, *The Federalist Papers* (1787–88).
4. Edmund Burke, *Letter to a Member of the National Assembly* (1791).
5. Milton Friedman, *Capitalism and Freedom* (1962).
6. Albert Szent-Györgyi, address at the Nobel Banquet, Stockholm (1937).
7. Deirdre McCloskey, *Bourgeois Dignity: Why Economics Can't Explain the Modern World* (2010).
8. St. Francis de Sales, *Introduction to the Devout Life* (1609).
9. John Adams, *A Dissertation on the Canon and Feudal Law* (1765).
10. Norman Cousins, *Human Options: An Autobiographical Notebook* (1981).
11. Douglass C. North and Robert Thomas, *The Rise of the Western World* (1973).
12. Aristotle, *Nicomachean Ethics* (ca. 340 BC).
13. Grace Hopper, address to the American Federation of Information Processing Societies (1967).
14. Deirdre McCloskey, *Bourgeois Dignity: Why Economics Can't Explain the Modern World* (2010).
15. Franklin D. Roosevelt, Second Inaugural Address (January 20, 1937).
16. Niall Ferguson, *Civilization: The West and the Rest* (2011).
17. Modern proverb, unattributed; contemporary folk usage.
18. World Bank, *Migration and Remittances Data* (2024); United Nations, *International Migration Report* (2024).
19. Benjamin Franklin, *Memoirs and Writings* (1774).

CHAPTER 6: ENDNOTES

1. Karl Marx and Friedrich Engels, *The Communist Manifesto* (1848).
2. James Madison, *The Federalist Papers* (Nos. 10 and 51). Liberty Fund edition.
3. Michael Ellman, *Planning Problems in the USSR*. Cambridge University Press, 1973.
4. Milton Friedman, *Capitalism and Freedom*. University of Chicago Press, 1962.

5. Vladimir Lenin, *The State and Revolution*. 1917.
6. Milton Friedman and Rose Friedman, *Free to Choose*. Harcourt, 1980.
7. Ludwig von Mises, "Economic Calculation in the Socialist Commonwealth." 1920.
8. Henry David Thoreau, *Walden* and *Civil Disobedience*. Various editions.
9. Robert Conquest, *The Harvest of Sorrow: Soviet Collectivization and the Terror-Famine*. Oxford University Press, 1986.
10. Aleksandr Solzhenitsyn, *The Gulag Archipelago*. Harper & Row, 1973–78.
11. Anne Applebaum, *Red Famine: Stalin's War on Ukraine*. Doubleday, 2017.
12. Patrick Henry, "Letter to Archibald Blair." 1775.
13. Stéphane Courtois et al., *The Black Book of Communism*. Harvard University Press, 1999.
14. Attribution note: The quotation ascribed to Voltaire—"find out who you are not allowed to criticize"—has disputed provenance.
15. Karl Marx, *Economic and Philosophic Manuscripts*. 1844.
16. James Madison, speech to the Virginia Constitutional Convention, 1788.
17. Richard Pipes, *Russia Under the Bolshevik Regime*. Vintage, 1995.
18. John F. Kennedy, Address on the Alliance for Progress, March 13, 1962.
19. Frank Dikötter, *Mao's Great Famine*. Walker & Company, 2010.
20. Winston S. Churchill, *Never Give In!* Speeches 1897–1963. Hyperion, 2003.

CHAPTER 7: ENDNOTES

1. Karl Marx and Friedrich Engels, *The Communist Manifesto*, 1848.
2. Frédéric Bastiat, *The Law*, 1850.
3. Stéphane Courtois et al., *The Black Book of Communism: Crimes, Terror, Repression*, Harvard University Press, 1999.
4. Frank Dikötter, *Mao's Great Famine: The History of China's Most Devastating Catastrophe, 1958–1962*, Walker & Co., 2010.
5. Adrian Rogers, Sermon on Economics and Freedom, Bellevue Baptist Church, 1984.
6. Ludwig von Mises, *Socialism: An Economic and Sociological Analysis*, Yale University Press, 1951.
7. Friedrich A. Hayek, *The Road to Serfdom*, University of Chicago Press, 1944.
8. Richard Pipes, *Property and Freedom*, Knopf, 1999.
9. Frank Dikötter, *Mao's Great Famine*, Walker & Co., 2010.
10. Stéphane Courtois et al., *The Black Book of Communism*, Harvard University Press, 1999.
11. Calvin Coolidge, *Speech on the 150th Anniversary of the Declaration of Independence*, Philadelphia, 1926.
12. Margaret Thatcher, *Speech to the Conservative Party Conference*, 1976.
13. John Locke, *Two Treatises of Government*, 1690.
14. John Adams, *A Defence of the Constitutions of Government of the United States of America*, 1787.

CHAPTER 8: ENDNOTES

1. Adam Smith, *The Theory of Moral Sentiments* (1759).
2. Ludwig von Mises, *Economic Calculation in the Socialist Commonwealth* (1920).
3. Thomas Sowell, *Knowledge and Decisions* (Basic Books, 1980).
4. Michael Polanyi, *The Tacit Dimension* (University of Chicago Press, 1966).

5. Hernando de Soto, *The Mystery of Capital: Why Capitalism Triumphs in the West and Fails Everywhere Else* (Basic Books, 2000).
6. János Kornai, *Economics of Shortage* (North-Holland, 1980).
7. James C. Scott, *Seeing Like a State: How Certain Schemes to Improve the Human Condition Have Failed* (Yale University Press, 1998).
8. Mancur Olson, *The Rise and Decline of Nations* (Yale University Press, 1982).
9. Israel Kirzner, *Competition and Entrepreneurship* (University of Chicago Press, 1973);
10. Anne Applebaum, *Red Famine: Stalin's War on Ukraine* (Doubleday, 2017).

CHAPTER 9: ENDNOTES

1. Walter Scheidel, *The Great Leveler: Violence and the History of Inequality from the Stone Age to the Twenty-First Century* (Princeton: Princeton University Press, 2017).
2. Calvin Coolidge, *The Price of Freedom: Speeches and Addresses* (New York: Charles Scribner's Sons, 1924).
3. Ludwig von Mises, *Human Action: A Treatise on Economics* (New Haven: Yale University Press, 1949).
4. Thomas Sowell, *The Vision of the Anointed* (New York: Basic Books, 1995).
5. Friedrich A. Hayek, "The Use of Knowledge in Society," *American Economic Review* 35, no. 4 (1945): 519–530.
6. Friedrich A. Hayek, *The Fatal Conceit* (Chicago: University of Chicago Press, 1988).
7. Adam Smith, *An Inquiry into the Nature and Causes of the Wealth of Nations* (London: W. Strahan and T. Cadell, 1776).
8. Alexis de Tocqueville, *Democracy in America* (Paris: Charles Gosselin, 1835).
9. Stéphane Courtois et al., *The Black Book of Communism: Crimes, Terror, Repression* (Cambridge, MA: Harvard University Press, 1999); Daron Acemoglu and James A. Robinson, *Why Nations Fail: The Origins of Power, Prosperity, and Poverty* (New York: Crown Business, 2012).
10. Thomas Jefferson, "Letter to Edward Carrington," May 27, 1788.
11. John Locke, *Second Treatise of Government* (London: Awnsham Churchill, 1690).
12. Michael Novak, *The Spirit of Democratic Capitalism* (New York: Simon & Schuster, 1982).

CHAPTER 10: ENDNOTES

1. Herbert Hoover, *Addresses upon the American Road* (1931).
2. Thomas Sowell, *Basic Economics* (2007).
3. Ludwig von Mises, *Economic Calculation in the Socialist Commonwealth* (1920).
4. Friedrich A. Hayek, *The Road to Serfdom* (1944).
5. Stephen Nickell, "Competition and Corporate Performance," *Journal of Political Economy* 104 (1996).
6. Friedrich A. Hayek, "The Use of Knowledge in Society," *American Economic Review* 35 (1945).
7. Barry Goldwater, *The Conscience of a Conservative* (1960).
8. Joseph Schumpeter, *Capitalism, Socialism, and Democracy* (1942).
9. Milton Friedman, *Capitalism and Freedom* (1962).
10. Aghion et al., "Competition and Innovation: An Inverted-U Relationship," *Quarterly Journal of Economics* (2005).

11. Hayek, *The Road to Serfdom*, ibid.
12. János Kornai, *Economics of Shortage* (1980).
13. IMF Country Report No. 19/297 (Venezuela, 2019).
14. William F. Buckley Jr., *Up from Liberalism* (1959).
15. Nicholas Bloom & John Van Reenen, "Measuring and Explaining Management Practices Across Firms and Countries," *QJE* (2007).
16. Ronald Reagan, "Address to the Phoenix Chamber of Commerce," March 30, 1961.
17. Friedrich A. Hayek, *Law, Legislation and Liberty* (1973).
18. János Kornai & Eric Maskin, "The Soft Budget Constraint," *Economics of Transition* (1999).
19. Milton Friedman & Anna Schwartz, *Free to Choose* (1980).
20. F. A. Hayek, *Individualism and Economic Order* (1948).
21. Ronald Reagan, ibid.
22. Megginson & Netter, "From State to Market: A Survey of Empirical Studies on Privatization," *Journal of Economic Literature* 39 (2001).
23. Hayek, *The Constitution of Liberty* (1960).
24. Friedrich Hayek & Milton Friedman collected essays in *IMF Transition Studies Series* (1995).

CHAPTER 11: ENDNOTES

1. Richard Pipes, *Communism: A History* (New York: Modern Library, 2001).
2. H. L. Mencken, *Prejudices: Third Series* (New York: Knopf, 1922).
3. R. W. Davies and Stephen G. Wheatcroft, *The Years of Hunger: Soviet Agriculture, 1931–1933* (New York: Palgrave Macmillan, 2004).
4. Sheila Fitzpatrick, *Stalin's Peasants: Resistance and Survival in the Russian Village after Collectivization* (Oxford: Oxford University Press, 1994).
5. Robert Conquest, *The Harvest of Sorrow: Soviet Collectivization and the Terror-Famine* (Oxford: Oxford University Press, 1986).
6. Anne Applebaum, *Red Famine: Stalin's War on Ukraine* (New York: Doubleday, 2017).
7. James C. Scott, *Seeing Like a State: How Certain Schemes to Improve the Human Condition Have Failed* (New Haven: Yale University Press, 1998).
8. Timothy Snyder, *Bloodlands: Europe Between Hitler and Stalin* (New York: Basic Books, 2010).
9. Ronald Reagan, Speech, Washington, DC (1964).
10. Anne Applebaum, *Red Famine*, ibid.
11. EBSCO Research Starters, "Great Famine Strikes the Soviet Union" (2023).
12. Jung Chang and Jon Halliday, *Mao: The Unknown Story* (New York: Knopf, 2005).
13. Frédéric Bastiat, *Economic Sophisms* (Paris, 1845).
14. Lynne Viola, *The Unknown Gulag: The Lost World of Stalin's Special Settlements* (Oxford: Oxford University Press, 2007).
15. James C. Scott, *Seeing Like a State*, ibid.
16. Anne Applebaum, *Red Famine*, ibid.
17. Peter Kenez, *A History of the Soviet Union from the Beginning to the End* (Cambridge: Cambridge University Press, 2016).
18. Richard Pipes, *Communism: A History*, ibid.
19. Murray N. Rothbard, *The Ethics of Liberty* (New York: New York University Press, 1982).

CHAPTER 12: ENDNOTES

1. Aleksandr Solzhenitsyn. *The Gulag Archipelago.* Harper & Row, 1973.
2. G.K. Chesterton. *The Illustrated London News.* 1928.
3. Czesław Miłosz. *The Captive Mind.* Knopf, 1953.
4. Ronald Reagan. Address to the Alabama State Legislature. March 15, 1982.
5. Whittaker Chambers. *Witness.* Random House, 1952.
6. Pope John Paul II. Address to the United Nations. October 2, 1979.
7. Karl Marx and Friedrich Engels. *The Communist Manifesto.* 1848.
8. Winston Churchill. Speech to the House of Commons. November 10, 1948.
9. Paul Froese. *The Plot to Kill God: Findings from the Soviet Experiment in Secularization.* University of California Press, 2008.
10. Barry Goldwater. Speech to the Republican National Convention. 1964.
11. Winston Churchill. Speech to the House of Commons. 1938.

CHAPTER 13: ENDNOTES

1. Hannah Arendt, *The Origins of Totalitarianism* (New York: Harcourt, 1951).
2. George Orwell, *The Prevention of Literature, Polemic* No. 2 (1946).
3. Karl Marx and Friedrich Engels, *The Communist Manifesto* (1848).
4. Anne Applebaum, *Twilight of Democracy* (New York: Doubleday, 2020).
5. Václav Havel, *The Power of the Powerless* (1978).
6. Aleksandr Solzhenitsyn, *The Gulag Archipelago* (Harper & Row, 1973).
7. Jung Chang and Jon Halliday, *Mao: The Unknown Story* (New York: Knopf, 2005).
8. Ayn Rand, *The Fountainhead* (New York: Bobbs-Merrill, 1943).
9. U.S. House Judiciary Committee, *Report on the Weaponization of the Federal Government* (Washington, D.C., 2023).
10. Michael Schellenberger et al., "The Twitter Files," *Substack* (2022).
11. Matt Taibbi, *Twitter Files Testimony,* U.S. Congress (March 2023).
12. House Select Subcommittee on the Weaponization of Government Report (2024).
13. Elon Musk interview, *CNBC,* May 2023.
14. Timothy Snyder, *On Tyranny* (New York: Tim Duggan Books, 2017).
15. Hannah Arendt, *Between Past and Future* (New York: Viking, 1968).
16. Justice Louis D. Brandeis, *Whitney v. California,* 274 U.S. 357 (1927).
17. Anne Applebaum, *Twilight of Democracy,* ibid.
18. BBC News, "Police Arrest Man for Offensive Tweet," *BBC.com,* 2022.
19. John Locke, *A Letter Concerning Toleration* (1689).
20. The Telegraph (London), "Britons Arrested for Online Speech Surge," 2023.
21. Thomas Jefferson, Letter to Charles Yancey (1816).
22. Anne Applebaum, *Twilight of Democracy,* ibid.
23. Justice Learned Hand, "The Spirit of Liberty" (Address, 1944).
24. Francis Fukuyama, *The End of History and the Last Man* (New York: Free Press, 1992).
25. Václav Havel, *The Power of the Powerless,* ibid.
26. Voltaire, *Essay on Tolerance* (1763).

CHAPTER 14: ENDNOTES

1. Erich Fromm, *Marx's Concept of Man.* Continuum, 1961.
2. Aleksandr Solzhenitsyn, *The Gulag Archipelago.* Harper & Row, 1973.
3. Richard Pipes, *Russia Under the Bolshevik Regime.* Vintage, 1994.

4. Karl Marx and Friedrich Engels, *The Communist Manifesto*. 1848.
5. Che Guevara, *"Socialism and Man in Cuba."* 1965.
6. Leszek Kołakowski, *Main Currents of Marxism*. Oxford University Press, 1978.
7. George Orwell, *Nineteen Eighty-Four*. Secker & Warburg, 1949.
8. Václav Havel, *The Power of the Powerless*. 1978.
9. Ludwig von Mises, *Socialism: An Economic and Sociological Analysis*. Yale University Press, 1951.
10. Bryan Caplan, "The Inadequacy of the New Socialist Man." *EconLog*. Library of Economics and Liberty, 2010.
11. Alexander Zinoviev, *Homo Sovieticus*. Grove Press, 1986.
12. C. S. Lewis, *God in the Dock*. Eerdmans, 1970.
13. Leszek Kołakowski, *Main Currents of Marxism*. Oxford University Press, 1978.
14. Richard Pipes, *Communism: A History*. Random House, 2001.
15. Leszek Kołakowski, *Is God Happy? Selected Essays*. Basic Books, 2013.
16. F. A. Hayek, *The Constitution of Liberty*. University of Chicago Press, 1960.
17. F. A. Hayek, *The Road to Serfdom*. University of Chicago Press, 1944.
18. Alexander Zinoviev, *Homo Sovieticus*. Grove Press, 1986.
19. Václav Havel, *The Power of the Powerless*. 1978.
20. Leszek Kołakowski, *Main Currents of Marxism*. Oxford University Press, 1978.
21. Aleksandr Solzhenitsyn, *The Gulag Archipelago*. Harper & Row, 1973.

CHAPTER 15: ENDNOTES

1. Karl Marx, *The Communist Manifesto*. 1848.
2. Lord Acton, *The History of Freedom and Other Essays*. Macmillan, 1907.
3. Ibid.
4. Ayn Rand, *The Virtue of Selfishness*. New American Library, 1964.
5. Ibid.
6. Ibid.
7. William E. Gladstone, *Speech on the Employers and Workmen Bill,* House of Commons, 1875.
8. Ibid.
9. Aleksandr Solzhenitsyn, *The Gulag Archipelago*. Harper & Row, 1973.
10. Thomas Sowell, *Civil Rights: Rhetoric or Reality?* William Morrow & Co., 1984.
11. Ibid.
12. Ibid.
13. Herbert Hoover, *Addresses Upon the American Road*. Charles Scribner's Sons, 1936.
14. Ibid.
15. Ibid.
16. Anne Applebaum, *Red Famine: Stalin's War on Ukraine*. Doubleday, 2017.
17. Ibid.
18. Ibid.

CHAPTER 16: ENDNOTES

1. Hannah Arendt, *The Origins of Totalitarianism* (Harcourt, 1951), 6–9.
2. Isaiah Berlin, *The Crooked Timber of Humanity* (Princeton University Press, 1990), 19–23.
3. Karl Marx and Friedrich Engels, *The German Ideology* (1846).
4. Aleksandr Solzhenitsyn, *The Gulag Archipelago* (Harper & Row, 1973), Vol. I.

5. Saint Bernard of Clairvaux, attributed proverb, c. 12th century.
6. Friedrich Hayek, *The Road to Serfdom* (University of Chicago Press, 1944), 57–60.
7. Václav Havel, *The Power of the Powerless* (1978), essay section I.
8. Jung Chang and Jon Halliday, *Mao: The Unknown Story* (Knopf, 2005), 413–418.
9. Solzhenitsyn, *The Gulag Archipelago*, Vol. II.
10. Karl Popper, *The Open Society and Its Enemies* (1945), 190–191.
11. Hayek, *The Road to Serfdom*, 78–80.
12. Arendt, *The Origins of Totalitarianism*, 306–310.
13. Nikolai Berdyaev, *The End of Our Time* (1933), 200–201.
14. Ibid.
15. Arendt, *The Origins of Totalitarianism*, 329–331.
16. Solzhenitsyn, *The Gulag Archipelago*, Vol. III.
17. Havel, *The Power of the Powerless*, section IV.
18. Koestler, *Darkness at Noon* (1940), Part Two.
19. Ayn Rand, *The Ayn Rand Column* (1981).
20. Rand, *Atlas Shrugged* (1957), 1050.
21. Berlin, *The Crooked Timber of Humanity*, 37.
22. Solzhenitsyn, *The Gulag Archipelago*, Vol. III.
23. Ronald Reagan, Speech, August 12, 1986, press transcript.
24. Hayek, *The Road to Serfdom*, 94.
25. Berlin, *Two Concepts of Liberty* (Oxford, 1958).
26. Arendt, *The Origins of Totalitarianism*, 389–390.
27. Havel, *The Power of the Powerless*, section V.
28. Koestler, *Darkness at Noon*, concluding passage.

CHAPTER 17: ENDNOTES

1. Karl Marx and Friedrich Engels, *The Communist Manifesto*, 1848.
2. Karl Marx, *A Contribution to the Critique of Hegel's Philosophy of Right*, 1844.
3. Aleksandr Solzhenitsyn, *The Gulag Archipelago* (New York: Harper & Row, 1973).
4. Leon Trotsky, *Their Morals and Ours* (New York: Pathfinder Press, 1938).
5. Fyodor Dostoevsky, *The Brothers Karamazov* (New York: Macmillan, 1912).
6. Robert Conquest, *The Great Terror* (London: Macmillan, 1968); Cambodian genocide archives under Pol Pot.
7. Traditional English proverb first recorded in George Herbert's *Jacula Prudentum*, 1651.
8. Documented examples: Soviet rationing under Stalin and Cuban ration system post-1959.
9. R. Pipes, *Communism: A History* (New York: Modern Library, 2001).
10. Calvin Coolidge, Address to the American Legion Convention, Omaha, Nebraska, October 6, 1925.
11. Friedrich A. Hayek, *The Road to Serfdom* (Chicago: University of Chicago Press, 1944).
12. Johann Wolfgang von Goethe, *Maxims and Reflections* (London: Dent & Sons, 1906).
13. Georg Christoph Lichtenberg, *The Waste Books* (New York: NYRB Classics, 2000).
14. Ludwig von Mises, *Human Action: A Treatise on Economics* (New Haven: Yale University Press, 1949).

15. Jostein Gaarder, *Sophie's World* (New York: Farrar, Straus and Giroux, 1994).
16. Patrick Henry, Speech before the Virginia Ratifying Convention, June 1788.
17. Ibid.
18. Samuel Adams, *The Writings of Samuel Adams*, Vol. 2, ed. Harry Alonzo Cushing (New York: G. P. Putnam's Sons, 1906).
19. Ibid.
20. Georg Wilhelm Friedrich Hegel, *Lectures on the Philosophy of History* (London: George Bell & Sons, 1902).
21. Ibid.
22. Aristotle, *Politics*, trans. Benjamin Jowett (Oxford: Clarendon Press, 1885).
23. Documented historical violations of human rights in Soviet and Maoist regimes; see Amnesty International archives.
24. Eleanor Roosevelt, *Tomorrow Is Now* (New York: Harper & Row, 1963).
25. Alexis de Tocqueville, *Democracy in America*, trans. Henry Reeve (New York: Vintage Books, 1945).
26. R. J. Rummel, *Death by Government* (New Brunswick: Transaction Publishers, 1994), on communist control of family life.
27. Pope John XXIII, *Mater et Magistra* (Vatican City: 1961).
28. Documentation of Soviet "Young Pioneer" and Maoist "Red Guard" indoctrination programs.
29. Confucius, *The Analects*, trans. Arthur Waley (London: George Allen & Unwin, 1938).
30. Benjamin Disraeli, *Sybil, or the Two Nations* (London: Henry Colburn, 1845).
31. Oscar Wilde, *Intentions* (London: Methuen & Co., 1891).
32. Historical evidence of neighborhood surveillance under East German Stasi and Cuban Committees for the Defense of the Revolution.
33. Tocqueville's analysis of labor and equality in *Democracy in America*, Vol. 2 (1840).
34. Alexis de Tocqueville, Ibid.
35. Lenin's "war communism" policies and Soviet labor quotas (1918–1921).
36. Thomas Sowell, *Basic Economics: A Common Sense Guide to the Economy* (New York: Basic Books, 2000).
37. Documented stagnation in USSR and Eastern Bloc innovation, e.g., Soviet computer industry, 1950–1980s.
38. Common 20th-century aphorism circulated in Cold War critiques of collectivism.
39. Friedrich A. Hayek, *The Road to Serfdom* (Chicago: University of Chicago Press, 1944).
40. Albert Einstein, "Science and Civilization," Address before the Conference on Science, 1933.
41. Case studies: Lysenkoism in Soviet biology; censorship of genetics and cybernetics under Stalin.
42. Salman Rushdie, *Imaginary Homelands: Essays and Criticism, 1981–1991* (London: Granta Books, 1991).
43. Historical accounts of artistic repression in Soviet, Chinese, and North Korean regimes (see UNESCO archives).

CHAPTER 18: ENDNOTES

1. Aleksandr Solzhenitsyn, *The Gulag Archipelago* (New York: Harper & Row, 1973).
2. Anne Applebaum, *Gulag: A History* (New York: Doubleday, 2003).
3. Richard Pipes, *Communism: A History* (New York: Modern Library, 2001).

4. Robert Conquest, *The Harvest of Sorrow: Soviet Collectivization and the Terror-Famine* (New York: Oxford University Press, 1986).
5. Stéphane Courtois et al., *The Black Book of Communism* (Cambridge: Harvard University Press, 1999).
6. Niall Ferguson, *Civilization: The West and the Rest* (New York: Penguin Press, 2011).
7. Pipes, *Communism: A History.*
8. Applebaum, *Gulag: A History.*
9. Courtois et al., *The Black Book of Communism.*
10. Solzhenitsyn, *The Gulag Archipelago.*

CHAPTER 19: ENDNOTES

1. Stéphane Courtois et al., *The Black Book of Communism* (Cambridge: Harvard University Press, 1999).
2. Ibid.
3. Ibid.
4. Rudolph Rummel, *Death by Government* (New Brunswick: Transaction Publishers, 1994).
5. Ibid.
6. Anne Applebaum, *Gulag: A History* (New York: Doubleday, 2003).
7. Aleksandr Solzhenitsyn, *The Gulag Archipelago* (New York: Harper & Row, 1973).
8. Robert Conquest, *The Harvest of Sorrow: Soviet Collectivization and the Terror-Famine* (New York: Oxford University Press, 1986).
9. Ibid.
10. Jung Chang and Jon Halliday, *Mao: The Unknown Story* (New York: Knopf, 2005).
11. Ibid.
12. Ben Kiernan, *The Pol Pot Regime: Race, Power, and Genocide in Cambodia under the Khmer Rouge* (New Haven: Yale University Press, 2002).
13. Richard Pipes, *Communism: A History* (New York: Modern Library, 2001).
14. Courtois et al., *The Black Book of Communism.*
15. George F. Kennan, *American Diplomacy* ***1900–1950*** (Chicago: University of Chicago Press, 1951).
16. Niall Ferguson, *Civilization: The West and the Rest* (New York: Penguin Press, 2011).
17. Pipes, *Communism: A History.*
18. Steven Pinker, *The Better Angels of Our Nature* (New York: Viking, 2011).
19. U.S. Department of Defense, *Korean War Veterans Memorial Fact Sheet* (Washington, D.C., 2015).
20. Ferguson, *Civilization: The West and the Rest.*
21. U.S. Department of Defense, *Vietnam Conflict Extract Data File* (Defense Casualty Analysis System, 2020).
22. Ibid.
23. Pinker, *The Better Angels of Our Nature.*
24. Václav Havel, *The Power of the Powerless* (Armonk, NY: M.E. Sharpe, 1985).
25. Pinker, *The Better Angels of Our Nature.*
26. Deirdre McCloskey, *Bourgeois Equality* (Chicago: University of Chicago Press, 2016).
27. Ibid.
28. Pinker, *The Better Angels of Our Nature.*

CHAPTER 20: ENDNOTES

1. Robert Conquest, *The Great Terror* (Oxford University Press, 1968).
2. John Locke, *Two Treatises of Government* (London, 1689).
3. Hannah Arendt, *The Origins of Totalitarianism* (Harcourt, 1951).
4. Anne Applebaum, *Gulag: A History* (Anchor Books, 2004).
5. Andrei Sakharov, *Memoirs* (Knopf, 1990).
6. Vaclav Havel, *The Power of the Powerless* (1978).
7. Aleksandr Solzhenitsyn, *The Gulag Archipelago* (Harper & Row, 1973).
8. George Orwell, *Collected Essays* (Secker & Warburg, 1946).
9. Anne Applebaum, *Gulag: A History* (Anchor Books, 2004).
10. Robert Conquest, *Reflections on a Ravaged Century* (Norton, 2000).
11. Thomas Paine, *The Rights of Man* (London, 1791).
12. Hannah Arendt, *The Origins of Totalitarianism* (Harcourt, 1951).
13. Aleksandr Solzhenitsyn, *The Gulag Archipelago* (Harper & Row, 1973).
14. Hannah Arendt, *Between Past and Future* (Viking, 1961).
15. Robert Conquest, *The Great Terror* (Oxford University Press, 1968).
16. Jung Chang and Jon Halliday, *Mao: The Unknown Story* (Knopf, 2005).
17. Jonathan D. Spence, *The Search for Modern China* (Norton, 1990).
18. Adrian Buzo, *The Making of Modern Korea* (Routledge, 2002).
19. Bradley K. Martin, *Under the Loving Care of the Fatherly Leader* (St. Martin's, 2004).
20. Anne Applebaum, *Twilight of Democracy* (Doubleday, 2020).
21. Vaclav Havel, *The Power of the Powerless* (1978).
22. Lech Wałęsa, *A Way of Hope* (Henry Holt, 1987).
23. Hannah Arendt, *Between Past and Future* (Viking, 1961).
24. Friedrich Hayek, *The Road to Serfdom* (University of Chicago Press, 1944).
25. Aleksandr Solzhenitsyn, *The Gulag Archipelago* (Harper & Row, 1973).

CHAPTER 21: ENDNOTES

1. Ludwig von Mises, Socialism: An Economic and Sociological Analysis (New Haven: Yale University Press, 1922).
2. Thomas Sowell, Basic Economics: A Common Sense Guide to the Economy (New York: Basic Books, 2000).
3. Friedrich A. Hayek, The Road to Serfdom (Chicago: University of Chicago Press, 1944).
4. Richard Pipes, Communism: A History (New York: Modern Library, 2001).
5. Milton Friedman, Capitalism and Freedom (Chicago: University of Chicago Press, 1962).
6. Anne Applebaum, Red Famine: Stalin's War on Ukraine (New York: Doubleday, 2017).
7. Lawrence W. Reed, Was Jesus a Socialist? (Washington, D.C.: Regnery Publishing, 2020).
8. Václav Smil, Energy and Civilization: A History (Cambridge, MA: MIT Press, 2017).
9. John Stuart Mill, Principles of Political Economy (London: John W. Parker, 1848).
10. Mises, Socialism. Ibid. for repeated references.
11. Larry McMurtry, quoted in 100 Quotes from the Global Financial Crisis: Lessons for the Future (London: ResearchGate Publishing, 2010).
12. Pipes, Communism: A History. Ibid.
13. Applebaum, Red Famine. Ibid.

14. Richard Sakwa, The Rise and Fall of the Soviet Union (London: Routledge, 1999).
15. Alec Nove, An Economic History of the USSR, 1917–1991 (London: Penguin Books, 1992).
16. Jung Chang and Jon Halliday, Mao: The Unknown Story (New York: Anchor Books, 2005).
17. Frank Dikötter, Mao's Great Famine: The History of China's Most Devastating Catastrophe, 1958–1962 (New York: Walker & Company, 2010).
18. Jared Diamond, Collapse: How Societies Choose to Fail or Succeed (New York: Viking Press, 2005).
19. Dikötter, Mao's Great Famine. Ibid.
20. Moisés Naím, The End of Power (New York: Basic Books, 2013).
21. Pavel Vidlák, "The Cuban Special Period," Cold War Studies Journal 14, no. 3 (2012).
22. Naím, The End of Power. Ibid.
23. U.S. Department of Agriculture, Cuba Agricultural Report (Washington, D.C.: USDA, 2020).
24. Francisco Toro, "Venezuela's Tragedy," Foreign Affairs 98, no. 2 (2019).
25. International Monetary Fund, World Economic Outlook: Venezuela Data Summary (Washington, D.C.: IMF, 2018).
26. Naím, The End of Power. Ibid.
27. Mehmet Murat İldan, "Goodreads Quotes on Economic Crises," Goodreads Archive (2021).
28. Friedman, Capitalism and Freedom. Ibid.
29. Naím, The End of Power. Ibid.
30. Pipes, Communism: A History. Ibid.
31. Hayek, The Road to Serfdom. Ibid.
32. Amity Shlaes, The Forgotten Man: A New History of the Great Depression (New York: Harper Perennial, 2007).
33. Alfred Müller-Armack, The German Social Market Economy (Berlin: Springer, 1960).
34. Friedman, Capitalism and Freedom. Ibid.
35. Mises, Socialism. Ibid.
36. Reed, Was Jesus a Socialist? Ibid.
37. Pipes, Communism: A History. Ibid.

CHAPTER 22: ENDNOTES

1. Robert Conquest, *The Harvest of Sorrow: Soviet Collectivization and the Terror-Famine* (Oxford: Oxford University Press, 1986).
2. Stéphane Courtois et al., *The Black Book of Communism: Crimes, Terror, Repression* (Cambridge, MA: Harvard University Press, 1999).
3. Anne Applebaum, *Red Famine: Stalin's War on Ukraine* (New York: Doubleday, 2017).
4. Ibid., drawing on Conquest's characterization of the Holodomor as deliberate political policy.
5. Conquest, *The Harvest of Sorrow* (Oxford: Oxford University Press, 1986).
6. Applebaum, *Red Famine* (New York: Doubleday, 2017).
7. Ibid.
8. Courtois et al., *The Black Book of Communism: Crimes, Terror, Repression* (Cambridge, MA: Harvard University Press, 1999).
9. Frank Dikötter, *Mao's Great Famine: The History of China's Most Devastating Catastrophe, 1958–1962* (London: Bloomsbury, 2010).

10. Jasper Becker, *Hungry Ghosts: Mao's Secret Famine* (New York: Free Press, 1996).
11. Ibid.
12. Dikötter, *Mao's Great Famine* (London: Bloomsbury, 2010).
13. Courtois et al., *The Black Book of Communism: Crimes, Terror, Repression* (Cambridge, MA: Harvard University Press, 1999).
14. Becker, *Hungry Ghosts: Mao's Secret Famine* (New York: Free Press, 1996).
15. Courtois et al., *The Black Book of Communism: Crimes, Terror, Repression* (Cambridge, MA: Harvard University Press, 1999).
16. Ibid.
17. Applebaum, *Red Famine: Stalin's War on Ukraine* (New York: Doubleday, 2017).
18. Aleksandr Solzhenitsyn, *The Gulag Archipelago* (New York: Harper & Row, 1973).
19. Ibid.
20. Courtois et al., *The Black Book of Communism: Crimes, Terror, Repression* (Cambridge, MA: Harvard University Press, 1999).
21. Conquest, *The Harvest of Sorrow: Soviet Collectivization and the Terror-Famine* (Oxford: Oxford University Press, 1986).
22. Becker, *Hungry Ghosts: Mao's Secret Famine* (New York: Free Press, 1996).
23. Dikötter, *Mao's Great Famine: The History of China's Most Devastating Catastrophe, 1958–1962* (London: Bloomsbury, 2010).
24. Courtois et al., *The Black Book of Communism: Crimes, Terror, Repression* (Cambridge, MA: Harvard University Press, 1999).
25. Applebaum, *Red Famine: Stalin's War on Ukraine* (New York: Doubleday, 2017).
26. Becker, *Hungry Ghosts: Mao's Secret Famine* (New York: Free Press, 1996).
27. Conquest, *The Harvest of Sorrow: Soviet Collectivization and the Terror-Famine* (Oxford: Oxford University Press, 1986).
28. Courtois et al., *The Black Book of Communism: Crimes, Terror, Repression* (Cambridge, MA: Harvard University Press, 1999).

CHAPTER 23: ENDNOTES

1. Pipes, Richard. *Communism: A History.* New York: Modern Library, 2001.
2. Ibid.
3. Burke, Edmund. *Thoughts on the Cause of the Present Discontents.* London, 1770.
4. Marx, Karl, and Friedrich Engels. *The Communist Manifesto.* 1848; Lenin, Vladimir. *The State and Revolution.* 1917.
5. Pipes, *Communism: A History.*
6. Orwell, George. *1984.* London: Secker & Warburg, 1949.
7. Hayek, Friedrich A. *The Road to Serfdom.* Chicago: University of Chicago Press, 1944.
8. Ibid.
9. Courtois, Stéphane, ed. *The Black Book of Communism.* Cambridge, MA: Harvard University Press, 1999.
10. Ibid.
11. Solzhenitsyn, Aleksandr. *The Gulag Archipelago.* New York: Harper & Row, 1973.
12. Conquest, Robert. *The Harvest of Sorrow.* Oxford: Oxford University Press, 1986.
13. Ibid.

14. Goldman, Wendy Z. *Women, the State, and Revolution.* Cambridge: Cambridge University Press, 1993.
15. Dikötter, Frank. *Mao's Great Famine.* New York: Walker & Company, 2010.
16. Hesburgh, Theodore. Quoted in *Time*, March 25, 1965.
17. Pipes, *Communism: A History.*
18. Dikötter, *Mao's Great Famine.*
19. Pipes, *Communism: A History.*
20. Tocqueville, Alexis de. *Democracy in America.* 1835.
21. Ibid.
22. Solzhenitsyn, *The Gulag Archipelago*; Conquest, *The Harvest of Sorrow.*
23. Havel, Václav. *The Power of the Powerless.* 1978.
24. Adams, John. *The Works of John Adams*, Vol. IX. Boston: Little, Brown, 1854.
25. Pipes, *Communism: A History.*
26. Gieseke, Jens. *The History of the Stasi.* New York: Berghahn Books, 2014.
27. Pipes, *Communism: A History.*
28. Reagan, Ronald. *Public Papers of the Presidents of the United States: Ronald Reagan, 1983.* Washington, D.C.: GPO, 1984.
29. Courtois, *The Black Book of Communism.*
30. Tocqueville, *Democracy in America.*
31. Washington, George. *Farewell Address.* 1796.
32. Coolidge, Calvin. *Foundations of the Republic.* 1926.
33. John Paul II. *Homily in Victory Square, Warsaw.* June 2, 1979.
34. Pipes, *Communism: A History.*

CHAPTER 24: ENDNOTES

1. Karl Marx and Friedrich Engels, *The Communist Manifesto* (London: Penguin Classics, 1998 [1848]).
2. Richard Pipes, *Property and Freedom* (New York: Vintage Books, 1999), 45–46.
3. Robert Conquest, *The Harvest of Sorrow: Soviet Collectivization and the Terror-Famine* (New York: Oxford University Press, 1986), 17–18.
4. Anne Applebaum, *Gulag: A History* (New York: Anchor Books, 2004), xxiii–xxv.
5. Aristotle, *Politics*, trans. Benjamin Jowett (New York: Modern Library, 1943), Book II.
6. Frank Dikötter, *Mao's Great Famine: The History of China's Most Devastating Catastrophe, 1958-1962* (New York: Walker & Company, 2010), 37–38.
7. Ibid., 102–104.
8. Ibid., 324–326.
9. Lord John Emerich Edward Dalberg Acton, *Lectures on Modern History* (London: Macmillan, 1906), 34.
10. Richard E. Feinberg, *Open for Business: Building the New Cuban Economy* (Washington, D.C.: Brookings Institution Press, 2016), 9–10.
11. Ibid., 19–20.
12. Carmelo Mesa-Lago, *Market, Socialist and Mixed Economies: Comparative Policy and Performance* (Baltimore: Johns Hopkins University Press, 2000), 172.
13. Abraham Lincoln, Speech at New Haven, Connecticut, March 6, 1860.
14. Francisco Rodríguez and Jeffrey Sachs, "Why Venezuela Collapsed and How It Can Recover," *Foreign Affairs* 97, no. 6 (2018): 72–84.

15. Ricardo Hausmann and Francisco Rodríguez, *Venezuela Before Chávez: Anatomy of an Economic Collapse* (University Park: Pennsylvania State University Press, 2014), 201.
16. Alejandro Grisanti, "Venezuelan Economic Crisis: The Collapse of a Petrostate," *Harvard Review of Latin America* 17, no. 3 (2018): 32–33.
17. Voltaire, *Philosophical Dictionary* (Paris: Garnier-Flammarion, 1964 [1764]), 237.
18. John Adams, *Discourses on Davila* (1790), in *The Works of John Adams*, ed. Charles Francis Adams (Boston: Little, Brown, 1854), Vol. VI, pp. 280-281.
19. Sir Edward Coke, *The Institutes of the Laws of England* (London: Company of Stationers, 1628).
20. Friedrich A. Hayek, *The Road to Serfdom* (Chicago: University of Chicago Press, 1944), 71–72.
21. Thomas Sowell, *Basic Economics: A Common Sense Guide to the Economy* (New York: Basic Books, 2000), 13–14.
22. Milton Friedman, *Capitalism and Freedom* (Chicago: University of Chicago Press, 1962), 36–37.
23. Ibid., 67.
24. Pipes, *Property and Freedom*, 312–314.
25. Ronald Reagan, "Address to the National Association of Realtors," March 28, 1984.

CHAPTER 25: ENDNOTES

1. Landes, David S. *The Wealth and Poverty of Nations*. W. W. Norton, 1998.
2. Smith, Adam. *The Wealth of Nations*. 1776.
3. Mokyr, Joel. *The Lever of Riches: Technological Creativity and Economic Progress*. Oxford University Press, 1990.
4. Sakharov, Andrei. *Progress, Coexistence, and Intellectual Freedom*. Norton, 1968.
5. Ibid.
6. Ibid.
7. Landes, *The Wealth and Poverty of Nations*.
8. Ibid.
9. Mokyr, *The Lever of Riches*.
10. Landes, *The Wealth and Poverty of Nations*.
11. Mokyr, *The Lever of Riches*.
12. Landes, *The Wealth and Poverty of Nations*.
13. Schumpeter, Joseph A. *Capitalism, Socialism and Democracy*. Harper & Brothers, 1942.
14. Ibid.
15. Drucker, Peter F. *Innovation and Entrepreneurship*. Harper & Row, 1985.
16. Ibid.
17. Ibid.
18. Jobs, Steve. Interview, *BusinessWeek,* May 1998.
19. Ibid.
20. Schumpeter, *Capitalism, Socialism and Democracy*.
21. Landes, *The Wealth and Poverty of Nations*.
22. Drucker, *Innovation and Entrepreneurship*.

CHAPTER 26: ENDNOTES

1. Murray Feshbach and Alfred Friendly, *Ecocide in the USSR: Health and Nature Under Siege* (New York: Basic Books, 1992), 3.
2. Garrett Hardin, "The Tragedy of the Commons," *Science* 162 (1968): 1244.
3. Philip Micklin, *The Aral Sea Disaster, Annual Review of Earth and Planetary Sciences* 35 (2007): 47–72.
4. Ibid.
5. Ibid.
6. Micklin, *The Aral Sea Disaster,* 70.
7. Zhores A. Medvedev, *The Legacy of Chernobyl* (New York: W. W. Norton, 1990), 12–15.
8. Feshbach and Friendly, *Ecocide in the USSR,* 219.
9. Ibid.
10. Medvedev, *The Legacy of Chernobyl,* 102.
11. Vaclav Smil, *China's Environmental Crisis: An Inquiry into the Limits of National Development* (Armonk, NY: M.E. Sharpe, 1993), 25–30.
12. Ibid.
13. Ibid., 142.
14. Ibid., 201.
15. Ibid.
16. Feshbach and Friendly, *Ecocide in the USSR,* 87.
17. Ibid., 90.
18. Alfred Friendly in Feshbach and Friendly, *Ecocide in the USSR,* 112.
19. Hardin, "The Tragedy of the Commons," 1243–1248.
20. Ibid.
21. Ronald Reagan, remarks on environmental policy, White House Archives, 1984.
22. U.S. Environmental Protection Agency, *Clean Air Act Overview* (Washington, D.C., 2023).
23. Feshbach and Friendly, *Ecocide in the USSR,* 248.
24. Ibid., 249.

CHAPTER 27: ENDNOTES

1. Hannah Arendt, *The Origins of Totalitarianism* (New York: Harcourt Brace, 1951), p. 323.
2. Robert Conquest, *The Great Terror: A Reassessment* (New York: Oxford University Press, 1990), p. 15.
3. C.S. Lewis, *The Humanitarian Theory of Punishment* (1949).
4. Paul Johnson, *Modern Times: The World from the Twenties to the Nineties* (New York: Harper & Row, 1983), p. 237.
5. Karl Marx and Friedrich Engels, *The Communist Manifesto* (1848).
6. Dietrich Bonhoeffer, *Letters and Papers from Prison* (New York: Macmillan, 1953), p. 139.
7. Richard Pipes, *Russia Under the Bolshevik Regime* (New York: Vintage, 1994), p. 204.
8. Frank Dikötter, *The Cultural Revolution: A People's History* (New York: Bloomsbury, 2016), p. 76.
9. Vaclav Havel, *The Power of the Powerless* (Prague, 1978), p. 41.
10. Fyodor Dostoevsky, *The Brothers Karamazov* (Moscow, 1880).
11. Hubertus Knabe, *The Stasi Files: East Germany's Secret Operations* (Berlin: Springer, 1999).
12. Whittaker Chambers, *Witness* (New York: Random House, 1952), p. 318.

13. T.S. Eliot, *The Idea of a Christian Society* (New York: Harcourt Brace, 1939).
14. Roger Scruton, *Culture Counts: Faith and Feeling in a World Besieged* (New York: Encounter Books, 2007).
15. Thomas Aquinas, *Summa Theologica* (1273), Part I-II, Q. 31, Art. 3.
16. Aleksandr Solzhenitsyn, *The Gulag Archipelago* (New York: Harper & Row, 1973).
17. Pope Benedict XVI, *Caritas in Veritate* (Vatican City: Libreria Editrice Vaticana, 2009).
18. Dimitry Pospielovsky, *A History of Soviet Atheism in Theory and Practice* (New York: St. Martin's Press, 1987).
19. Carlos Eire, *Waiting for Snow in Havana* (New York: Free Press, 2003), p. 102.
20. Anne Applebaum, *Gulag: A History* (New York: Anchor, 2004), p. 484.
21. Viktor Frankl, *Man's Search for Meaning* (Boston: Beacon Press, 1946).
22. Adrian Buzo, *The Guerrilla Dynasty: Politics and Leadership in North Korea* (Boulder: Westview Press, 1999).
23. Milton Friedman, *Capitalism and Freedom* (Chicago: University of Chicago Press, 1962), p. 11.
24. John Stuart Mill, *On Liberty* (London: John W. Parker and Son, 1859).

CHAPTER 28: ENDNOTES

1. Arendt, Hannah. *The Origins of Totalitarianism.* Harcourt Brace, 1951.
2. Koestler, Arthur. *Darkness at Noon.* Macmillan, 1940.
3. Rand, Ayn. *The Fountainhead.* Bobbs-Merrill, 1943.
4. Scruton, Roger. *Culture Counts: Faith and Feeling in a World Besieged.* Encounter Books, 2007.
5. Pipes, Daniel. *Communism and Revolution.* Houghton Mifflin, 1968.
6. Conquest, Robert. *The Great Terror: A Reassessment.* Oxford University Press, 1990.
7. Sowell, Thomas. *Intellectuals and Society.* Basic Books, 2009.
8. Hawking, Stephen. *Black Holes and Baby Universes.* Bantam Books, 1993.
9. Orwell, George. *Essays and Journalism.* Penguin Classics, 1984.
10. Applebaum, Anne. *Iron Curtain: The Crushing of Eastern Europe, 1944–1956.* Anchor Books, 2013.
11. Chang, Jung; and Jon Halliday. *Mao: The Unknown Story.* Knopf, 2005.
12. Chang, Jung. *Wild Swans: Three Daughters of China.* Simon & Schuster, 1991.
13. Hollander, Paul. *Political Pilgrims: Western Intellectuals in Search of the Good Society.* Transaction Publishers, 1998.
14. Orwell, George. *Essays and Journalism.* Penguin Classics, 1984.
15. Solzhenitsyn, Aleksandr. *The Gulag Archipelago.* Harper & Row, 1973.
16. Applebaum, Anne. *Iron Curtain: The Crushing of Eastern Europe, 1944–1956.* Anchor Books, 2013.
17. Judt, Tony. *Postwar: A History of Europe Since 1945.* Penguin Press, 2005.
18. Havel, Václav. *The Power of the Powerless.* M. E. Sharpe, 1985.
19. Orwell, George. *Essays and Journalism.* Penguin Classics, 1984.
20. Arendt, Hannah. *The Origins of Totalitarianism.* Harcourt Brace, 1951.
21. Becker, Jasper. *Hungry Ghosts: Mao's Secret Famine.* Free Press, 1996.
22. Kiernan, Ben. *The Pol Pot Regime: Race, Power, and Genocide in Cambodia under the Khmer Rouge.* Yale University Press, 2002.
23. Snyder, Timothy. *Bloodlands: Europe Between Hitler and Stalin.* Basic Books, 2010.
24. Sowell, Thomas. *Intellectuals and Society.* Basic Books, 2009.

25. Applebaum, Anne. *Iron Curtain: The Crushing of Eastern Europe, 1944–1956.* Anchor Books, 2013.
26. Malia, Martin. *The Soviet Tragedy: A History of Socialism in Russia, 1917–1991.* Free Press, 1994.
27. Scruton, Roger. *Culture Counts: Faith and Feeling in a World Besieged.* Encounter Books, 2007.
28. Solzhenitsyn, Aleksandr. *Warning to the West.* Farrar, Straus and Giroux, 1976.
29. Scruton, Roger. *Culture Counts: Faith and Feeling in a World Besieged.* Encounter Books, 2007.
30. Arendt, Hannah. *Between Past and Future: Eight Exercises in Political Thought.* Viking Press, 1961.
31. Carr, E. H. *The Bolshevik Revolution, 1917–1923.* W. W. Norton, 1985.
32. Davies, Norman. *Europe: A History.* HarperCollins, 1996.
33. Shaw, George Bernard. *Man and Superman.* Penguin Classics, 2001.
34. Havel, Václav. *The Power of the Powerless.* M. E. Sharpe, 1985.
35. Judt, Tony. *Postwar: A History of Europe Since 1945.* Penguin Press, 2005.
36. Orwell, George. *Nineteen Eighty-Four.* Secker & Warburg, 1949.
37. Havel, Václav. *The Power of the Powerless.* M. E. Sharpe, 1985.
38. Arendt, Hannah. *Between Past and Future: Eight Exercises in Political Thought.* Viking Press, 1961.
39. Solzhenitsyn, Aleksandr. *Warning to the West.* Farrar, Straus and Giroux, 1976.
40. Peterson, Jordan B. *Maps of Meaning: The Architecture of Belief.* Routledge, 1999.

CHAPTER 29: ENDNOTES

1. Woodrow Wilson, The New Freedom (New York: Doubleday, 1913).
2. John A. Rohr, To Run a Constitution: The Legitimacy of the Administrative State (University Press of Kansas, 1986).
3. Federal Reserve Act of 1913, Public Law 63-43.
4. U.S. Bureau of Labor Statistics (BLS), Historical Consumer Price Index for All Urban Consumers, 1913 data series.
5. U.S. Department of the Treasury, Report of the Director of the Mint, 1913 (GPO, 1914).
6. World Gold Council, "Gold Prices 1940–2025," accessed October 2025.
7. Milton Friedman and Anna J. Schwartz, A Monetary History of the United States, 1867–1960 (Princeton University Press, 1963).
8. Congressional Research Service (CRS), Federal Reserve: Structure, Functions, and History, updated 2024.
9. Woodrow Wilson, speech at New York Press Club, May 19, 1912.
10. U.S. Department of Commerce, Statistical Abstract of the United States, 1910 edition.
11. Internal Revenue Service (IRS), History of the U.S. Tax System, IRS Historical Archive.
12. Tax Foundation, Facts and Figures 2024: How Does Your State Compare?, 2024 edition.
13. Lord Acton, letter to Bishop Creighton, April 5, 1887, in Essays on Freedom and Power (Boston: Beacon Press, 1948).
14. Amity Shlaes, The Forgotten Man: A New History of the Great Depression (New York: HarperCollins, 2007).
15. Robert Higgs, Crisis and Leviathan: Critical Episodes in the Growth of American Government (Oxford University Press, 1987).

16. Thomas Jefferson, letter to Albert Gallatin, June 1816, in The Writings of Thomas Jefferson, vol. 15 (Washington, 1904).
17. Social Security Act of 1935, Public Law 74-271.
18. U.S. Social Security Administration, The 1935 Act and Its Historical Background, SSA History Series.
19. Board of Trustees, 2024 Annual Report of the Social Security Trust Funds, Washington, D.C.
20. Thomas Paine, Dissertations on First Principles of Government (London, 1795).
21. National Labor Relations (Wagner) Act of 1935, Public Law 74-198.
22. Federal Election Commission (FEC), Political Contributions and Labor Organizations, FEC Data Portal, 2024.
23. Pew Research Center, "Union Membership and Middle Class Income Trends," August 2023.
24. Calvin Coolidge, address to the American Federation of Labor Convention, October 4, 1919.
25. Lyndon B. Johnson, "Special Message to the Congress Proposing the War on Poverty," March 16, 1964.
26. Senator John Kennedy, remarks to Senate Budget Committee, April 25, 2017, Congressional Record.
27. U.S. Department of Health and Human Services, Welfare Indicators and Risk Factors, Annual Report 2023.
28. U.S. Bureau of Labor Statistics, Labor Force Participation Rate 1960–2024, Series LNS11300000.
29. Aristotle, Politics, Book V, trans. Benjamin Jowett (Oxford University Press, 1885).
30. Environmental Protection Agency (EPA), History and Organization Overview, EPA Archive.
31. U.S. Code Title 5, Administrative Procedure Act of 1946, 5 U.S.C. § 551–706.
32. Harvey A. Silverglate, Three Felonies a Day: How the Feds Target the Innocent (New York: Encounter Books, 2009).
33. Ronald Reagan, speech to National Association of Counties, March 6, 1981.
34. Department of Education Organization Act of 1979, Public Law 96-88.
35. U.S. Department of Education, About ED — Overview, ed.gov, accessed October 2025.
36. U.S. House Committee on the Judiciary, Letter to Attorney General Garland on Parents and School Boards, October 4, 2021.
37. George Orwell, Nineteen Eighty-Four (London: Secker & Warburg, 1949).
38. Patient Protection and Affordable Care Act of 2010, Public Law 111-148.
39. Barack Obama, remarks on health care reform, White House Press Office, June 15, 2009.
40. FactCheck.org, "Obama's $2,500 Premium Reduction Promise," Annenberg Public Policy Center, 2014.
41. Kaiser Family Foundation, Health Insurance Premiums and Cost Sharing Under the ACA, Issue Brief, 2023.
42. Congressional Budget Office (CBO), Repeal Efforts and Fiscal Impact of the Affordable Care Act, April 2022.
43. P. J. O'Rourke, Parliament of Whores (New York: Atlantic Monthly Press, 1991).
44. Federal Reserve Bank of St. Louis, Economic Impact of COVID-19 Lockdowns, FRED Blog, 2023.
45. National Institutes of Health (NIH), Timeline of COVID-19 Policy Guidance, 2021.
46. U.S. Department of Education, Learning Loss Report 2023: Post-Pandemic Assessment.

47. Friedrich A. Hayek, The Road to Serfdom (University of Chicago Press, 1944).
48. World Economic Forum, Measuring Stakeholder Capitalism: Metrics and ESG Disclosure, 2020.
49. Bloomberg Intelligence, Global ESG Assets May Hit $40 Trillion by 2030, Market Analysis, June 2024.
50. PwC Global, The State of ESG Reporting 2023, PricewaterhouseCoopers, 2023.
51. Christopher Rufo, "Capitalism with a Woke Face," City Journal, Spring 2022.
52. U.S. Chamber of Commerce, DEI and Corporate Compliance Frameworks, Policy Brief 2024.
53. Christopher F. Rufo, address at National Conservatism Conference, Orlando, FL, 2022.
54. Robert Higgs, Crisis and Leviathan (Oxford University Press, 1987), conclusion chapter.
55. Paul Kengor, Dupes: How America's Adversaries Have Manipulated Progressives for a Century (ISI Books, 2010).
56. James Burnham, The Managerial Revolution (New York: John Day Company, 1941).
57. Heritage Foundation, Restoring Limited Government: Principles and Policy Roadmap, Policy Report 2024.

CHAPTER 30: ENDNOTES

1. Kiernan, Denise. *The Girls of Atomic City: The Untold Story of the Women Who Helped Win World War II*. New York: Simon & Schuster, 2013.
2. Pitney, John J., Jr. *The Politics of Blue Dog Democrats*. Washington, DC: Brookings Institution Press, 2005.
3. Schlesinger, Arthur M., Jr. *The Age of Roosevelt*. Boston: Houghton Mifflin, 1957.
4. Key, V.O., Jr. *Politics, Parties, and Pressure Groups*. New York: Crowell, 1958.
5. Emerson, Ralph Waldo. *Essays: First Series*. Boston: James Munroe, 1841.
6. Reagan, Ronald. First Inaugural Address, January 20, 1981.
7. Phillips, Kevin. *The Emerging Republican Majority*. New Rochelle: Arlington House, 1969.
8. Wilentz, Sean. *The Rise of American Democracy: Jefferson to Lincoln*. New York: W.W. Norton, 2005.
9. Schlesinger, Arthur M., Jr. *The Age of Roosevelt*. Boston: Houghton Mifflin, 1957.
10. Foner, Eric. *Reconstruction: America's Unfinished Revolution, 1863–1877*. New York: Harper & Row, 1988.
11. Kazin, Michael. *The Populist Persuasion: An American History*. Ithaca: Cornell University Press, 1995.
12. Skocpol, Theda. *Protecting Soldiers and Mothers: The Political Origins of Social Policy in the United States*. Cambridge: Harvard University Press, 1992.
13. Kennedy, David M. *Freedom from Fear: The American People in Depression and War, 1929–1945*. New York: Oxford University Press, 1999.
14. Cooper, William J., Jr. *Liberty and Slavery: Southern Politics to 1860*. Columbia: University of South Carolina Press, 2000.
15. Calhoun, John C. Speech in the U.S. Senate, 1850.
16. Donald, David Herbert. *Lincoln*. New York: Simon & Schuster, 1995.
17. Foner, Eric. *Reconstruction: America's Unfinished Revolution, 1863–1877*. New York: Harper & Row, 1988.
18. Foner, Eric. *Reconstruction: America's Unfinished Revolution, 1863–1877*. New York: Harper & Row, 1988.

19. Woodward, C. Vann. *The Strange Career of Jim Crow*. New York: Oxford University Press, 1955.
20. Bensel, Richard Franklin. *The Political Economy of American Industrialization, 1877–1900*. Cambridge: Cambridge University Press, 2000.
21. Perman, Michael. *The Road to Redemption: Southern Politics, 1869–1879*. Chapel Hill: University of North Carolina Press, 1984.
22. Tillman, Benjamin R. Speech, 1900.
23. Parsons, Elaine Frantz. *Ku Klux: The Birth of the Klan during Reconstruction*. Chapel Hill: University of North Carolina Press, 2015.
24. Woodward, C. Vann. *The Strange Career of Jim Crow*. New York: Oxford University Press, 1955.
25. Lofgren, Charles A. *The Plessy Case: A Legal-Historical Interpretation*. New York: Oxford University Press, 1987.
26. Yellin, Eric S. *Racism in the Nation's Service: Government Workers and the Color Line in Woodrow Wilson's America*. Chapel Hill: University of North Carolina Press, 2013.
27. Hamby, Alonzo L. *Beyond the New Deal: Harry S. Truman and American Liberalism*. New York: Columbia University Press, 1973.
28. Carmines, Edward G., and James A. Stimson. *Issue Evolution: Race and the Transformation of American Politics*. Princeton: Princeton University Press, 1989.
29. Wiebe, Robert H. *The Search for Order, 1877–1920*. New York: Hill and Wang, 1967.
30. Cooper, John Milton, Jr. *Woodrow Wilson: A Biography*. New York: Knopf, 2009.
31. Leuchtenburg, William E. *Franklin D. Roosevelt and the New Deal, 1932–1940*. New York: Harper & Row, 1963.
32. Roosevelt, Franklin D. Radio Address, October 31, 1936.
33. Sunstein, Cass R. *The Second Bill of Rights: FDR's Unfinished Revolution*. New York: Basic Books, 2004.
34. Leuchtenburg, William E. *Franklin D. Roosevelt and the New Deal, 1932–1940*. New York: Harper & Row, 1963.
35. Patterson, James T. *Grand Expectations: The United States, 1945–1974*. New York: Oxford University Press, 1996.
36. McGerr, Michael. *A Fierce Discontent: The Rise and Fall of the Progressive Movement in America, 1870–1920*. New York: Free Press, 2003.
37. Rodgers, Daniel T. *Atlantic Crossings: Social Politics in a Progressive Age*. Cambridge: Harvard University Press, 1998.
38. Rodgers, Daniel T. *Atlantic Crossings: Social Politics in a Progressive Age*. Cambridge: Harvard University Press, 1998.
39. Katznelson, Ira. *Fear Itself: The New Deal and the Origins of Our Time*. New York: Liveright, 2013.
40. Bloom, Allan. *The Closing of the American Mind*. New York: Simon & Schuster, 1987.
41. Pells, Richard H. *The Liberal Mind in a Conservative Age: American Intellectuals in the 1940s and 1950s*. New York: Harper & Row, 1985.
42. Brinkley, Alan. *The End of Reform: New Deal Liberalism in Recession and War*. New York: Knopf, 1995.
43. Esping-Andersen, Gøsta. *The Three Worlds of Welfare Capitalism*. Princeton: Princeton University Press, 1990.
44. Zelizer, Julian E. *The Fierce Urgency of Now: Lyndon Johnson, Congress, and the Battle for the Great Society*. New York: Penguin Press, 2015.
45. Truman, Harry S. Speech on the Fair Deal, January 5, 1949.
46. Rodgers, Daniel T. *Atlantic Crossings: Social Politics in a Progressive Age*. Cambridge: Harvard University Press, 1998.

47. Friedman, Milton. *Capitalism and Freedom*. Chicago: University of Chicago Press, 1962.
48. McCullough, David. *Truman*. New York: Simon & Schuster, 1992.
49. Hacker, Jacob S., and Paul Pierson. *American Amnesia: How the War on Government Led Us to Forget What Made America Prosper*. New York: Simon & Schuster, 2016.
50. Lowi, Theodore J. *The End of Liberalism: The Second Republic of the United States*. New York: W.W. Norton, 1979.
51. Shlaes, Amity. *Great Society: A New History*. New York: Harper, 2019.
52. Johnson, Lyndon B. Great Society Speech, University of Michigan, May 22, 1964.
53. Friedman, Milton. *Capitalism and Freedom*. Chicago: University of Chicago Press, 1962.
54. Shlaes, Amity. *Great Society: A New History*. New York: Harper, 2019.
55. Moynihan, Daniel P. *Maximum Feasible Misunderstanding: Community Action in the War on Poverty*. New York: Free Press, 1969.
56. Collins, Robert M. *More: The Politics of Economic Growth in Postwar America*. New York: Oxford University Press, 2000.
57. Davies, Gareth. *From Opportunity to Entitlement: The Transformation and Decline of Great Society Liberalism*. Lawrence: University Press of Kansas, 1996.
58. Kimball, Roger. *The Long March: How the Cultural Revolution of the 1960s Changed America*. San Francisco: Encounter Books, 2000.
59. Kimball, Roger. *The Long March: How the Cultural Revolution of the 1960s Changed America*. San Francisco: Encounter Books, 2000.
60. Bloom, Allan. *The Closing of the American Mind*. New York: Simon & Schuster, 1987.
61. Groseclose, Tim. *Left Turn: How Liberal Media Bias Distorts the American Mind*. New York: St. Martin's Press, 2011.
62. Kengor, Paul. *Dupes: How America's Adversaries Have Manipulated Progressives for a Century*. Wilmington: ISI Books, 2010.
63. Lasch, Christopher. *The Culture of Narcissism: American Life in an Age of Diminishing Expectations*. New York: W.W. Norton, 1979.
64. Marini, John. *The Progressive Revolution in Politics and Political Science*. Lanham: Rowman & Littlefield, 2005.
65. Wilson, James Q. *Bureaucracy: What Government Agencies Do and Why They Do It*. New York: Basic Books, 1989.
66. Hamburger, Philip. *Is Administrative Law Unlawful?*. Chicago: University of Chicago Press, 2014.
67. Applebaum, Anne. *Iron Curtain: The Crushing of Eastern Europe, 1944–1956*. New York: Doubleday, 2012.
68. Zuboff, Shoshana. *The Age of Surveillance Capitalism*. New York: PublicAffairs, 2019.
69. Marini, John. *The Progressive Revolution in Politics and Political Science*. Lanham: Rowman & Littlefield, 2005.
70. Sowell, Thomas. *Intellectuals and Society*. New York: Basic Books, 2009.
71. Hamburger, Philip. *Is Administrative Law Unlawful?*. Chicago: University of Chicago Press, 2014.
72. Gottfried, Paul. *The Strange Death of Marxism: The European Left in the New Millennium*. Columbia: University of Missouri Press, 2005.
73. Murray, Charles. *Losing Ground: American Social Policy, 1950–1980*. New York: Basic Books, 1984.
74. Hayek, Friedrich A. *The Road to Serfdom*. Chicago: University of Chicago Press, 1944.

75. Lifton, Robert Jay. *Thought Reform and the Psychology of Totalism*. New York: W.W. Norton, 1961.
76. Gramsci, Antonio. *Selections from the Prison Notebooks*. New York: International Publishers, 1971.
77. Hayek, Friedrich A. *The Road to Serfdom*. Chicago: University of Chicago Press, 1944.
78. Sowell, Thomas. *Intellectuals and Society*. New York: Basic Books, 2009.
79. Tocqueville, Alexis de. *Democracy in America*. New York: Knopf, 1945.
80. Arnn, Larry P. *The Founders' Key: The Divine and Natural Connection Between the Declaration and the Constitution*. Nashville: Thomas Nelson, 2012.

CHAPTER 31: ENDNOTES

1. Allan Bloom, *The Closing of the American Mind*. New York: Simon & Schuster, 1987.
2. Ibid.
3. Roger Kimball, *Tenured Radicals: How Politics Has Corrupted Our Higher Education*. New York: Harper & Row, 1990.
4. Commonly attributed to Abraham Lincoln; attribution disputed in scholarly sources.
5. Ibid.
6. Karl Marx and Friedrich Engels, *The Communist Manifesto*. London: 1848.
7. Martin Jay, *The Dialectical Imagination*. Berkeley: University of California Press, 1973.
8. Ibid.
9. Max Horkheimer and Theodor W. Adorno, *Dialectic of Enlightenment*. New York: Herder & Herder, 1972.
10. Will Durant, *The Story of Civilization, Vol. I*. New York: Simon & Schuster, 1935.
11. Ibid.
12. E. D. Hirsch Jr., *The Schools We Need and Why We Don't Have Them*. New York: Doubleday, 1996.
13. Kimball, *Tenured Radicals*. Ibid.
14. John Stuart Mill, *On Liberty*. London: Parker & Son, 1859.
15. Ibid.
16. Hirsch, *The Schools We Need*. Ibid.
17. Nelson Mandela, *Long Walk to Freedom*. Boston: Little, Brown, 1994.
18. Ibid.
19. Greg Lukianoff and Jonathan Haidt, *The Coddling of the American Mind*. New York: Penguin Press, 2018.
20. Ibid.
21. Yevgeny Yevtushenko, *Selected Poems*. New York: Penguin, 1962.
22. Kimball, *Tenured Radicals*. Ibid.
23. Ibid.
24. Aphorism attributed to Aristotle; traditional maxim on intellectual openness.
25. Ibid.
26. Lukianoff and Haidt, *The Coddling of the American Mind*. Ibid.
27. Ibid.
28. Ibid.
29. Ibid.
30. Ibid.

31. Herbert Marcuse, *One-Dimensional Man*. Boston: Beacon Press, 1964.
32. Ibid.
33. Herbert Marcuse, "Repressive Tolerance," in *A Critique of Pure Tolerance*. Boston: Beacon Press, 1965.
34. Bloom, *The Closing of the American Mind*. Ibid.
35. Kimball, *Tenured Radicals*. Ibid.
36. Ibid.
37. Ibid.
38. Paulo Freire, *Pedagogy of the Oppressed*. New York: Continuum, 1970.
39. Ibid.
40. Henry A. Giroux, *Theory and Resistance in Education*. South Hadley, MA: Bergin & Garvey, 1983.
41. Ibid.
42. Ibid.
43. Terry M. Moe, *Special Interest: Teachers Unions and America's Public Schools*. Washington, D.C.: Brookings Institution Press, 2011.
44. Ibid.
45. Ibid.
46. Martin Luther King Jr., "The Purpose of Education." *The Maroon Tiger*, Jan.–Feb. 1947.
47. Ibid.
48. Moe, *Special Interest*. Ibid.
49. Ibid.
50. Freire, *Pedagogy of the Oppressed*. Ibid.
51. Ibid.
52. Moe, *Special Interest*. Ibid.
53. Ibid.
54. Thomas Sowell, *The Vision of the Anointed*. New York: Basic Books, 1995.
55. Ibid.
56. Ibid.
57. Ibid.
58. Ibid.
59. Ibid.
60. Ibid.
61. Ibid.
62. Ibid.
63. Ibid.
64. Benjamin Franklin, aphorism quoted in Fred R. Shapiro, *The Yale Book of Quotations*. New Haven: Yale University Press, 2006.
65. Neil Gross and Solon Simmons, *The Social and Political Views of American Professors*. Washington, D.C.: American Enterprise Institute, 2007.
66. Ibid.
67. Ibid.
68. Lukianoff and Haidt, *The Coddling of the American Mind*. Ibid.
69. Ibid.
70. Kimball, *Tenured Radicals*. Ibid.
71. Bloom, *The Closing of the American Mind*. Ibid.
72. Ibid.
73. Ibid.
74. Ibid.

CHAPTER 32: ENDNOTES

1. G. Michael Hopf, *Those Who Remain* (CreateSpace, 2016).
2. Thomas Sowell, *The Quest for Cosmic Justice* (New York: Free Press, 1999).
3. F. A. Hayek, *The Road to Serfdom* (Chicago: University of Chicago Press, 1944).
4. Milton Friedman, *Free to Choose* (New York: Harcourt, 1980).
5. C. S. Lewis, *The Abolition of Man* (Oxford: Oxford University Press, 1943).
6. George Orwell, *Collected Essays, Journalism and Letters* (London: Secker & Warburg, 1968).
7. Voltaire, *Questions sur l'Encyclopédie* (Geneva, 1770).
8. Thomas Sowell, *Knowledge and Decisions* (New York: Basic Books, 1980).
9. Democratic Socialists of America, *What We Believe* (National Platform, 2020).
10. United Nations, *Agenda 2030: Sustainable Development Goals* (New York: UN, 2015).
11. Gerald R. Ford, Address to a Joint Session of Congress (Washington, DC, August 12, 1974).
12. Milton Friedman, *Free to Choose* (New York: Harcourt, 1980).
13. F. A. Hayek, *The Road to Serfdom* (Chicago: University of Chicago Press, 1944).
14. John Philpot Curran, Speech upon the Right of Election of Lord Mayor of Dublin (Dublin, July 10, 1790).
15. George Orwell, *Collected Essays, Journalism and Letters* (London: Secker & Warburg, 1968).
16. Joseph Goebbels, *Michael: A German Destiny in Diary Form* (Munich: Zentralverlag der NSDAP, 1929).
17. George Orwell, *Collected Essays, Journalism and Letters* (London: Secker & Warburg, 1968).
18. Ibid.
19. George Orwell, *Collected Essays, Journalism and Letters* (London: Secker & Warburg, 1968).
20. Edmund Burke, *Reflections on the Revolution in France* (London: J. Dodsley, 1790).
21. Calvin Coolidge, Speech to the American Society of Newspaper Editors (Washington, DC, January 17, 1925).
22. Milton Friedman, *Free to Choose* (New York: Harcourt, 1980).
23. F. A. Hayek, *The Road to Serfdom* (Chicago: University of Chicago Press, 1944).
24. Aldous Huxley, *Ends and Means* (London: Chatto & Windus, 1937).
25. George Orwell, *Collected Essays, Journalism and Letters* (London: Secker & Warburg, 1968).
26. Thomas Sowell, *Knowledge and Decisions* (New York: Basic Books, 1980).
27. Thomas Sowell, *The Quest for Cosmic Justice* (New York: Free Press, 1999).
28. Abraham Lincoln, Address at the Sanitary Fair, Baltimore (April 18, 1864).

CHAPTER 33: ENDNOTES

1. Samuel Johnson, *The Rambler No. 178* (London: J. Payne, 1751).
2. Friedrich A. Hayek, *The Constitution of Liberty* (Chicago: University of Chicago Press, 1960).
3. Fyodor Dostoevsky, *The Brothers Karamazov* (St. Petersburg: The Russian Messenger, 1880).
4. Thomas Sowell, *Knowledge and Decisions* (New York: Basic Books, 1980).

5. Ibid.
6. Confucius, *The Analects*, trans. Arthur Waley (London: George Allen & Unwin, 1938).
7. Friedrich A. Hayek, *The Constitution of Liberty* (Chicago: University of Chicago Press, 1960).
8. Thomas Sowell, *Knowledge and Decisions* (New York: Basic Books, 1980).
9. Thomas Paine, *The Rights of Man* (London: J. S. Jordan, 1791).
10. Samuel Johnson, *The Rambler No. 178* (London: J. Payne, 1751).
11. Friedrich A. Hayek, *The Constitution of Liberty* (Chicago: University of Chicago Press, 1960).
12. Voltaire, *Le Siècle de Louis XIV* (Paris: Garnier Frères, 1751).
13. Thomas Sowell, *Knowledge and Decisions* (New York: Basic Books, 1980).
14. Ibid.
15. Albert Einstein, "The Peril of Modern Man," speech delivered at Princeton University (Princeton, NJ, 1946).
16. Friedrich A. Hayek, *The Constitution of Liberty* (Chicago: University of Chicago Press, 1960).
17. Thomas Sowell, *Knowledge and Decisions* (New York: Basic Books, 1980).
18. *The Holy Bible*, 2 Corinthians 3:17, King James Version (Cambridge: Cambridge University Press, 1769).
19. Friedrich A. Hayek, *The Constitution of Liberty* (Chicago: University of Chicago Press, 1960).
20. Thomas Sowell, *Knowledge and Decisions* (New York: Basic Books, 1980).

CHAPTER 34: ENDNOTES

The following works informed the definitions, historical parallels, and linguistic analyses used throughout this chapter. Each provides insight into how language has been used—both past and present—to manipulate thought and mask authoritarian aims.

1. Orwell, George. *Politics and the English Language*. London: Horizon, 1946.
2. Hayek, F. A. *The Road to Serfdom*. Chicago: University of Chicago Press, 1944.
3. Sowell, Thomas. *The Quest for Cosmic Justice*. New York: Free Press, 1999.
4. Burke, Edmund. *Reflections on the Revolution in France*. London: J. Dodsley, 1790.
5. Thatcher, Margaret. Interview. Thames Television, 1980.
6. Ibid. (Orwell, *Politics and the English Language*.)
7. Hayek, F. A., *The Road to Serfdom*, op. cit.
8. Friedman, Milton. *Free to Choose*. New York: Harcourt, 1980.
9. Churchill, Winston. Speech to the House of Commons, October 22, 1945.
10. Burke, Edmund, *Reflections on the Revolution in France*, op. cit.
11. Harvard University. *Office for Equity, Diversity, Inclusion, and Belonging: Glossary of Terms*. Cambridge, MA, 2022.
12. U.S. Department of Education. *Advancing Diversity, Equity, Inclusion, and Accessibility in Higher Education*. Washington, DC, 2022.
13. United Nations. *Agenda 2030: Sustainable Development Goals*. New York: UN, 2015.
14. Klaus Schwab. *The Great Reset*. Geneva: World Economic Forum, 2020.
15. World Economic Forum. *Stakeholder Capitalism Metrics*. Geneva: WEF, 2020.
16. BlackRock. *ESG Integration Framework*. New York: BlackRock, 2020.

17. Orwell, George. *Politics and the English Language.* London: Horizon, 1946.
18. Hayek, F. A. *The Road to Serfdom.* Chicago: University of Chicago Press, 1944.
19. Sowell, Thomas. *Knowledge and Decisions.* New York: Basic Books, 1980.
20. Burke, Edmund. *Reflections on the Revolution in France.* London: J. Dodsley, 1790.
21. Thatcher, Margaret. Interview. Thames Television, 1980.
22. Friedman, Milton. *Free to Choose.* New York: Harcourt, 1980.
23. Orwell, George, *Politics and the English Language,* op. cit.
24. Churchill, Winston. Speech to the House of Commons, October 22, 1945.
25. Confucius. *The Analects.* Trans. Arthur Waley. London: George Allen & Unwin, 1938.
26. Solzhenitsyn, Aleksandr. *Live Not by Lies.* Moscow, 1974.
27. Hayek, F. A., *The Road to Serfdom,* op. cit.
28. Lincoln, Abraham. Speech at Springfield, Illinois, 1858.

CHAPTER 35: ENDNOTES

1. Lippmann, *Public Opinion* (New York: Harcourt Brace, 1922), p. 29.
2. Vladimir I. Lenin, *Collected Works* (Moscow: Progress Publishers, 1963), vol. 13, p. 301.
3. Edward Bernays, *Propaganda* (New York: Ig Publishing, 1928), p. 37.
4. George Orwell, "Politics and the English Language," *Horizon* (London, 1946).
5. Ibid.
6. Taibbi, Matt. "The Twitter Files." Twitter archive, Dec 2022–Jan 2023.
7. George Orwell, *1984* (London: Secker & Warburg, 1949), p. 262.
8. Ibid.
9. Media Bias/Fact Check Survey, "Political Leaning of Major Outlets," 2023.
10. Sharyl Attkisson, *Slanted* (New York: HarperCollins, 2020), p. 114.
11. Ibid.
12. Lippmann, *Public Opinion*, p. 56.
13. Bernays, *Propaganda*, p. 42.
14. Ibid.
15. Attkisson, *Slanted*, p. 237.
16. Taibbi et al., "The Twitter Files," Dec 2022.
17. Jay Bhattacharya et al., *The Great Barrington Declaration*, Oct 2020.
18. *The New York Post*, "Biden Secret Emails," Oct 14 2020.
19. Mozilla Foundation, "YouTube Regrets Report," July 2021.
20. Wikipedia Foundation Transparency Report, 2024.
21. Mark Twain, *Autobiography of Mark Twain* (Berkeley: University of California Press, 1959), p. 89.
22. Ibid.
23. Edward Bernays, *Propaganda*, p. 53.
24. Schoch et al., "Coordination Patterns Reveal Online Political Astroturfing," *Nature Scientific Reports* (2022).
25. *Los Angeles Times*, "Crowds for Hire," Oct 21 2018.
26. Stanford Internet Observatory, *Rally Forge Takedown Report*, Oct 2020.
27. *The Washington Post*, "Who's Behind Reopen America Groups," May 2020.
28. U.S. Department of Justice, *Internet Research Agency Indictment*, Feb 16 2018.
29. Bernays, *Propaganda*, p. 96.
30. H. L. Mencken, *Notes on Democracy* (New York: Knopf, 1926), p. 21.
31. Ibid.

32. *The Wall Street Journal*, "Facebook Knows It Promotes Division," Sep 2021.
33. *Los Angeles Times*, "Crowds for Hire," Oct 21 2018. *Ibid.*
34. Procter & Gamble Earnings Report, Feb 2019.
35. CNBC, "Nike Sales Jump After Kaepernick Campaign," Sep 2018.
36. *Folha de São Paulo*, "Sleeping Giants Brasil and Ad Boycotts," May 2020.
37. Orwell, *1984*, p. 309.
38. U.S. Federal Election Commission Report, "2024 Presidential Results," Dec 2024.
39. Winston Churchill, speech at the House of Commons, Nov 1947 (quoted in context of truth and democracy).

CHAPTER 36: ENDNOTES

1. Allan Bloom, *The Closing of the American Mind* (New York: Simon & Schuster, 1987), preface.
2. Roger Kimball, *Tenured Radicals: How Politics Has Corrupted Our Higher Education* (New York: Harper & Row, 1990), p. 11.
3. Benjamin Franklin, quoted in *Poor Richard's Almanack*, 1758.
4. Saint Augustine, quoted in *Sermons on the New Testament Lessons*, trans. R.G. MacMullen (London: Rivingtons, 1844), Sermon 18.
5. *The Black Book of Communism: Crimes, Terror, Repression*, ed. Stéphane Courtois (Cambridge: Harvard University Press, 1999).
6. William J. Bennett, *The Book of Virtues* (New York: Simon & Schuster, 1993).
7. Thomas Sowell, *A Conflict of Visions: Ideological Origins of Political Struggles* (New York: Basic Books, 2007).
8. Hubert H. Humphrey, speech before the Democratic National Convention, Chicago, 1968.
9. Bloom, *The Closing of the American Mind*, IBID.
10. Kimball, *Tenured Radicals*, IBID.
11. Foundation for Individual Rights and Expression (FIRE), *2026 College Free Speech Rankings* (Philadelphia, 2026).
12. National Association of Scholars (NAS), *DEI Mandate Reports* (New York, 2025).
13. American Council of Trustees and Alumni (ACTA), *What Will They Learn? 2024–2025 Edition* (Washington, 2025).
14. Parents Defending Education, *Incident Tracker* (Arlington, VA, 2025).
15. U.S. Department of Education, "End DEI Portal Announcement," Press Release, March 2025.
16. Sharyl Attkisson, *The Smear: How Shady Political Operatives and Fake News Control What You See, What You Think, and How You Vote* (New York: Harper, 2017).
17. Walter Lippmann, *Public Opinion* (New York: Harcourt, Brace & Company, 1922).
18. George Orwell, *Politics and the English Language* (London: Horizon, 1946).
19. Attkisson, *The Smear*, IBID.
20. Edward S. Herman and Noam Chomsky, *Manufacturing Consent: The Political Economy of the Mass Media* (New York: Pantheon, 1988).
21. Federal Bureau of Investigation, "Astroturfing and Online Manipulation," Public Affairs Bulletin (Washington, 2024).
22. Columbia Journalism Review, "Paid Protests and Astroturf Activism," Vol. 61, No. 2 (2023).
23. C.S. Lewis, *The Abolition of Man* (New York: Macmillan, 1947).

24. Attkisson, *The Smear*, IBID.
25. Viktor E. Frankl, *Man's Search for Meaning* (Boston: Beacon Press, 1959).
26. Kimball, *Tenured Radicals*, IBID.
27. Herbert I. Schiller, *Mind Managers* (Boston: Beacon Press, 1973).
28. STOPit Solutions, *School Safety Reporting App Documentation* (2024).
29. Anderson Software, *report it® — School Safety & Security Solutions* (2024).
30. Elker Systems, *Anonymous Reporting for Schools and Universities* (2025).
31. Parents Defending Education, *Incident Tracker*, IBID.
32. U.S. Department of Education, *End DEI Portal Announcement*, IBID.
33. Turning Point USA, *Professor Watchlist* (Scottsdale, AZ, 2025).
34. Leadership Institute, *Campus Reform News Archive* (Arlington, VA, 2025).
35. FIRE, *2026 College Free Speech Rankings*, IBID.
36. ACTA, *What Will They Learn?*, IBID.
37. Milton Friedman, *Free to Choose* (New York: Harcourt, 1980).
38. Thomas Sowell, *Basic Economics: A Common Sense Guide to the Economy* (New York: Basic Books, 2014).
39. Attkisson, *The Smear*, IBID.
40. Mark Twain, quoted in *Notebooks and Journals*, Vol. I, ed. Frederick Anderson (Berkeley: University of California Press, 1975), p. 347.
41. Friedman, *Free to Choose*, IBID.
42. Sowell, *A Conflict of Visions*, IBID.
43. William J. Bennett, *Our Sacred Honor* (New York: Simon & Schuster, 1997).
44. Thomas Paine, *The American Crisis*, No. 1 (Philadelphia: 1776).
45. C.S. Lewis, *The Screwtape Letters* (London: Geoffrey Bles, 1942).
46. Winston S. Churchill, speech at the House of Commons, June 4, 1940.
47. Federal Election Commission, *Guide to Voting and Participation* (Washington, 2024).
48. Pew Research Center, *Trends in Political Discourse and Civic Engagement* (2023).
49. U.S. Senate Office of Public Records, *Constituent Communication Procedures* (Washington, 2024).
50. Federal Election Commission, *Campaign Finance and Individual Contribution Report* (2024).
51. Boycott List Report, *Economic Pressure and Political Change* (New York: 2024).
52. U.S. Constitution, Art. I, § 2, and Art. II, § 4 (Recall and Impeachment Clauses).
53. National Archives, *Bill of Rights: First Amendment Protections* (Washington, 2023).
54. American Bar Association, *Civic Responsibility and Jury Duty* (2024).
55. FIRE, *2026 College Free Speech Rankings*, IBID.
56. Sowell, *A Conflict of Visions*, IBID.
57. National Association of Scholars, *DEI Mandate Reports*, IBID.

CHAPTER 37: ENDNOTES

1. *Communist Party USA*, "About the Party," CPUSA.org, accessed October 2025.
2. Influence Watch, "Communist Party USA," Capital Research Center, June 2024.
3. Democratic Socialists of America, "About DSA," DSAUSA.org, accessed October 2025.

4. Influence Watch, "Democratic Socialists of America," Capital Research Center, May 2024.
5. Party for Socialism and Liberation, "Who We Are," PSLweb.org, accessed October 2025.
6. *Liberation News,* "The Party for Socialism and Liberation Program," PSL Publications, 2024.
7. Workers World Party, "About Workers World Party," Workers.org, accessed October 2025.
8. *Workers World* Editorial Board, "Marxism, Anti-Imperialism and U.S. Struggles," *Workers.org,* April 2024.
9. Patrisse Cullors, interview by Jared Ball, *The Real News Network,* June 2020 ("We are trained Marxists ...").
10. Associated Press, "Black Lives Matter Group Raises $90 Million, Plans Expansion," February 23, 2021.
11. Congressional Research Service, "Antifa as a Domestic Movement: Background and Context," CRS Report R46459, August 2020.
12. Rose City Antifa, "Who We Are," RoseCityAntifa.org, accessed October 2025.
13. Karl Marx, *The Eighteenth Brumaire of Louis Bonaparte,* 1852.
14. Shmuel Almog, *Antisemitism Through the Ages,* Oxford University Press, 1990.
15. Paul Johnson, *A History of the Jews,* Harper & Row, 1987.
16. Kenneth L. Marcus, *The Definition of Anti-Semitism,* Oxford University Press, 2015.
17. Natan Sharansky and Gil Troy, *Never Alone: Prison, Politics, and My People,* PublicAffairs, 2020.
18. International Socialist Organization, "Letter to Members Announcing Dissolution," March 2019, *Socialist Worker Archive.*
19. David North, "The Collapse of the ISO and the Crisis of the Pseudo-Left," *World Socialist Web Site,* April 15, 2019.
20. "It's Going Down," "Red Guards Austin Announces Dissolution," September 2020.
21. Ben Norton, "The Rise and Fall of the Red Guards: A Maoist Experiment in U.S. Cities," *Grayzone Project,* December 2021.
22. *W.E.B. Du Bois Clubs of America: Organizational Statement,* Communist Party USA Archives, 1964.
23. U.S. Senate Internal Security Subcommittee, *Investigation of Communist Front Youth Organizations: Hearings on the Du Bois Clubs of America,* 1966.
24. U.S. House Committee on Oversight and Accountability, *Preliminary Report on Domestic Communist Affiliations and Funding Sources,* June 2025.
25. CPUSA, "Membership Dues and Support Structure," CPUSA.org; DSA National Bylaws Article II, DSAUSA.org.
26. Thousand Currents, "2020 Independent Auditor's Report and Financial Statements," August 2020; Tides Foundation, IRS Form 990 (2023).
27. *People's World,* "Annual Fund Drive Announcement," April 2024; *Liberation News,* "Support Our Work," PSLweb.org.
28. Federal Election Commission, "Democratic Socialists of America PAC Filings," FEC.gov, accessed October 2025; OpenSecrets.org, "Democratic Socialists of America Political Action Committee," 2024 Cycle Report.
29. U.S. House Committee on Oversight and Accountability, Letter to Neville Roy Singham and Associated Entities, June 13, 2025; IBID.
30. Vasili Mitrokhin and Christopher Andrew, *The Mitrokhin Archive: The KGB in Europe and the West,* Penguin Press, 1999.

31. U.S. House Select Committee on China, *Preliminary Findings on United Front Activities and Foreign Influence Operations,* July 2024.
32. Office of the Director of National Intelligence, *Global Influence Report 2023,* Section III, "Information Operations and Ideological Penetration."
33. CharityWatch, "Black Lives Matter Global Network Foundation: Financial Review and Audit Summary," April 2023; Associated Press, "BLM Leader Faces Questions Over Use of Donor Funds," May 2022.

CHAPTER 38: ENDNOTES

1. Friedrich A. Hayek, *The Road to Serfdom* (Chicago: University of Chicago Press, 1944), p. 3.
2. George Orwell, *Politics and the English Language* (London: Horizon Press, 1946).
3. Milton Friedman, *Capitalism and Freedom* (Chicago: University of Chicago Press, 1962), p. 15.
4. Democratic Socialists of America, "Elected Officials," DSA National Website, 2025.
5. New York State Assembly, "Assembly Member Zohran K. Mamdani Biography," Official State Website, 2024.
6. *Texas Tribune,* "Greg Casar and the Progressive Wing in Texas Politics," 2023.
7. Eugene V. Debs, *Speech to the Socialist Party Convention,* St. Louis, 1919.
8. Anne Applebaum, *Gulag: A History* (New York: Doubleday, 2003), p. xxiii.
9. Richard Pipes, *Communism: A History* (New York: Modern Library, 2001), p. 27.
10. Aleksandr Solzhenitsyn, *The Gulag Archipelago,* Vol. I (New York: Harper & Row, 1973), p. 168.
11. Thomas Sowell, *Basic Economics* (New York: Basic Books, 2014), p. 210.
12. Robert Conquest, *The Harvest of Sorrow: Soviet Collectivization and the Terror-Famine* (New York: Oxford University Press, 1986), p. 8.
13. Alexis de Tocqueville, *Democracy in America,* Vol. I (New York: Vintage Classics, 1945), p. 254.
14. James Madison, *The Federalist Papers,* No. 10 (New York: 1787).
15. Karl Marx and Friedrich Engels, *Manifesto of the Communist Party* (London: 1848), p. 14.
16. Vladimir Lenin, *State and Revolution* (Moscow: Progress Publishers, 1917), p. 23.
17. C. S. Lewis, *The Abolition of Man* (New York: Harper Collins, 1943), p. 34.
18. Thomas Sowell, *The Vision of the Anointed* (New York: Basic Books, 1995), p. 83.
19. U.S. Department of Justice, *United States v. Robert Menendez et al.,* Indictment, 2023.
20. Franklin D. Roosevelt, *The Four Freedoms Speech,* January 6, 1941, Voices of Democracy Project, University of Maryland.
21. Alexis de Tocqueville, *Democracy in America,* Vol. I (New York: Vintage Classics, 1945), p. 301.
22. James Madison, *The Federalist Papers,* No. 51 (New York: 1787).
23. Anne Applebaum, *Twilight of Democracy: The Seductive Lure of Authoritarianism* (New York: Doubleday, 2020), p. 17.
24. United States Department of State, *Foreign Disinformation and Propaganda Report,* 2023.
25. John Adams, "Letter to the Massachusetts Militia," 1798, National Archives: Founders Online.

26. C. S. Lewis, *The Weight of Glory* (New York: Harper Collins, 1949), p. 56.
27. Abraham Lincoln, "Speech at Edwardsville, Illinois," September 11, 1858.
28. John Stuart Mill, *On Liberty* (London: John W. Parker & Son, 1859), p. 45.
29. Dwight D. Eisenhower, "Speech to the American Legion," St. Louis, August 24, 1955.
30. Anne Applebaum, *Iron Curtain: The Crushing of Eastern Europe 1944–1956* (New York: Doubleday, 2012), p. 4.
31. Friedrich A. Hayek, *Law, Legislation and Liberty,* Vol. I (Chicago: University of Chicago Press, 1973), p. 68.
32. Ryszard Legutko, *The Demon in Democracy: Totalitarian Temptations in Free Societies* (New York: Encounter Books, 2016), p. 33.
33. Samuel Adams, "Essay Signed 'Candidus,'" *Boston Gazette,* October 14, 1771, in *The Writings of Samuel Adams,* ed. Henry Alonzo Cushing, Vol. III (New York: G. P. Putnam's Sons, 1907), 236–237.
34. Ronald Reagan, "Speech at the Republican National Convention," July 17, 1980.
35. George Washington, *First Inaugural Address,* April 30, 1789, *The Papers of George Washington: Presidential Series,* Vol. 2 (Charlottesville: University of Virginia Press, 1987), 1–8.
36. Edmund Burke, *Reflections on the Revolution in France* (London: J. Dodsley, 1790), p. 89.
37. John Adams, *A Defence of the Constitutions of Government of the United States* (London: C. Dilly, 1787).
38. Thomas Jefferson, *Notes on the State of Virginia* (Philadelphia: Prichard and Hall, 1787), p. 154.
39. Winston S. Churchill, "Speech at the House of Commons," October 22, 1945.
40. Samuel Adams, "Essay Signed 'Candidus,'" *Boston Gazette,* October 14, 1771, in *The Writings of Samuel Adams,* ed. Henry Alonzo Cushing, Vol. III (New York: G. P. Putnam's Sons, 1907), 236–237.
41. George Washington, *First Inaugural Address,* April 30, 1789, *The Papers of George Washington: Presidential Series,* Vol. 2 (Charlottesville: University of Virginia Press, 1987), 1–8.